FROM THE PINEY WOODS

FROM THE PINEY WOODS

PJ HAMILTON

Plus One

publishing

From the Piney Woods
Published by Plus One Publishing
San Antonio, Texas, U.S.A.

HAMILTON, PJ, Author
FROM THE PINEY WOODS
PJ HAMILTON

Library of Congress Control Number: 2024919963

ISBN: 979-8-9916035-0-8, 979-8-9916035-2-2 (paperback)
ISBN: 979-8-9916035-3-9 (hardcover)
ISBN: 979-8-9916035-1-5 (digital)

BODY, MIND & SPIRIT / Inspiration & Personal Growth
SELF-HELP / Journaling
BIOGRAPHY & AUTOBIOGRAPHY / Women

Editing: Lisa Shrewsberry (shrewsberry5live@gmail.com)
Book Design: Amit Dey (amitdey2528@gmail.com)
Publishing Management: Susie Schaefer (FinishTheBookPublishing.com)

QUANTITY PURCHASES: Schools, companies, professional groups, clubs, and other organizations may qualify for special terms when ordering quantities of this title.
For information, email support@plus1publishing.com

DEDICATION

To my beloved son, Kyle…

In the pages of this book lies not just a story, but the essence of a journey shaped and inspired by you. You are the heartbeat of my life's narrative, the driving force behind every word written and every lesson learned. Your presence has transformed me, guiding me to depths of understanding and heights of love I never knew possible.

You, Kyle, are the reason for the person I am today. Your laughter has been my music, your challenges, my lessons, and your love, my unwavering light. This book is a testament to the incredible impact you have had on my life. It is because of you that I have found the strength to grow, the courage to face the unknown, and the wisdom to embrace life's complexities. With every page turned, know that it is your spirit that breathes life into this story.

With all my love and gratitude,
Mom

TABLE OF CONTENTS

A NOTE FROM THE AUTHOR

Dear Reader,

As PJ Hamilton, a name I chose to represent the many facets of my journey, I welcome you to the pages of *From the Piney Woods*. This book, a tapestry of my life's trials and triumphs, is an offering of hope and a testament to faith's healing power.

My story, etched in the shadows of abandonment and neglect, is not unique. There are many who have wandered through similar woods, entangled in thorns of shame and battles with self-worth. But in these shared struggles, there is a universal truth—our past does not define us; it prepares us.

Each chapter of this book unfolds from a journal entry, fragments of my soul laid bare in therapy sessions. These reflections are more than just recounting a troubled past; they are stepping stones towards a future illuminated by faith and self-discovery.

I wrote this book to serve as a beacon for those lost in their own piney woods. Therapy, for me, was a journey of rediscovery, a path back to a faith that I thought I had lost. It taught me that our scars are not just reminders of our past pain but also markers of our strength.

In sharing my story, I hope you find the courage to face your own, to seek solace in counseling, to lean into your faith, and to understand that every experience, no matter how painful, has the potential to shape you into someone stronger, wiser, and more compassionate.

As you journey through these pages, you may find echoes of your own struggles and aspirations. May you realize that you are not alone and that the path to healing, though rugged, is also a road to profound growth and self-acceptance.

Embrace your past, lean into your faith, and walk confidently into the person you are meant to be. Your story, like mine, is one of resilience and hope. Let it unfold, let it heal, and let it shine.

With warmth and understanding,
PJ Hamilton

Journal Entry, August 18, 1992

Settling onto a well-worn leather sofa in a dimly lit room, I offer a half-hearted smile to the woman seated behind a desk of rich mahogany. It strikes me as odd—aren't psychiatrists supposed to have a chair by the sofa, ready for the patient to spill their thoughts while lying back? Yet, here I am, meeting Barbara, my first-ever psychologist.

We exchange pleasantries, and then she asks that all-too-familiar question, "So, what brings you here today, PJ?"

It's a broad question, one that could eat up our entire hour. Armed with sarcasm, I reply, "Can you erase the memories of a terrible childhood and all the bad decisions I made just to get away from it?"

Barbara offers a warm smile, suggesting I start from my earliest memory; she casually mentions that I should journal my thoughts post-session, bringing them along next time. Journaling? As if I'm not swamped enough already, I thought. Here I am, a 26-year-old single mom juggling three jobs to provide for my toddler, Kyle. Therapy wouldn't even be on my radar if it weren't for my previous job footing the bill—a settlement of sorts for a sexual harassment issue involving my boss's superior. But hey, why not give this therapy thing a chance?

Besides, I think to myself, Barbara could use a new sofa. Why not help her out? After all, it's not like I'm the one paying...

Taking a deep breath, I begin to peel back the layers of my past, exposing the raw memories that have haunted me. I got my start in the piney woods of East Texas, my childhood unfolding in the rolling hills, dense forests, and shimmering lakes. I can almost hear the echoes of those early years—the laughter, the tears, and the moments of pain that left forever marks on my soul.

As I speak, Barbara listens intently, her eyes never leaving mine. I recount the tales of growing up in Nacogdoches, Texas, in a lively household with three brothers and three sisters. I tell her about the simple joys of childhood, the mischief, and the discipline that often followed. I describe the vibrant community and the warmth of Southern hospitality that enveloped our lives. We sit on the surface of those idyllic memories for just a moment, the icebreakers of one's life.

But beneath the surface lies a darker truth punctuated by the constant tension between my parents—the yelling, the hitting, and the way we watched it all. I dig deep to reveal the confusion and pain of being thrust into the muck of adult relationships at an early age, bearing the stains of fear and insecurity into adulthood.

As I delve into my story, beyond the depth where breathing is easy, I realize that these memories are more than just fragments of the past; they are the stubborn foundation of my present struggles with depression, low self-esteem, and shame. Each memory is a piece of the puzzle, and Barbara begins to see what has brought me to this point.

By the end of our session, I've shared more than I ever thought I would or could in just an hour. Barbara's compassionate presence and gentle encouragement have made it easier to be transparent. She nods thoughtfully, making notes and occasionally asking questions to draw out more details.

Leaving her office, I feel a strange mixture of exhaustion and relief. The process has begun, and while it won't be easy, I know that facing my past is the first step towards healing. As I drive home, I think about the journal Barbara suggested. It's not such a bad idea after all. Writing my story could be the key to understanding—and eventually outrunning—the shadows of my childhood... but that's the thing about shadows. Sometimes, they're hard to outpace.

Chapter 1

PINE SCENTED MEMORIES

The piney woods were a world apart in the vast landscape of the Lone Star State. Here, in this lush region, the warmth of Southern hospitality thrived, as did the bustling logging industry that was the heartbeat of local life. Sawmills dotted the landscape, supported by a network of ports, railroads, and family farms, each playing a pivotal role in the vibrant community.

In East Texas, large families were as common as biscuits and gravy at breakfast or squirrel dumplings at supper. My family was no exception. Nestled in the small community in Nacogdoches, ours was a lively household. I was the fifth of seven children born to my parents. Before the divorce, our childhood was a cluster of innocent and simple joys.

Growing up with three brothers and three sisters, it was easy to blend in, a blessing that often allowed me to sneak away with mischievous escapades—swimming in the street gutters after a heavy rain or daringly jumping off the house roof, trying to see how far I could leap before crashing to the ground. Of course, not all our adventures went unnoticed. Often, getting caught meant a swift and stinging encounter with a switch from the large bush in our front yard. Each of us had contributed to the bushes near-barren state, having been sent to pluck our very own switch for a spanking. Despite attempts to outrun her, none of us could ever match our Momma's speed; her discipline was as swift as her feet. In the car, she somehow managed to quell our backseat bickering and kicking with one hand while driving face forward with the other on the wheel.

Momma was the sole daughter among three brothers. Fiery red hair and a mere five feet in stature, she more than made up for her size with her fierce temper and strong will. At sixteen, she married our Daddy, the result of a whirlwind romance with one of those "boys down the road" much to her father's dismay.

"I told him, 'I don't care what you say, Daddy. I'm marrying him!' And that's exactly what I did," Momma would often recount, her hazel-green eyes gleaming with defiance.

Her father was a man with a great sense of humor who loved to laugh, and he adored my Granny, always teasing her playfully. He drove a logger truck, hauling pine trees down the mountain to the local lumber yards. Momma often shared stories of her childhood adventures with him.

"Daddy used to let me ride with him in the truck," she'd reminisce, a smile tugging at her lips. He'd say, "C'mon, darlin', keep me company while I work." Then Momma explained, "I started smoking because he'd have me roll his cigarettes and light them for him while he drove, I've been smoking ever since!"

I never met my grandfather, as he passed before I was born, but Momma often spoke of him with a wistful, far-off look. He died of cancer at just forty-nine, on her baby brother's thirteenth birthday. Her eyes would mist over as she remembered the man who had been both her hero and her greatest teacher, and she'd quickly turn away, hiding her tears from our young, curious eyes.

Despite her fiery temper, Momma had a softer side, especially when talking about her own childhood. "Your granddaddy was a hard man," she'd say, "but he always told me, 'You've got the spirit of a wildcat, darlin', and don't let anyone tame it." This saying became a mantra for her, something she passed down to us as she raised us with the same wildcat spirit, instilling in us resilience and strength.

These memories, a blend of joy, mischief, and the sting of discipline, are the threads of my early years in the piney woods—a time of simplicity, family, and the profound imprint of a mother's love and strength.

Momma was a striking woman, but the years of endless chores etched lines of fatigue onto her once youthful face. Her days were a relentless cycle of laundry, washing endless piles of clothes and diapers, then hanging them to dry on the clothesline. She bathed the babies in the old kitchen sink and spent hours over the stove, cooking meals that filled our modest home with warm, comforting aromas.

Daddy was scarce in our daily lives, often absent for long stretches. But I vividly recalled the excitement buzzing through us whenever he returned. He was a tall man, over six feet, with a strong frame and thick, black hair that matched the depth of his brown eyes. Those eyes, I remembered, could twinkle with mirth one moment and darken like storm clouds the next, reflecting his unpredictable moods.

One of my fondest memories was when Daddy picked up his guitar, settling onto the porch as the sun dipped below the pine trees. His fingers danced over the strings, coaxing out melodies that seemed to float through the air, blending with the sounds of the evening. "This here is what real music sounds like," he'd say with a grin, nodding toward the radio as if challenging it to compete with his tunes. "You kids pay attention. This is not the noise they play on the radio nowadays."

His music was magic, casting a spell over us that made the world feel right, if only for a moment. Those moments were rare, like finding a hidden path in the woods that only he knew.

But Daddy's mood could change as quickly as the wind shifted through the trees. Once, while he was playing, I accidentally knocked over his coke bottle, sending it rolling across the porch. The music stopped abruptly. He stared angrily at me for a moment, his brow furrowing as his head cocked to the side. "Can't you be more careful, girl?" he snapped, his voice sharp enough to cut through the night air. I froze, my heart pounding as I mumbled an apology, feeling the warmth of the evening vanish like a fleeting dream.

His eyes softened slightly, but the tension lingered in the air, leaving me wary of his unpredictable nature. "Just...watch what you're doin' next time," he added, the guitar resting silently on his knee as he reached for his coke.

It wasn't until much later that I fully understood the impact of his absence and his temper on our lives. In retrospect, I realized how Daddy's visits—so full of music and stories, yet so fleeting—taught me about the complexities of love and the dual nature of those we hold dear. His guitar playing was a cherished memory, but it was also a reminder of the bittersweet moments that defined my childhood, where love and uncertainty danced hand in hand under the starlit sky.

On the rare occasions when he took us along, Daddy would drive to the nearby town of Lufkin. During these trips, he would visit a string of lady "friends" or catch up with his family, often leaving us to wait in the car while he disappeared for hours.

"Be good, kids," he'd say before vanishing into the unknown, the car door shutting with a familiar thud. "I'll be back before you know it."

Daddy had been one of ten siblings, most of whom were brothers. His family was large and spread out across the area, which meant he was often busy visiting one relative or another. "Got to check on your Uncle JD," he'd explain. "He's been having a tough time lately."

His visits to Lufkin were a complex web of social obligations and personal pursuits. He had a knack for making friends everywhere he went, and he thrived on the attention and camaraderie he found in these interactions. "They're good people," he'd often say, referring to his many acquaintances and relatives in Lufkin. "You'd like them if you met them."

These trips were part of why Daddy was gone so much, as he juggled maintaining relationships with his expansive family and his friends in town. The allure of socializing often pulled him away from home, leaving us to manage without him for long stretches. It was a reality we had come to accept, though it left a void that was hard to fill.

Despite these absences, Daddy's return was always a mix of excitement and dread. He would arrive home with a booming voice and a playful ruffle of our hair, but there was always an underlying tension that hung in the air. His mood could shift suddenly, his jovial exterior giving way to something darker.

"Where the hell have you been?" Momma would confront him, her voice a mix of frustration and anger. "We needed you here!"

His eyes narrowed; storm clouds gathered. "Don't start, woman. I do what I can," he'd retort, his tone defensive and dismissive.

5

The arguments between Momma and Daddy could erupt out of nowhere, often over money or his absences. We'd watch, wide-eyed and silent, as their voices rose, and accusations flew across the room. Sometimes the fights turned physical, a blur of anger and chaos. Daddy's sturdy frame would loom over Momma and, though she was small, her fiery spirit matched his intensity.

"Get your hands off me, Fate!" Momma would shout, struggling against him.

Breaking glass or the thud of something hitting the wall became an all-too-familiar soundtrack in our home. These moments left us trembling in our rooms, clutching each other in the darkness, trying to drown out the noise.

When the storm passed, Daddy would leave again, slamming the door behind him. The silence that followed was heavy, filled with unspoken fears and constant worry about what might happen next. Momma would try to gather herself, her anger simmering beneath the surface, her eyes tired and distant.

"We'll be okay, kids," she'd assure us, though her voice wavered with uncertainty. "Just keep your heads down, and we'll get through this."

His single sister, our only aunt, was a distant figure we never had the chance to meet. Daddy spoke of her fondly, but she lived far away, beyond the reach of our occasional trips to Lufkin. "Your Aunt Lucille's doing well out in Dallas," he'd mention in passing. "Maybe one day we'll go visit her."

Despite his frequent absences, Daddy's influence lingered, casting a shadow over our lives that was equal parts absence and presence. We learned to make do, finding comfort in one another and in the routines, we built around his sporadic visits. We clung to the hope that each time he walked out the door, he wouldn't return with the storm clouds brewing overhead, and instead, he'd be the father we wished he could be.

In East Texas, large families were the norm. It seemed like everyone in that area was connected by a vast web of kinship spanning the rolling hills and pine forests. "Inbred as a pine tree," folks liked to joke, since everyone was just a distant cousin or two away from everyone else. This tangled family tree made for interesting reunions, where you'd meet a new relative every time.

The question of why Momma and Daddy stayed together despite their evident discord often puzzled me. Surely, there must have been a spark, at least seven times, one each evidenced by the seven of us children. But love and liking are curious things, especially seen through the eyes of a child in a large family. As the fifth child in our brood of seven, I was thrust early into the world of grown-up truths, including the mysteries of the "birds and the bees." My older brothers, always looking for a bit of mischief, had taken it upon themselves to educate their younger siblings. They seemed to relish unveiling these secrets, eagerly anticipating our reactions.

But I wasn't about to give them the satisfaction of seeing me flustered. So, when they explained the facts of life, expecting me to be shocked, I showed indifference. "I know!" I declared boldly, before scampering away. Only in solitude did I allow myself to express the shock and bewilderment that such revelations truly brought. In those moments, alone with my thoughts, I grappled with the complexities of adult relationships, a world as vast and perplexing as the piney woods surrounding our home.

Chapter 2

GRANNY'S MAGIC BALM

My first-grade year was like a daily treasure hunt, full of little adventures, whether walking to school or riding the bus home, threading through the towering pine trees of Nacogdoches. These majestic trees stood like silent sentinels over my imaginative daydreams, where I ventured into distant lands and epic tales.

One chilly autumn afternoon, while waiting for the bus, I discovered a new game to keep warm. I had forgotten my coat, so to combat the cold, I started pushing my knee back and forth between a brick wall and a steel post, enjoying the brief warmth each friction-filled slide offered. Absorbed in the comfort it brought, I didn't realize I was pushing too far until my leg got stuck. The more I wiggled, the more my knee swelled, trapping me even tighter.

Seeing my predicament, Mrs. Perkins, the school secretary who always looked as though she'd been caught in a windstorm, quickly dialed the Volunteer Fire Department. "Hurry up, please!" she urged into the phone, peering anxiously down the road. "The bus is going to arrive any second, and we've got a child stuck here."

Before long, Jethro and Jim Bob from the fire department arrived, their arrival marked by hearty laughs that filled the air. "Well, what do we have here? A little chick caught in a rabbit hole?" Jethro joked as they surveyed the situation. He had a big wad of chewing tobacco on his lip and kept spitting on the wall behind me; it was disgusting. With a combination of grease and ice, they began their rescue, their movements grand and theatrical.

As they worked, the bus pulled up and the driver, spotting the commotion, leaned out the window with a curious grin. "You boys better not be greasing up my seats now!" he called out, chuckling.

Jethro laughed back, wiping his hands on a rag, "Don't you worry. We'll make sure the kid doesn't slide right off your seats. But hey, if you need tips on cleaning grease, I've got a few good ones!"

Finally free, I climbed onto the bus, greasy and a bit disheveled. As I passed the bus driver, he winked and whispered, "Got any of that magic grease left for a squeaky door?" The whole bus erupted into laughter at the banter, adding to my embarrassment.

I slunk into the nearest seat, my cheeks burning hotter than the afternoon sun. The whispers and giggles of my classmates swirled around me, mixing with the rustling of the pine trees outside. It felt as if the entire forest was in on the joke. As the bus pulled away, I made a silent vow amid the laughter: I'd master my brother's ten-speed bike to avoid these bus rides—and the spotlight—forever.

First thing when I got home, I asked to borrow my brother's bike. It was far too big for me, but my stubbornness wouldn't let that stop me. He agreed, thinking I wouldn't manage to ride it anyway. I dragged it to Virginia Street, known for its steep hills, lined with houses all along the ride downhill. Memories of my old bike, crushed under Daddy's car, came flooding back. I had earned the worst spanking for leaving it in the driveway—his huge hands were always more dreaded than the switch.

Virginia Street was picturesque, especially during the fall. As I pedaled down, the hills were scattered with vibrant piles of leaves, a mix of bright oak leaves and the ever-present pine needles from the towering pine trees. Residents had raked them into heaps to either burn or bag, transforming the street into a patchwork of autumn hues. We loved to jump in these piles of leaves, except when there were too many prickly pinecones hidden within, turning a playful leap into a painful landing.

Energized by the crisp air and the rustle of leaves under the bike's tires, I felt a surge of freedom that made my earlier embarrassment on the bus fade into the background. The thrill of descending Virginia Street on a bike that was too large for me, dodging the occasional pinecone, was the perfect way to reclaim my day.

Things were perfect until, as I raced down the hill, I realized the brakes didn't work with the pedals like my old bike. In a panic, I crashed into a heap of leaves to stop, with no idea the brakes were on the handlebars. I pushed the bike home, tears streaming down my face. But they weren't tears of pain from the crash; they were from the dread of facing my classmates' sneers on the bus the next day. I decided to confide in Granny when I got home. She always had a way of putting things into perspective. She'd probably remind me that summer was just around the corner, and soon enough, the school bus—and its sneering occupants—would be a distant memory.

Granny, my mother's mom, lived right next door, yet stepping into her house was like entering a different realm. Our home buzzed with the chaotic energy of seven kids—running, shouting, and wrestling, a relentless whirlwind of activity. In stark contrast, Granny's place existed in a serene bubble, an oasis of tranquility and meticulous order. Her house was a sanctuary where calm reigned. The gentle swish of her broom sweeping the wooden floors was almost rhythmic, a soothing backdrop to the peace that pervaded her space. The air was infused with the comforting blend of fresh soap and brewed tea, each breath bringing a sense of order and calm.

Our occasional sleepovers at Granny's were a special treat. We'd drift off to sleep under sheets fresh off the clothesline, their clean, airy scent lulling us into the most peaceful slumber. Waking up there was another kind of magic, especially the smell of toast. Granny had this art of buttering toast perfectly, right to the very edges, and somehow, it was the best toast I'd ever tasted.

The fragrances of summer at Granny's were etched in my memory—toast, of course, but also honeysuckle, magnolias, fig-trees, blackberries, and sunflowers. During summer rains, the streets outside would turn into rivers, and we'd swim in them, laughing and splashing as Momma kept an eye on us. Sometimes, the rain would fall even as the sun shone brightly, and Daddy would say, "The devil's beating his wife!"

In Granny's kitchen, a bowl of ceramic fruit always caught my eye. Among the collection, there was a banana with tape around it, a silent testimony to some mishap. Nobody admitted to breaking it, but I had my suspicions—my older sister Karen knew more than she let on. These small mysteries and moments at Granny's house wove together a tapestry of simple yet profound joys from my childhood.

Granny's house, just next door to ours, was nestled beyond a lush expanse of green grass speckled with delicate white flowers that swayed gently in the breeze. This vibrant patch served as our daily pathway, a natural bridge from the endless energy of our home to the serene calm of Granny's doorstep. We used to pick so many of these white flowers to bring to Granny, our hands could hardly carry the thick cluster of them. She would then put them in a colorful plastic glass she had saved from her snuff, a smelly powder she dipped and put in her mouth, transforming our simple offerings into a fragrant display that brightened her kitchen. She always acted surprised and over-joyed to receive yet another batch of these flowers.

On the cool cement of Granny's front porch, where chairs were unnecessary, we sat directly on the cement porch steps, our backs against the slightly rough surface, absorbing the tranquil atmosphere. This quiet nook became our special place for bond-ing and meaningful lessons.

Light streamed through crisp, clean linen curtains, casting soft patterns on her worn but immaculately kept furniture. The chairs and couches, though showing signs of age, were spotless and inviting, each cushion and armrest lovingly maintained. On her shelves rested stacks of romance novels from the late 'sixties, their spines creased from years of loving re-reads. These books, filled with tales of distant times and grand passions, seemed to echo the quiet, enduring charm of the room they adorned. In Granny's house, the world outside with its noise and chaos felt miles away, replaced by an atmosphere of timeless tranquility and the lingering scent of lavender and tea.

Granny would carefully roll my long, thick, brown hair into curls, securing each with a bobby pin. As she did so, she seized the opportunity to impart a crucial life lesson. "You're stepping into second grade soon, Sweetie, and it's time you learned how to spell 'Nacogdoches.' It's a big word, isn't it?" she explained, articulating each letter as she twisted a strand of my hair. "N-A-C-O-G-D-O-C-H-E-S." We repeated it together, the letters flowing as smoothly as the wind that rustled the white flowers.

"Now, let's try it again," Granny encouraged, her hands artfully arranging another curl. She paused, her eyes meeting mine with a look of earnest intent. "Remember, Sweetie," she said as she sectioned another piece of my hair, "the road to hell is paved with good intentions. It's not just what you mean to do that matters, but what you do. Actions speak louder than words." Her fingers worked deftly, twisting, and securing, as her words wove a tapestry of guidance.

Every now and then, we'd pause as a neighbor wandered past, exchanging greetings with Granny, who was well known for her wisdom and warmth. Once alone again, she would continue, "People are like these flowers," gesturing towards the white blooms across the yard. "Each petal represents a stage in their life. And like spelling this big word, life is about taking things one step, one letter at a time."

Sitting there on Granny's porch, surrounded by the beauty of nature and the word Nacogdoches embedded in my mind, I felt a profound sense of pride and connection. Granny's lessons went beyond spelling. I realized it was Granny's wisdom and guidance that truly served as the magic balm, soothing the wounds of life's harsh realities, and helping me find a path forward through the rough terrain.

Chapter 3

SEVEN VOICES AMONG THE PINES

I returned to the vibrant tapestry of life that surrounded me, woven together by the voices of my siblings. Each of us, like branches of a tree, contributed our own distinct tune to the symphony of our shared lives, bound by family ties and shared experiences, forming a chorus of unique voices among the pines.

Richard, the family's resident prankster and the third child born, was always up to something, often whistling catchy tunes to keep everyone on their toes. I was always begging him to teach me how to whistle. One day, his mischief got the better of him, and he proposed a challenge to me. "Hey, if you learn to whistle like me, you gotta do it during Sunday prayer at church. To thank God," he added with a mischievous grin. Richard was tall and thin, with freckles and striking light brown hair and red highlights that seemed to flare in the sun like a warning sign.

"And what if Momma gets mad?" I asked, wary of his schemes.

He chuckled, "Then that means the devil's got her, and you should whistle even louder to save her soul!"

With Richard's guidance, I quickly picked up whistling. The following Sunday, as we sat in the church, the smell of old booze from folks "across the river" who had mingled the previous night, mixing with hymns, I saw my chance. As everyone bowed their heads in prayer, I started whistling softly. Instantly, Momma's eyes snapped open, and she gave me that stern "shut up now" look.

Thinking I was doing the righteous thing, I whistled louder to save her soul. Momma's frown deepened, and before I knew it, she had grabbed my arm and was leading me briskly to the back room for a spanking.

"But Richard told me to do it to save you from the devil!" I protested as Momma prepared my punishment.

Soon after, when the truth came out, Richard was dragged out of his hiding and found himself sharing my fate. Through the stern looks and impending discipline, I couldn't help but notice a few suppressed smiles among our siblings. They knew, as did I, that Richard's pranks often ended this way, but they also made our Sunday gatherings even more memorable from the strictures of our very dry town.

Karen, the fourth child and Daddy's darling, was as different from me as night is from day. Momma often dressed us like twins, and while we might have looked alike, our temperaments were worlds apart. I was the sensitive, shy type, whereas Karen was bold and unbothered by others' opinions. Richard, the third-born, was another of Daddy's favorites. Granny often remarked that Karen and Richard were born during a time when Daddy wanted children, implying the rest of us were... surprises.

One afternoon, under the oppressive heat of the Texas sun, the usual vibrancy of our household gave way to a tension that swelled to a boiling point. Karen and I peered from our bedroom window, an unintended front-row seat to the unfolding drama in the driveway where Momma and Tommy, a new figure in our lives, were engaged in a casual car repair on her 1957 Chevy.

Tommy, with his long, dirty blonde hair tied back in a loose ponytail, seemed relaxed and at ease with Momma, laughing and joking as they worked. His worn jeans and faded T-shirt spoke of a casual, carefree attitude, but there was a sharpness in his eyes, a keen awareness that contradicted his laid-back appearance. He had quickly become a regular presence around our house, not just because of his sleek convertible and charming demeanor, but also because he often bought candy and soda for us and took us for joy rides in his convertible with the top down.

The calm was shattered when Lynn, the second born and eldest son, approached with deliberate, heavy steps. Having just finished high school, he was no longer a boy but a young man, his presence more formidable than ever. Lynn had thick, coarse brown hair that never stayed down because of a cowlick in the front. He wore glasses and had a larger build than the rest of us. His intense brown eyes burned with a constant inner fire, and his robust stature made him an imposing figure. His emergence alone was enough to shift the air, the previous lightness dissipating as he towered over Momma, his voice booming with contained rage, "He needs to leave, now!"

Momma straightened up, wiping her hands on her jeans. Her face, usually composed, was flushed as she shot back, "If you don't like it, Lynn, you can just leave!" Their voices escalated, bouncing off the garage walls, causing Karen to squeeze my hand, her face pinched with worry as we watched the confrontation spiral.

Lynn stormed off, only to return moments later with a chilling calmness and a pistol in his grip. The transformation in the yard was instant; the earlier banter replaced by a heavy silence. Momma's fear was obvious as she rushed inside, her voice quivering with urgency as she called the police, "I need the police here—now!"

Tommy, standing up, his concern morphing into resolve, stepped towards Lynn. "Put that down, man," he said, his voice steady but forceful.

Lynn, his jaw set and his eyes dark with fury, tossed the pistol aside and lunged at Tommy with balled fists. The sound of scuffling feet and grunts filled the air as they grappled, dust kicking up around them.

It was then that Granny appeared, her usually serene face etched with worry. She moved quickly for her age, her voice trembling as she tried to intervene, "Stop this, both of you!"

Momma, emerging from the house, intercepted Granny. "He's just a friend, Mama! Stay out of this!" Her hand flailed in her agitation, accidentally scratching Granny, leaving a mark that began to well with blood.

Granny recoiled, one hand to her face, her expression one of shock as she whispered, "Patsy..."

Karen and I were motionless, the scene before us a nightmarish play. The sharp sound of sirens grew louder, slicing through the chaos as police cars rolled in. Officers moved quickly, pulling Lynn and Tommy apart. Lynn, his thick build heaving with each breath, his face a mixture of rage and despair, was handcuffed. Granny's protests were loud and painful. "He's, my grandson! Family doesn't call the police!" she cried.

The officers were firm, one of them, a tall man with a stern face, replying, "Ma'am, we have to keep everyone safe here."

As Lynn was led away, Granny's eyes followed him, her expression a complex mix of sorrow and disbelief. Momma stood by, her body tense, her face a canvas of mixed emotions—relief, regret, and a fierce protectiveness.

Karen and I turned away from the window, the weight of what we had witnessed settling around us like a heavy blanket. The complexities of adult relationships, the intense passions, and the sharp divides had spilled over, leaving us kids to survive the aftermath of a family storm.

That night, as Karen and I lay in our beds, the sound of Momma's crying echoed through the house. It was a sound that tugged at my heart, compelling me to leave the safety of my bed. I tiptoed into her room and crawled in beside her, trying in my small way to offer comfort. I gently rubbed her face and hair, and slowly, her sobs subsided.

As I drifted off to sleep, nestled next to her, Momma's whisper cut through the silence. "My sweet baby girl, I will miss you," she murmured, her voice thick with emotion. Her words hung in the air, heavy with unspoken meaning. Confusion and worry clouded my young, six-year-old mind. Where was she going? The question lingered, unanswered, as sleep finally claimed me with our family's storm.

Chapter 4

DIVIDED ROADS—MOMMA'S WAY

The events of that day were the tipping point for Momma. The burden of raising seven children on her own, without any help from Daddy, weighed heavily upon her. Her relationship with her own mother hadn't recovered since her father died; I never witnessed them hug or even touch one another. The town's whispering about Daddy's blatant philandering with other women only compounded her isolation and pain.

The night after Lynn challenged Tommy, feeling trapped and desperately wanting her own life to start over, Momma reached a bold decision. It was time to think about her own happiness—to hell with everyone else's opinions or expectations, even those of her children.

Days later, she made good on her words and packed our belongings into her car. It was a whirlwind of activity, a flurry of suitcases and whispered conversations, as she prepared to change the course of our lives. Her movements were hurried but focused, each item stowed away signaled her resolve to escape the stifling environment that had once been her sanctuary, to forge a new path for herself and her children, one where her own happiness was a priority. This new resolve brought an air of determination, and a sense of liberation absent in the years consumed by selfless mothering.

Momma told us she was taking us to Daddy's place in Lufkin on her own way to Huntsville. She planned to take Cherrie, our youngest sister, with her to Huntsville because Daddy claimed Cherrie wasn't his child. The resemblance Cherrie bore to Tommy, with her dirty blonde hair, did stand in stark contrast to the rest of us who shared Daddy's darker hair. As I sat in the car, a strange sense of relief washed over me, grateful, in a child's way, that my hair color aligned with Daddy's. It was a small comfort in a world that suddenly felt uncertain and fragmented. And dangerous.

At the mention of Lufkin, memories pulled me back to one of Daddy's many visits to see one of his lady friends; he had us in tow, Karen, and me. As his surprise guests, we found ourselves at an imposing two-story house, its weathered shutters and wrap-around porch filled with secrets, nestled among dense pine trees in a neglected part of Lufkin. We had never met this lady before, and why he brought us along is a mystery I'll never know. The house stood stark against the backdrop of poverty that marked the area, its air thick with the mingling scents of mildew and pine needles— a poignant reminder of the pervasive dampness of East Texas.

Inside, we were met with the staleness of old cigarette smoke and the smell of urine. It was a peculiar and uneasy night, made worse when Daddy vanished into a bedroom with his lady friend, the door clicking shut behind them, sealing them away for what seemed like an eternity. Karen and I sat on the floor outside the door when the presence of the woman's children, strangers to us, mirrored the hostility of the mean kids from our school, increasing our discomfort.

One was a boy with a scowl perpetually etched into his brow and the other, a glaring girl with narrow eyes; both made no efforts to hide their disdain for us. Their whispers filled the corners of the dimly lit hallway, their words were sharp and cutting.

"Why do *they* even have to be here, Mom's friend or not?" the boy muttered, loud enough for us to hear.

The girl scoffed, eyeing us up and down. "Just here to snoop around. *They* do not belong here."

Feeling the weight of their unwelcoming gaze, Karen tugged at my sleeve, her voice barely a whisper. "Let's get out of here."

Seeking escape from the tense atmosphere, Karen and I walked down a dark hallway where we met a little blue-eyed boy with a secretive air about him. He emerged from the shadows, running into a back bedroom. We found him and noticed that this little boy was covered in bruises, with strange round circles marking his face. This boy, seeming as out of place as we felt, showed us how to crawl out of a window and onto the roof. The roof was steep and slick with dew, yet it offered a strange sort of sanctuary. We followed him up, cautiously navigating the incline.

Once on the rooftop, the contrast between the suffocating indoor air and the crisp night breeze was like a breath of freedom. Karen and I sat with the boy, our legs dangling over the edge, gazing up at the stars that speckled the dark sky.

Karen whispered, "It's like Granny said, remember? About the stars?"

I nodded, smiling faintly. "Yeah, that each one is someone who lived a good life. They get to shine up there forever."

"And the bad ones?" Karen's voice was soft, thoughtful.

"They just disappear... like ghosts, never to be seen or heard," I murmured, glancing down at our quiet companion.

The boy looked up, his eyes reflecting the starlight. "I think it's nicer to be a star," he spoke quietly.

We each fell into a thoughtful silence, counting stars and whispering about the lives they might have lived, finding comfort in Granny's tales and the cool night air. We climbed back into the dark bedroom and laid on the floor to sleep, the little boy curled up next to us for warmth. As my mind quieted toward sleep, I wondered to myself how he kept warm on other nights.

On our departure to Lufkin, I thought to myself with trepidation, "Was this the same house?" This time, it was Momma taking us to Daddy with the intention of dropping us off there, possibly for good. The notion sat like a rock in my stomach. I remembered leaving that one lady's house with Daddy the next morning, and how good it felt to escape its dark embrace, the relief like it was all a bad dream settling as the house shrank away to so much fog in the distance.

Now, Momma was driving us back toward this town and toward an unwritten chapter of our lives, one where we were not in control of the pen. I couldn't help but feel a mix of apprehension and maybe a little curiosity. What awaited us in Lufkin, and what did this new journey mean for our family? Filled with more questions than answers, I counted each mile taking us further from the life we had always known.

The car was enveloped in silence, a quiet weighing heavily in the air. It was just four of us—Karen, our baby brother Kent, Cherrie, and me. The older siblings, Ann, Lynn, and Richard, stayed behind in Nacogdoches, carving out their own paths rather than joining us on this uncertain journey.

As we pulled into the driveway of a house unfamiliar to us, not the one Daddy had previously taken us to—whew! —Momma instructed us to go inside. With a brief, almost hurried assurance that she would be back soon, Momma and Cherrie left us standing there with just one suitcase between us.

As Momma drove away, leaving us with Daddy, the road felt more divided than ever, a testament to the choices and separations that had reshaped our family.

The reality of our situation began to sink in—we were a family divided, about to become part of another divided family. We walked through the front door, entering a kitchen where we were greeted by the new situation Daddy had chosen—a stepmother, Dorothy, and her three children from a previous marriage, Alana, Bobby, and Tanya. The atmosphere was unfamiliar, the faces new, and the sense of belonging we once took for granted seemed to have vanished.

As I looked around at these new faces, I couldn't help but wonder what life would be like with them. Would Alana, Bobby, and Tanya be fun to play with? Would we be able to find common ground and forge new bonds? Or would the differences and the unspoken tensions of a blended family prove to be too challenging?

Standing in that kitchen, I tried to be hopeful, but all I felt was scared. This was more than just a physical relocation; it was a step into a world of new dynamics, relationships, and experiences. It marked the beginning of a year that would undoubtedly shape our lives in profound and lasting ways.

Karen, sensing my unease, leaned in and whispered, "Do you think we'll be okay here, PJ?"

I squeezed her hand, trying to muster more confidence than I felt. "We have to be," I replied quietly. "We'll stick together, no matter what. We always do, right?"

She nodded, her eyes scanning the room as she tried to smile. "Right. If we have each other, we can handle anything."

Our shared smile was a small beacon of hope, a silent pact in the middle of so much uncertainty.

Chapter 5

THE COST OF SILENCE

The harsh realities of our new life, new house, and new family structure began to reveal themselves as soon as Daddy left for work. Dorothy, my stepmother, was a tall, lanky woman with a strikingly unfeminine appearance. Her dirty blonde hair was tied in a loose ponytail, messy strands hanging down in her face, giving her a perpetually unkempt look. Her blue eyes were as cold as ice, and a large hole in her left cheek, a reminder of a mole that had once been removed, punctuated her stern appearance.

Her boyish features were accentuated by her angular face and large hands, which always seemed to hold a cigarette. The smoke curled around her like a menacing cat as she moved about the kitchen, cigarette dangling from her lips, becoming an almost permanent fixture to her demeanor.

She set down bowls of rice before us at the kitchen table, a space that felt anything but welcoming. Dorothy's voice was as clipped and cold as her appearance. "Eat up," she instructed, gesturing to the bowls filled with rice, sugar, butter, and milk— a combination unfamiliar and strange to our palates.

I exchanged a wary glance with my sister Karen, feeling the weight of our new reality pressing down on us. Our baby brother, Kent, in his innocent longing for the familiar, kept asking for beans to accompany his rice.

"Where's the beans?" he asked, his voice small and hopeful.

Dorothy's expression hardened. "We don't have beans here," she replied curtly, flicking ash from her cigarette with a sharp motion. "This ain't your Momma's house."

At home, Momma would prepare pinto beans and rice with cornbread, turning this simple meal into something special. She had a way of making even the most mundane dishes feel like a treat, sometimes even adding sweet mayonnaise to delight us.

But here, in this unfamiliar kitchen with Dorothy standing over us, those comforts seemed worlds away. We sat in silence, the absence of Momma's warmth and the reality of our new life settling in with each spoonful of the strange meal.

Our new stepsiblings, Alana, Tanya, and Bobby, glared at us from the other side of the table, their expressions ranging from curious to openly hostile. Alana, the oldest, had her mother's sharp features with an added air of superiority. Tanya, the youngest, with her freckled cheeks and bright red hair, appeared indifferent, while Bobby, the middle child, seemed to take pleasure in our discomfort, smirking as he whispered to his sisters.

I felt the tension in the room, knowing that we were outsiders in this house, strangers in what was supposed to be our new home. This was only the beginning of the challenges we would face under Dorothy's roof, where kindness was scarce, and every day felt like a struggle for acceptance and belonging.

Dorothy's delayed response was swift and shocking. She slapped Kent, the force of her hit sending him tumbling off his chair. "I said eat what's in front of you!" she snapped, her voice cold and unforgiving.

Karen and I sat there, petrified, as we witnessed this act of violence. Our stepsiblings, scowling at us since our arrival, exchanged knowing glances, their lips curling into smiles for the first time.

"See what happens when you don't listen?" Alana taunted, her eyes glinting with satisfaction.

Dorothy, with alarming roughness, grabbed Kent by one arm. He let out a frightened yelp as she yanked him to his feet. "Stop whining!" she barked, dragging him toward the back room. The cigarette dangled from her lips, a trail of smoke following her like the ghost-cat.

Kent's cries faded as Dorothy pulled him further away. "Please, no! I want my Momma!" he sobbed.

Karen turned to me, her voice barely above a whisper. "What do we do?"

I shook my head, feeling helpless and scared. "I don't know," I replied, my voice trembling. "I don't know what to do."

The scene felt surreal, a stark contrast to the warmth and care we were used to from Momma, unpredictable as she could be. We had jumped out of the frying pan and into the fire with Dorothy, and now we knew it. Her kitchen table, with its chipped paint and wobbly legs, was more than just a place for meals; it stood as a symbol of the drastic change in our lives, a shabby and unstable situation we had never asked for.

As Karen and I sat there, frozen in disbelief, the aftermath of Hurricane Dorothy lingered in the air. The sense of being unwelcome, of being out of place, was evident, paired with a profound sense of loss and longing for the home we once knew.

Karen whispered, her voice barely audible, "I can't believe this is happening."

I shook my head, my voice a mix of fear and disbelief. "It's like a bad dream we can't wake up from."

Our efforts to avoid the hostile atmosphere of the house led us to hide away, seeking solace in each other's company. But as night fell and we were told to share a bed with Tanya and Alana, our sense of safety further diminished. Earlier that evening, the sleeping arrangements had become a subject of heated discussion. Tanya and Alana expressed their frustration to Dorothy in the dimly lit living room, illuminated by the eerie glow of numerous candles placed throughout the house. These candles, positioned near every cigarette ashtray, were useful not only for lighting new cigarettes but for casting disconcerting shadows that flickered across the walls.

"Why do Karen and PJ have to sleep with us? There's hardly enough room as it is!" Alana complained, her annoyance obvious, "It's not fair! They're not even our real sisters. Why can't they sleep somewhere else?" Tanya added, her voice tinged with bitterness.

Dorothy, her patience thinning, responded sternly, waving her hand dismissively. "Enough! You four will just have to make do. We don't have space to spare, and that's that. Now get ready for bed and no more arguments," she decreed, her voice echoing slightly.

Reluctantly, we followed Tanya and Alana through the house to the bedroom. As we entered, the small full-sized bed, barely large enough for two, became visible. Several cats that had been sleeping on it jumped out, startled by our approach, and disappeared into the shadows. The room was cramped, the air filled with the scent of old fabric and the faintest hint of cat urine.

We arranged ourselves in the bed such that two of us slept at one end and the other two at the opposite end, with our legs and feet touching in the middle. I tried to smile at our new roommates, hoping to befriend them and get them to smile. No such luck—their faces remained unyielding and cold.

That night, whispers in the dark soon turned cruel. I was jolted awake by a searing pain and struggled to comprehend the cause. It was hot candle wax, deliberately poured on me by Tanya and Alana. My screams echoed in the room as I saw them standing over us, their faces devoid of remorse. Deciding to take matters into their own hands, they issued a chilling ultimatum– "Find another place to sleep, or face worse…"

Karen and I retreated to a corner of the room on a makeshift bed of dirty clothes. The night was long and uncomfortable. As I lay my head in Karen's lap, a position that once brought comfort during long car rides, it now served as a meager consolation in this hostile environment. The floor became our refuge, a place free from the threat of hot wax but not from the ongoing intimidation.

"Do you think we'll ever feel safe again?" I whispered, trying to find some solace in Karen's presence.

"I don't know," she replied softly, stroking my hair. "But we have to stay strong, okay?"

As the night unfolded, Karen and I realized we hadn't seen Kent since our arrival. We thought he might be sleeping in Daddy and Dorothy's bedroom, in a crib, but we never saw or heard him.

"Where is Kent?" I asked, worry creeping into my voice. "And why haven't we seen him?"

Karen shook her head, her expression troubled. "I have no idea. It scares me that we haven't heard anything. I thought maybe they'd at least let us see him."

The uncertainty of his whereabouts added to our growing distress. Karen contemplated telling Daddy about what was happening and our concerns for Kent, but the threats from our stepsiblings grew more sinister.

"If you say anything to your Daddy," Tanya warned, her eyes cold and threatening, "Bobby will smother Kent in his sleep."

I felt a chill run through me at the threat, and I looked at Karen, fear etched on her face. "What are we going to do?" I asked, my voice barely above a whisper.

Karen sighed, her resolve hardening. "We keep quiet, for now. We can't risk Kent getting hurt. We'll just have to watch and wait for the right moment."

We clung to each other in the darkness, our minds racing with thoughts of Kent and the danger that loomed over us. The fear of what might happen if we spoke out kept us silent, and the weight of our unspoken worries settled heavily on our small shoulders as we tackled the treacherous terrain of our new life.

That night, after everyone else had fallen asleep, I lay awake in our corner on the floor, haunted by the thought of Kent and his safety. I couldn't shake the feeling that I needed to know he was okay.

I took a deep breath and whispered to Karen, "I need to check on him. I have to make sure Kent's alright."

Karen nodded, her eyes heavy with exhaustion and worry. "Just be careful," she murmured, her voice barely above a whisper.

Slowly, I tiptoed out of our makeshift bed on the floor, careful not to disturb Tanya and Alana, who were sprawled across the bed. I moved quietly through the house, the shadows casting long shapes in the dim light.

I made my way through the kitchen, my heart pounding as I headed in the direction Dorothy had taken Kent in earlier. I approached a closed door and opened it slowly, mindful not to make a sound that might wake anyone.

As I peered into the dark room, I noticed a small television playing an old black-and-white movie, the volume turned down low. I paused for a moment, letting my eyes adjust to the darkness. In the faint glow of the TV, I could make out a large king-size bed with what must have been Dorothy sleeping in it, her form silhouetted against the flickering screen. But there was no sign of Daddy. Where was he, anyway?

My gaze shifted to the corner of the room where I spotted a baby crib. Relief washed over me as I saw Kent, sound asleep, though the sight of him lying there with no blanket or sheets, just a bare mattress, tugged at my heart.

I crept closer, careful not to make a sound, and reached out to check if he was breathing. I sighed with relief as I felt his warm breath on my hand.

"Oh, Kent," I whispered softly, fighting the urge to pick him up and carry him away from this nightmare. "I wish I could take you away from here." But deep down, I knew better.

As I stood by the crib, my eyes were drawn to a door behind it that was slightly ajar. Curiosity got the better of me, and I peered into the room it led to.

There, I saw Bobby sleeping, his body twitching as if caught in the grips of a nightmare. His presence so close to Kent's crib sent a chill down my spine.

"He could hurt him so easily," I thought, my mind racing. I knew I couldn't risk telling anyone about what was happening. It was too easy for Bobby to make good on their threats.

Quietly, I tiptoed back out of the bedroom, the weight of fear heavy in my chest. I returned to our cold spot on the floor, curling up next to Karen. "We can't tell anyone, Karen," I whispered, tears brimming in my eyes. "There's no one we can go to for help. No one." Karen squeezed my hand in silent solidarity, and together we cried ourselves to sleep, the darkness of the night echoing our despair and helplessness.

As Daddy left the next morning, he paused at the door, his face unreadable and tired. "Behave for Dorothy, I have to work late again," he commanded. His tone was dismissive, his eyes briefly meeting mine before he turned away.

I murmured, still in shock from the incident the morning previous. "Dad, she hit Kent..."

He paused, half-turned, and replied flatly, "You kids just need to learn to listen, then."

His words and the swift closing of the door behind him sealed the cold reality to which we were confined. Karen and I exchanged a look, a mix of fear and resolve passing between us. We understood in that moment that any hope for protection from Daddy was as absent as the warmth in Dorothy's kitchen.

Chapter 6

SILENT WOUNDS

The new school year would start soon, the stifling heat fueled the tensions in our new home. One afternoon, as the cicadas droned relentlessly outside, Tanya and Alana cornered me in the sweltering hallway. The heat was oppressive, pressing down on us as Tanya leaned in, her voice low and threatening. "I've got a deal for you," Alana said, her voice unusually soft. Hope flickered briefly in my heart—they were offering a truce. She led me to a dimly lit room where Bobby was waiting, his face marred by a black eye and bruises that made my stomach churn.

"Your Daddy found out what we did and beat Bobby badly," Alana whispered, her eyes glinting with a mixture of fear and vengeance. "Now, Bobby wants to get back at him... through you."

The air thickened with dread as Bobby stepped forward, his grin disturbing. "Just let me hit you a few times, and I won't touch Kent," he bargained, his tone menacing.

Terrified but desperate to protect Kent, I agreed. After all, I had two older brothers so I learned how to take a hit or two, how bad could it be? They shoved me into a tiny bathroom, locking the door behind them. The assault was brutal—slaps threw me to the ground, and blows rained down on my back and head. I curled into a tight ball, the cold tile against my cheek, my arms shielding my head as best I could. I never felt such pain, each blow striking a different part of my body. I thought to myself, "When will this end? Am I going to die?"

When they finally grew tired, their laughter echoed off the walls as they left, leaving me alone with my pain and fear. After a while, I managed to stand, facing my reflection in the cracked bathroom mirror. My nose was bloodied, my eyes swollen—a stark reminder of the brutal reality of my new life. Walking was painful, and I didn't know how to hide this from Karen. When I found her in the kitchen, she took one look at me and knew instantly I was hurt. "That jerk! Why is he so evil?" she stated with dismay. That night, back in our dark corner on the floor, I lay awake, the echoes of my sobs swallowed by the night. I told Karen everything and we came up with a strategy for surviving Bobby's attacks—to curl up and wait it out. I knew that her fierce temper and desire to protect me could make things worse for Kent. Was it Karen who had told Daddy about us sleeping on the floor? I wondered.

Each time Bobby was punished, I knew what was coming. I braced myself for the inevitable—the bathroom would become my prison again. Bobby, with his broad shoulders and that permanent scowl etched across his face, always seemed to carry the weight of Daddy's rejection on his back. And I paid for it.

The door would creak open, and there he'd be, fists clenched, eyes blazing with the fury he couldn't unleash on anyone else. "Get in here," he'd growl, his voice low but terrifying. My stomach twisted with dread, but I didn't dare protest. Resistance only made things worse.

As soon as the door clicked shut, the tension in the small, cramped bathroom would suffocate me. Bobby towered over me, his breath hot and heavy, his rage radiating off him. The first blow would be a punch in the stomach, and I'd bite my lip to stop the scream that tried to escape. I had learned early on that crying only made it last longer. Each slap, punch, kick, or shove carried the weight of everything he hated—Daddy, life, me.

"I told you to stay outta my way!" Bobby would hiss, his voice trembling with rage. His words barely registered, though, as I focused on survival, curling up, making myself as small as possible, hoping he'd get tired quickly.

The walls of that bathroom saw more than any child should endure. The tile was cold against my skin, my body aching from the impact of his punches and kicks, but the worst part was the waiting—the moments before each beating when I could feel the violence coming but couldn't do a thing to stop it.

Every encounter with Bobby left me more hardened, less trusting. I'd stagger out of the bathroom afterward, my face bruised, my body sore, and something inside me just…numb. The innocence I once had was fading, replaced by a hardened shell, the survival instincts of someone too young to have learned them.

"One day, this will be over," I'd whisper to myself, trying to believe it. But deep down, I wasn't sure. Every time I faced that bathroom door, a piece of my childhood slipped away, lost in the brutality of those moments.

"Listen up, you two," Tanya hissed, her eyes darting around to ensure no one else could hear. "Ask Daddy for money, and then give it to us."

Alana crossed her arms, adding, "And don't think about keeping any of it. We'll know."

Karen bit her lip, anxiety flickering across her face. She glanced at me, and I nodded silently, too frightened to argue. We both knew that, for some reason, Daddy always seemed more inclined to fulfill our requests than theirs, but we didn't realize that his compliance was only deepening our troubles.

Later that day, I found Daddy under the kitchen sink, grumbling to himself as he fixed a leak. The moment felt tense, like walking a tightrope. I hesitated, then took a deep breath and asked, "Daddy, can we have some money to buy ice cream?"

He looked up, wiping his brow with the back of his hand. "Sure, pumpkin," he replied with a small smile, reaching for his wallet, and handing me a few bills without a second thought. "Get something nice for you and Karen."

The relief I felt at his easy consent was quickly overshadowed by the dread of what was to come. I could almost feel Karen's tension beside me as we turned away.

Handing the money to Tanya felt like feeding a beast, one that grew more threatening each day. Tanya snatched the bills from my hand, her lips curling into a smirk. "Good girl," she sneered. "You did good."

In this house, where hostility overshadowed kindness, Karen and I faced each day with caution, always mindful of the looming threats over our heads. Soon, Tanya and Alana began demanding that we fetch ice cream from the Dairy Queen just a block away. They seemed to enjoy sending us on these errands, to assert their control.

"We want two Blizzards, and make sure they don't melt on the way back, or you'll regret it," Alana instructed one sweltering afternoon, her tone sharp.

Karen and I didn't mind the errands initially, as it seemed like we were just getting treats for ourselves, which might look innocuous to Daddy if he noticed. As we sprinted down the street, the cold treats threatening to drip down our hands, Karen whispered to me, "Do you think they'll ever leave us alone?"

I shook my head, panting from the heat and the fear. "I don't know. But we can't let them melt," I replied, my voice a mix of determination and dread.

We resisted the urge to lick the ice cream, knowing well that any sign of melting would ignite more anger from Tanya and Alana— an outcome we desperately wanted to avoid. Each sprint back from Dairy Queen became a tense race against the sun, our hearts pounding not just from the running but from the fear of the consequences if we failed in our task. "Faster, PJ," Karen urged, her breath coming in short gasps. "We can't let them catch us with melting ice cream. Who knows what they will do to Kent?" This small act of fetching ice cream, seemingly harmless, was covered with the heavy burden of potential risks, further emphasizing the constant state of vigilance and submission we lived in.

I remembered the songs we sang about Jesus and how much God loved all the little children during Vacation Bible School at church, a special event we attended each summer. There, yummy cookies and fruit punch made it a perfect week, a stark contrast to our usual sporadic Sunday visits, which I always dreaded. The dread came partly because it meant I had to brush my long, thick brown hair, a task I skillfully avoided by brushing just the very outside to make it look neat while hiding a mass of knots underneath. Mom would often find me wrestling with the tangles and threaten, "I'm going to cut it all off if you don't take better care of it." Her voice was stern as she tried to tame my unruly hair. She never did cut it until I started getting frequent headaches, and Granny suggested it might be because of the weight of my heavy hair. So, it was cut short. No more painful tangles, but I hated my new look.

Ann, seeing my distress, said she had prayed for my headaches to go away. "God made it happen," she told me, trying to offer comfort. "Sometimes bad things happen in order for things to get better."

I didn't fully understand it then, but this thought revisited me each time harsher circumstances in our new home happened. "Did this mean that things would get better?" I often wondered.

Things took a more menacing turn over a pair of pink socks. Tanya, coveting the lace-trimmed socks my Momma had given me—one of my few cherished possessions—demanded them.

"Give me those socks," Tanya ordered, her eyes filled with envy.

I shook my head, clutching them tightly. "No, they're mine! Momma gave them to me," I replied, my voice defiant yet scared.

Tanya's expression turned dark. "If you won't give them up, you'll regret it," she hissed menacingly.

That night, they locked me in the hall closet, a dark, cramped space with an attic door above. They had filled my mind with stories of the devil that lived there, ready to devour me if I dared to make a sound. "You'll never last the night," Alana taunted, closing the closet door and leaving me in darkness. Paralyzed with fear, I remained motionless and silent, too terrified to call for help. Exhaustion eventually took over, and I fell asleep, spending the entire night in that closet.

The next morning, Karen, frantic with worry, found me. "PJ! Are you okay? I looked everywhere for you!" she exclaimed as she opened the closet door, her face flooded with relief and concern.

I blinked against the sudden light from the hallway, the contrast blinding after the darkness. "I'm okay," I croaked, my voice barely audible.

"What happened?" Karen asked, helping me out of the cramped space.

"They locked me in," I whispered, my voice trembling. "I didn't mean to fall asleep. I was just so scared." Her discovery brought an end to my night of terror, but the ordeal wasn't over. We cleaned up quietly, erasing any evidence of the incident and the accident I had had, unable to reach the bathroom. We agreed not to tell anyone, fearing it might only worsen our situation. "Will this nightmare ever end?" I wondered aloud as we straightened the house, trying to return it to normal.

Karen put her arm around me. "We just have to be strong, PJ. We'll get through this somehow," she assured me, her voice filled with determination.

"Where is Jesus in all this?" I muttered, more to myself than to Karen. I had sung "Jesus loves me" to myself in that dark closet, just like I used to in church, yet it felt like no one was there to save me. "Maybe He doesn't love me like the other little children." I said with tears in my eyes.

We needed to find a way to survive, to endure this life that felt more like a bad dream. As we continued our daily routines, Ann's words about hardship and change lingered in my mind, a faint hope that, in time, things would indeed get better.

Karen and I discovered a secret place—a hollowed-out tree with enough space to climb inside and ascend to the top. One hot afternoon, we stumbled upon it while exploring the edges of our yard. "Look at this, Karen!" I called out, peering into the wide trunk. "I bet we could fit inside!"

Karen's eyes lit up with curiosity. "Let's see how high we can climb!" In that tree, we found a semblance of peace, a brief escape from the relentless cruelty of our reality. It was our sanctuary, a place where we could be just kids, if only for a moment, away from the harsh world that awaited us beyond its protective bark.

Inside, the air was cool and earthy, a stark contrast to the oppressive heat outside. It became our refuge, our haven from the horrors of the house. Hidden within its trunk, I would climb as high as possible and cry, longing for the comforting presence of my oldest sister, Ann, wishing she were there to stroke my hair and soothe my fears.

"Do you think Ann misses us?" I asked Karen one day as we sat perched in our secret spot.

Karen nodded, her voice wistful. "I'm sure she does. But she's got her own life now."

Ann's absence weighed heavily on my heart. Her memory represented another missing piece of normalcy and love in a life that had become anything but.

I remember the day I first saw her with Ernie, her boyfriend, at her apartment. I had innocently ridden my bike over, as I often did, only to walk in on them kissing. "Ann!" I exclaimed, startled by the scene before me.-

Ann jumped, pulling away from Ernie, her cheeks flushed. "Oh, shoot! PJ, what are you doing here?"

Her reaction was a stark reminder of how much our lives were changing. "I just wanted to see you," I said, feeling a bit awkward. "I miss you, Ann."

She softened, coming over to give me a hug. "I miss you too, PJ," she said, smoothing my hair. "But things are different now. You know that, right?"

I nodded, understanding, yet not fully accepting. Ann's move to her own apartment and her journey into adulthood, with college and a relationship, contrasted sharply with the tumultuous lives we were living. She was stepping into a new phase of life, one filled with hope and possibilities, while the rest of us seemed to be sinking deeper into chaos. "Is Ernie nice?" I asked, glancing over at him.

Ann chuckled, her face lighting up. "Yeah, he's nice. You'll like him."

Ernie waved, giving me a friendly smile. "Hey there, PJ. Heard a lot about you."

Despite the warmth of their home, the visit left me with a bittersweet feeling. As I rode my bike back to our own chaotic world, I couldn't shake the sense of being left behind, the gap between our lives growing wider with each passing day. In the tree, with Karen beside me, I clung to the hope that things might change, that we could find our own way out of the darkness. But for now, the hollow tree was our haven, our shared secret, and the one place where we could let our imaginations soar and find comfort in each other.

We also thought about Lynn and how he had his own battles to face. After a stint in jail, he had moved in with a friend, eager to escape the hostile environment at home. His relationship with Daddy was strained, marred by constant conflict and aggression, especially when Richard, seeking attention and Daddy's favorite, would tattle on him.

"Why do you always have to make things worse, Richard?" Lynn snapped one evening after a particularly heated argument with Daddy.

"I'm just telling him what he needs to know," Richard retorted, his thin frame tense with defiance. Despite Richard's bravado, there was always a vulnerability in his eyes, a hint of the young boy thrust too early into the responsibilities of adulthood.

I remembered the disturbing scenes of both parents punishing the boys, their anger toward each other spilling over onto them. Richard, on the other hand, refused to join us in Lufkin.

His disdain for Dorothy was evident. Still in high school, he juggled his studies with a job and his newfound interest in playing the guitar. But beneath his independent exterior was a deep-seated resentment towards Momma for abandoning him. His loneliness was evident, a young boy thrust too early into the responsibilities of adulthood.

Despite his anger and the distance, he tried to maintain, I suspected that Daddy was keeping an eye on Richard, offering some support. Richard had Granny next door in addition to occasional visits from Daddy, who brought food and anything else he might need.

"Hey, got you some groceries and I brought you some new guitar strings," Daddy would say during his visits, trying to bridge the gap with practical support, even if his presence was fleeting.

"Yeah, thanks," Richard muttered, his gratitude tinged with the residual bitterness of feeling left behind.

"Have you been practicing?" Daddy asked, trying to spark a conversation.

Richard shrugged; his eyes focused on the guitar strings in his hands. "I try to, when I'm not working."

Daddy nodded, his expression softening for a moment. "Keep it up. You've got talent, kid."

These reflections on my siblings, each dealing with their own struggles and paths, filled me with a mix of sadness and longing. Our family, once a chaotic but united front, was now scattered, each of us grappling with the fallout of our fractured home in our own ways. The longing for a semblance of the love and security we once shared was a constant ache in my heart.

"I wish things were different," I confided to Karen one afternoon as we sat under our favorite tree. "I miss when we were all together, even if it was crazy."

Karen's gaze was distant. "Me too, PJ. We may never see happiness again."

In those moments, I realized that no matter how far apart we were, the bond we shared as siblings was unbreakable, a thread of love and resilience that kept us connected despite the distance and difficulties.

Chapter 7

A MOTHER'S INTERVENTION

The occasional visits from Momma with little Cherrie became like beacons of light in the dark world we lived in. Staying at a hotel, just the five of us, felt like a brief escape to a happier, safer place. "Look what I've brought you!" Momma exclaimed each time, her arms filled with gifts. Her eyes reflected a mix of joy and underlying guilt. Her presence filled us with a sense of hope and anticipation, a break from the harsh reality of Daddy's house.

She often talked about moving us to Huntsville, painting a picture of a new life away from Daddy's house. "It'll be a fresh start for all of us," she would say, her voice tinged with a hopeful tone that seemed more for her reassurance than ours.

Despite everything, Karen and I chose to keep the truth from Momma. We could tell she felt bad, and her visits seemed to be her way of easing her own guilt and shame. "We shouldn't worry her more, right?" Karen whispered to me one night, her face shadowed by the dim hotel lamp. "It's already hard enough for her."

"Yeah, and we can't risk Kent getting hurt," I murmured in agreement, feeling the weight of our secret tighten around my heart.

Even though we never saw Kent at Daddy's house, Momma always brought him with her to the hotel. Kent was almost five years old, but he had stopped talking completely. I remembered how he used to chatter away, full of stories and questions before the move to Daddy's. Now, his silence was a stark contrast to the lively boy he once was, but Momma didn't seem to notice the change. Karen tried to coax him, saying, "Can you say 'mama', Kent?" But he just stared with wide eyes, clutching his stuffed bear tightly.

Momma laughed, brushing off our concerns. "He's just shy, give him some time," she said, ruffling Kent's thick, brown, curls. But I saw the way Karen looked at him, worry etched into her face.

Cherrie was growing, too. She had more freckles on her face than any of us, and her dirty blonde hair was getting long and straight as a board, but thin at the same time. She was hyper and ran all over the place, her energy a stark contrast to Kent's silence. She was always laughing, her freckled face lighting up as she darted around the room.

"Cherrie, slow down!" Momma would call out, a smile tugging at her lips despite the chaos. "You're gonna wear yourself out." Cherrie would giggle, pausing only for a moment before resuming her play.

"Can't catch me!" she'd tease, dodging around the furniture. We wanted to enjoy the time with Momma and Cherrie while we could, savoring these moments of reprieve. Each goodbye was a silent pact between us not to share the darker parts of our lives, to protect her as much as she wanted to protect us.

When it was time to return to Daddy's, each farewell with Momma became a heart-wrenching struggle. As she prepared to leave, I felt the familiar surge of desperation and sadness. "Please, don't go yet," I whispered, my voice choked with emotion as I clung to her, feeling the warmth of her embrace for what seemed like the last time.

Momma hugged me tighter, her own eyes glistening with unshed tears. "Oh, my sweeties, I wish I could take you with me now," she murmured, her voice heavy with sorrow.

As she released us and walked back to her car, I fought the overwhelming urge to run after her, to scream out everything. I wanted to shout with every fiber of my being, "Momma, they hurt us, and it's not safe for us here!" But the words stuck in my throat as I watched her car pull away, disappearing down the road.

Turning to walk back into the house, my heart felt heavy with unspoken fears. I knew Alana, Tanya, and Bobby were lurking inside, eager to snatch away any joy we might have found in Momma's gifts. It was a fleeting moment of happiness to enjoy the gifts while we could, but we were all too soon baptized in a colder reality. Karen squeezed my hand, her presence a small comfort against the returning dread. "Let's stay strong," she said softly, her voice a mix of resilience and resignation. The emotional toll of the farewell hung in the air like a thick fog, marking the end of our brief escape and the return to our uncertain lives.

Starting second grade added a layer of unease to the complex landscape of my life. The classroom was intimidating and, at times, painful. Our teacher, Mrs. Gamble, enforced strict discipline with a wooden ruler for minor infractions like forgetting homework or speaking out of turn. The sharp pops of the ruler on our hands were a common ordeal, often leaving blisters and marks. It was a harsh introduction to a world where the warmth of home was replaced by the cold sting of authority.

One afternoon, as I sat at the kitchen table with Momma during one of her visits, she noticed the blisters on my hands. She frowned, reaching for my hand.

"What happened here?" she asked, her voice soft yet edged with concern.

I hesitated, then admitted, "Mrs. Gamble hits us with a ruler when we forget our homework."

Momma's eyes narrowed with indignation, but I could see a flicker of annoyance, too. "Oh, really?" she said, her tone a mix of anger and exasperation. "You know, you really should try to remember your homework. I can't keep coming down here to sort out every little issue," she added, her voice suggesting such matters were more an inconvenience to her than anything else.

Despite her initial reluctance, Momma decided to accompany me to school the next day. I could tell she was driven by the visible evidence of the harsh discipline I endured. As we approached Mrs. Gamble before class, the tension in the air was thick.

"Mrs. Gamble," Momma began sternly, "I want to talk about how you're treating my child." Mrs. Gamble looked up, taken aback by the confrontation.

She adjusted her glasses nervously and started to defend her actions. "It's standard practice for…"

"I don't care what's standard," Momma cut her off, her voice rising with fierce determination. "You will not lay another finger on my child. Are we clear? No more rulers, no more marks."

Mrs. Gamble, visibly shaken and intimidated by Momma's protective demeanor, quickly agreed to stop the physical punishment. Her earlier confidence seemed to shrink under Momma's unwavering gaze.

After that tense encounter, I began receiving the reading award every week, a stark turnaround from my earlier treatment. Mrs. Gamble was eager to avoid any further confrontations, perhaps out of fear of repercussions or maybe because she realized there was somebody who loved me enough to fight for me.

During one of Momma's visits after school had started, she brought me a bag of school supplies. Her gesture felt a bit perfunctory, as if she were checking off a box on her to-do list. "Here's some stuff for school," she said nonchalantly, handing us the bag. "Make sure you use these to keep up with your work. I can't keep fixing things for you."

"Thanks, Momma," I replied, recognizing her love had its limits but grateful for what she could give. As she hugged us goodbye, her parting words were brief and to the point: "Take care of your things and try not to get into trouble. I've got enough on my plate."

With the new supplies in hand but a hollow feeling inside, Karen and I faced school with determination. Momma's visits and the lingering sense of her love felt increasingly overshadowed by her focus on her own needs, leaving us to face the complexities of our young lives with a growing sense of independence and resilience.

School did bring a sweet distraction in the form of a blonde-haired, blue-eyed boy who sat across from me in class. He had a playful habit of tapping my toes with his, calling them "toe-kisses," which always sent a wave of heat across my cheeks each time he flashed a smile at me. "Stop it," I'd whisper, grinning despite myself. "I can't help it," he'd tease back, his eyes twinkling with mischief.

One morning, as Karen and I walked to school with our stepsiblings, we approached a hill leading to an overpass. The bottom of the hill was a mess of green slime from a constant leak that dribbled over the sidewalk. It was slippery, slimy, and unavoidable. "I bet I can jump it," I declared, feeling bold.

"PJ, don't!" Karen warned, but I was already running.

In my attempt to jump over it, reminiscent of my earlier escapades, I slipped and fell into the wet mess, my pants soaked and tinted green. With no time to walk back and change, I was mortified at the prospect of arriving at school with a wet backside, echoing the embarrassment I felt in first grade when I got my knee stuck between a pole and a wall. This time, thankfully, there was no need for the fire department, but the anticipation of my peers' laughter weighed heavily on me.

"Great," I muttered, trying to brush off the slimy mess. "Just great." Mrs. Gamble, noticing my condition, sent me to the front office and called Dorothy, who responded with her usual indifference.

"I have to work," she said flatly, offering no help.

The school nurse offered me a pair of jeans that were comically large, barely staying up as I walked back to class. As I rounded the corner, my heart lifted in sheer relief and joy at the sight of Momma, holding a fresh outfit for me to change into.

"Hey, sweetheart," Momma said warmly, her presence washing away my embarrassment. "Let's get you cleaned up." She even took the time to brush my hair and tie it into a ponytail, adding with a smile, "How about a touch of my lipstick? Just for today."

As she carefully applied the lipstick, I gazed into the mirror, the transformation from a morning of mishaps to a moment of unexpected joy with Momma's surprise visit, making it all feel like a distant memory. I couldn't recall ever feeling such happiness and relief in her presence. This unsolicited rescue was a rare and cherished gesture that warmed my heart deeply, reminding me of the layers of love hidden beneath our complicated family dynamics.

As the school year ended, the joy of daily distractions faded, and the impending summer loomed over us like a dark cloud. The absence of school meant more time at home, more time exposed to the unpredictable cruelty and physical abuse that marred our daily lives.

Karen and I dreaded the coming months, knowing that the respite provided by school hours would be replaced by long days under the watchful and often hostile eyes of Alana, Tanya, and Bobby. The thought of another summer filled with fear and pain was almost unbearable, and we clung to each other, our bond a small beacon of hope in the threatening storm.

"Maybe we can find a way out," Karen said one evening, her voice barely above a whisper. "Maybe things will get better." I nodded, clinging to that fragile hope, even as doubt crept in. The summer stretched ahead of us, a daunting challenge we could only face together.

The weekend after my embarrassing fall, I came home to hear Dorothy on the phone in the kitchen. Momma must have called because I could hear her voice too. Dorothy spoke with her usual indifference, "Yeah, I told the school I can't be there. I have work to do. Those kids need to handle their own mess."

I paused by the door, not wanting to intrude but also too curious to walk away. I heard Momma's voice, slightly raised, cutting through Dorothy's words. "I'm sure you're busy, Dorothy, but those kids are trying their best. You might want to help them when they need it."

Dorothy scoffed, lighting a cigarette. "They're not my responsibility, Patsy."

Momma's tone softened but carried an edge. "They are while they're in your house."

Hearing her defend us, even a little, made something tighten in my chest. It wasn't much, but it was more than I'd ever expected from Momma in a conversation with Dorothy. I slipped away before they saw me, the words lingering like a soft promise. Maybe things wouldn't change overnight, but Momma was there. She knew, she noticed, and in some small way, she tried to fight for us, even if it was just in conversation.

That evening, as I lay in bed beside Karen, I whispered what I'd overheard. "Momma talked to Dorothy about us."

Karen turned toward me, surprised, and there was a flicker of hope in her eyes. "Really?" she asked.

"Yeah," I nodded, "she was saying we're trying and that we need help."

Karen let out a soft sigh, "Maybe she'll keep trying."

"Maybe," I agreed, holding onto that hope. We lay there in the dark, side by side, the quiet warmth of our shared understanding making the night feel a little less cold.

Chapter 8

BREAKING FREE

We had three dogs that lived outside in the backyard, which were fenced and wrapped around the side of the house. One afternoon, I noticed Bobby pulling something off their backs and wrapping it in a piece of paper before setting it on fire. Curious and horrified, I crept closer to see what he was doing.

"What are you doing, Bobby?" I asked, my voice trembling.

"Watch this," Bobby said with a twisted grin, holding up the paper-wrapped object. "It's a tick, filled with the dogs' blood. When the fire hits, it explodes."

I watched in disgust as he set the paper on fire, and the tick exploded with a small pop. Bobby enjoyed this very much, while I thought it was so gross.

As each dog walked away from me, I could see hundreds of white, blood-filled ticks raised on their backs. It was terrible. We had ticks on us, too. Their invasive presence was so painful; I felt so bad for the dogs.

One evening, I gathered the courage to ask Daddy for help. "Daddy, can you do something about the dogs? They have so many ticks."

He barely looked up from his newspaper. "I don't want anything to do with those dogs. I didn't want them anyway." Disheartened, I did everything I could to avoid seeing the dogs, torn between wanting to help them and not knowing how. The sight of them covered in ticks haunted me, and I wished I could do something to ease their suffering.

Then, one day, they were just gone. The backyard felt emptier, and I was left with a mix of relief and guilt, wondering what had happened to them and if they had found some peace away from the torment of ticks. Bobby stormed up to me, his face twisted with anger.

"You killed my dogs..." he accused, his voice low and menacing.

"What? I didn't..." I stammered, confused, and scared.

"Mom told me you said something to your Daddy. So, he took them 'hunting,' and now they're gone," Bobby spat out, his eyes filled with hatred. "A life for a life," he added ominously.

I felt a chill run down my spine as I saw the intensity of his anger. I knew he meant every word. Trembling, I ran to find Karen.

"Karen! Bobby's blaming me for the dogs," I cried. "He said Daddy took them hunting and now they're gone," I said, my voice shaking. "He says it's all my fault!"

Karen's eyes widened in fear. "We have to tell Momma. Maybe she'll come and get us," she said, trying to stay calm but clearly just as frightened. We clung to the hope that Momma would arrive soon and take us away from this place, away from Bobby's threats and the cruelty that surrounded us.

That night, after Bobby's threat about the dogs, the darkness brought a new level of horror. I woke to the feeling of something burning hot being poured on us, and a scream tore from my throat as pain seared through my skin.

Bobby stood over us, his face twisted with glee as, once again, red-hot candle wax was poured onto our bodies. "It's the dogs' blood," he sneered, his voice filled with malice. Karen and I cried out in pain, trying to shield ourselves from his relentless torment.

But he wasn't finished. As I lay there, paralyzed by fear and agony, Bobby wrapped a rope around my neck and began dragging me across the room, laughing maniacally. "You're just like those dogs, PJ. Worthless and easy to get rid of," he taunted, his grip tightening.

I struggled against the rope trying to breathe, tears streaming down my face. "Please, Bobby, stop! You're hurting me, I can't breathe!" I cried, my voice breaking with desperation.

I heard Karen gasp, her voice barely audible. "Please, Bobby, stop it!" she pleaded, her hands clutching the edge of the bed in desperation.

Just then, I heard footsteps approaching, a flicker of hope igniting in my chest. Surely it was Daddy coming to stop this madness. But when the door opened, it was Dorothy who stood there, a cigarette dangling from her lips, her blue eyes cold and amused.

"What's going on here?" Dorothy drawled, her voice dripping with indifference. She took in the scene, Bobby with the rope and the wax, and smirked. "Don't wake your Daddy," she warned, her voice a mockery of concern. "You'll have hell to pay if you do. Continue with your fun, but quietly."

She turned and left, the door clicking shut behind her, leaving us trapped in Bobby's cruelty. My heart sank as I realized there would be no rescue tonight, only the continuation of our torment. "I'm so scared," Karen whimpered, her voice breaking. "I wish Momma would come and take us away from here."

"Just keep breathing" I thought to myself. I don't remember the horror ending, everything went black.

The next morning, I was left bruised and exhausted, the events of the night before weighing heavily on my mind as I tried to get the hardened wax out of my hair. Bobby peeked in. "Oh. You're still alive." he said casually, coolly.

But a glimmer of hope came in the form of Momma's unexpected call. "Pack all your things. Your Momma is coming, she's moving you to Huntsville." Dorothy said, her voice cold and unfeeling.

Karen and I didn't need to be told twice. We scrambled to gather our belongings, stuffing everything we owned into the single suitcase we'd brought with us to Lufkin. There was no time to waste and no time to look back.

Journal Entry - August 25, 1992

Reflecting on my past, the move from Lufkin with Daddy to Huntsville with Momma stands out as a turning point filled with both hope and trauma. Therapy with Barbara has been a lifeline, guiding me through these turbulent memories. She often talks about a divine plan that encompasses all our experiences—a concept that offers both comfort and confusion, especially as I grapple with the profound feelings of shame and brokenness that stem from that period.

During our sessions, Barbara suggested trying antidepressants to complement our therapy. The thought of medication is uncertain, but if it can help lift the weight of my emotions, I'm willing to give it a try. Revisiting those memories has been painful. The trauma of living with Daddy in Lufkin, marked by neglect and abuse, left deep scars. The transition to Huntsville with Momma, though a relief in many ways, brought its own set of challenges.

When we first arrived in Huntsville, the change was overwhelming. Momma was determined to create a better life for us, but the wounds from Lufkin were still fresh. Starting school in this unfamiliar environment was intimidating. I remember feeling lost and unsure, trying to adapt while carrying the memories of my past.

During this time, I experienced something that shifted my perspective dramatically. Visiting a friend's home for the first time, I was struck by the contrast to my own life. Their house was clean, organized, and filled with warmth and comfort—a sharp contrast to my home. It was a moment of profound realization that not everyone lived the way I did.

For the first time, I felt a deep sense of shame and anger. I resented the filth and disorder that defined my home life. The seeds of hate and resentment began to grow as I recognized the neglect and the differences between my world and theirs. This realization was painful, stirring emotions I hadn't fully understood before. Emotions I would carry throughout my life, even now with the personal loss of Kyle's father with a divorce. Guilt and shame gnaw at me daily. Was I not good enough? Could I have done something different? This self-blame is a heavy burden, making me feel inadequate as both a partner and a mother. I worry about the impact his absence will have on Kyle and fear that I am responsible for this void in his life.

Despite these struggles, my commitment to Kyle remains unwavering. He is my driving force, my reason to push through the pain and uncertainties. I am determined to provide him with a life filled with love and stability, something I fear I failed to do by not being able to keep his father in our lives. I don't want Kyle to experience the kind of childhood I had—marked by fear and neglect.

As I prepare to delve deeper into my memories of those initial days in Huntsville and starting school, I hope to uncover the strength and resilience that got me through. This journey in therapy is not just about healing myself;

it's about becoming the mother Kyle needs—strong, loving, and whole. It's about overcoming my guilt, breaking the cycle of pain, and building a brighter future for us both, without fear.

Those early days in Huntsville, my initial experiences with Momma, and the challenges of starting school in a new place is where my journey towards believing the lies began, where the harsh realities of my home life clashed with the outside world, and where the seeds of hate began to take root.

Chapter 9

PLAYING HOUSE

The move to Huntsville with Momma marked the beginning of a new chapter, one that promised a semblance of the happiness for which we'd been yearning. Momma managed to rent a mobile home about ten miles outside of Huntsville, nestled in a small trailer park where the homes stood in a neat row, like soldiers at attention. Karen and I shared one bedroom, while Kent and Cherrie occupied the other. Kent, who had fallen silent during our time in Lufkin, brightened up in this unfamiliar environment. Momma, with a mix of hope and concern, asked him if he liked his new room. He nodded, still not ready to speak.

That summer had been all about moving away from Daddy's place in Lufkin and settling into our new life with Momma in Huntsville. As the summer ended, the new school year brought a mix of relief and anxiety. Karen's tension with Momma surfaced quickly. When Momma asked about Kent's silence, Karen's response had been sharp and laced with underlying resentment. "Nothing, Momma, because we protected him since you weren't there."

I could sense the conflict brewing. As Karen stormed off, I broke down and told Momma everything about our time in Lufkin. Her reaction was one I hadn't expected.

"Why didn't you tell me before?" Momma yelled, tears streaming down her face.

"We were scared!" I replied, my voice trembling. "Karen said we couldn't tell anyone."

Karen, emerging from the bedroom, confronted Momma with the harsh truth about why we had kept silent. "They threatened Kent's life, Momma. We were terrified!"

Momma's demeanor shifted from anger to heartbreak. She pulled me into her arms, repeatedly apologizing. "I'm so sorry, baby! I'm so sorry I wasn't there to protect you."

All I could think about was comforting her, assuring her that we had managed, despite everything. Kent's innocent request for food broke the heavy atmosphere, and I quickly shifted to a cheerful tone, hoping to lift his spirits. Momma cooked us a meal of fried eggs and homemade biscuits, a simple yet incredibly comforting feast.

For the first time in a long time, we felt safe, and the relief of having shared our burdens with Momma added to the warmth of the moment. However, Momma's expression, distant and tinged with anger, made me anxious. Remembering her confrontation with my teacher, Mrs. Gamble, I worried about what she might do to Daddy and Dorothy. Voicing my concern, I pleaded with her not to do anything drastic. Her response, though cryptic, was reassuring.

"I won't kill them honey, but just remember that what goes around comes around…seven times fold." I wondered what she meant by that, but at that moment, I was just relieved to hear her say she wouldn't retaliate.

In that small mobile home in Huntsville, surrounded by my siblings and Momma, I felt a glimmer of hope. Despite the uncertainties and the past struggles, for the first time in a long while, I felt like we might just be okay. In those days, with

Momma working tirelessly as a waitress at a restaurant called The Kettle; Karen and I were often left to look after Kent and Cherrie. Momma didn't seem to like her job much. She would come home weary, her feet aching from standing all day, and her face lined with fatigue.

She often shared her frustrations with us, saying, "I work on my feet all day long, and the people I work with are always wanting me to work more hours." Her coworkers frequently pressured her to take on additional shifts, but she couldn't because of her commitment to us. "I need to be here for you kids," she would say, her voice a mix of determination and exhaustion. The responsibility of caring for Kent and Cherrie fell to Karen and me, and while we did our best, it was a challenging time for all of us, trying to balance the demands of our family with the absence of our overworked Momma.

Our childhood was far from typical, marked by responsibilities and fears too big for our young shoulders. One of our most vivid and frightening memories began on an otherwise ordinary day. The sun had just begun to set, casting long shadows across our small house, when a man from down the road—someone who quickly became the source of our nightmares—approached our home. We were inside, playing with Kent and Cherrie, when we heard footsteps crunching on the gravel outside. Peering through the window, we saw him moving methodically around the house, checking each window and door, his intentions clear.

Panic set in as he tested the lock on the front door. Our hearts pounded, and we felt trapped, unsure of what to do. Karen, though just as scared as the rest of us, managed to summon a burst of bravery. She ran to the window and shouted, "We've got a gun, mister!" Her voice, filled with a mix of fear and determination, echoed through the evening air. To our immense relief, her words stopped him in his tracks. He hesitated, glanced around nervously, and then retreated down the road.

In the aftermath of that terrifying encounter, we struggled to cope with the lingering fear. To make it more manageable, we created the "Mean Man" game. It became our way of transforming our fear into something less threatening, something we could control. We'd run and hide, screaming, "The Mean Man is coming! The Mean Man is coming!" The game, filled with laughter and excitement, provided a brief respite from the constant anxiety that plagued us.

Despite these games and moments of childhood imagination, the stark reality of our situation couldn't be ignored. We were just kids, thrust into roles far beyond our years. We found ourselves as caretakers, protectors, and, in many ways, parents to our younger siblings. The weight of these responsibilities was heavy, and the fear of another encounter with the "Mean Man" always loomed in the back of our minds.

When Momma finally returned home from work, exhausted from her day, we gathered the courage to tell her what had happened.

"Momma, you'll never believe…," I began, my voice still shaky from the adrenaline of the encounter.

She sighed heavily, rubbing her temples as she sat down at the kitchen table. "What now, Honey?"

"There was a man trying to get in! Karen scared him off by yelling we had a gun!" I explained, hoping for some comfort.

Karen chimed in, "We were so scared, Momma! He was trying every door and window!"

Momma looked at us with tired eyes, the weariness of her day apparent. "I'm sure it was nothing," she dismissed, waving her hand as if brushing away an annoying fly. "Just someone passing by. You're all fine, aren't you?"

"But Momma, what if he comes back?" I insisted, feeling the frustration build.

"I don't have time for this, kids! I've got work to do and mouths to feed. I can't worry about every little thing that happens when I'm not here!" she replied sharply.

Her words stung, leaving us feeling like a burden rather than a joy. It was clear that our fears and experiences were secondary to the exhaustion she experienced from work. Karen and I exchanged glances, the weight of our existence pressing down on us, as we realized we had to make it in this world on our own. Momma's fatigue and indifference were yet another reminder of the isolation we felt in our young lives.

Our environment was chaotic, lacking the structure and guidance that only a parent could provide. Each day began with Momma waking up before dawn, slipping quietly out of the house to begin her long shift at The Kettle.

"I'll be back late," she whispered before leaving, her voice tinged with exhaustion.

Karen and I were left to get ourselves and our younger siblings ready for school. Our mornings were a flurry of activity— scrambling to find clean clothes, packing lunches, and making sure Kent and Cherrie were fed and dressed. One of the most stressful parts of our routine was waiting for Cherrie's daycare shuttle to arrive.

"Please let it come before the bus," Karen would mutter under her breath, checking the clock for the hundredth time. If the daycare shuttle didn't arrive before the bus, we would have to miss school. The anxiety was nerve-wracking, knowing our entire day depended on whether Cherrie's ride showed up on time.

One morning, as I rummaged through the laundry basket, I heard Kent scream, "I don't want to wear those shoes!" He flung them across the room, his small face red with anger.

Karen, already stressed from trying to make breakfast, snapped back, "Kent, just put them on! We don't have time for this!" Her sharp tone made him cry harder, and I could see the frustration building in her eyes.

Cherrie spilled cereal all over the floor. "I'm hungry!" she wailed, tears streaming down her face.

I grabbed a towel to clean up the mess, my patience wearing thin. "Cherrie, calm down. I'll get you more cereal," I said, trying to soothe her while feeling the pressure of the morning rush.

School provided a brief escape from the chaos at home, but it also highlighted the stark differences between our lives and those of our classmates. Seeing their orderly routines and attentive parents often made our situation feel even more desperate. After school, we returned to an empty house and a list of never-ending chores.

"Let's get this done before Momma gets home," Karen would say, her voice carrying a sense of urgency. Despite our best efforts, the dishes piled up, laundry overflowed, and the house was never quite clean. "I hate this," Karen confided to me one night after we had put Kent and Cherrie to bed. "We shouldn't have to do all of this."

I nodded in agreement, feeling the weight of her words. "I know," I whispered. "It's not fair."

The responsibility of looking after our siblings, the constant worry about our safety, and the longing for a semblance of normalcy shaped us in profound and lasting ways. We were angry and confused little children, raising other angry and confused children, all while trying to survive a world that seemed relentlessly harsh and unforgiving.

Chapter 10

RICHARD'S RETURN

Life in Huntsville came with its own challenges, but one weekend, Richard showed up unexpectedly while Momma was at work. He had graduated high school early and gotten a job doing construction work in Nacogdoches. We were so excited to see him, and for the first time in a long while, I felt safe.

"Richard!" I shouted, running to hug him as he stepped inside the door. He grinned widely, hugging me back. "Hey there, cutie! I missed you guys," he said, ruffling my hair. Karen and Kent ran over, their faces lighting up at the sight of him.

"What are you doing here?" Karen asked, her voice filled with excitement. "Thought I'd come by and see my favorite siblings," Richard replied, setting down the guitar he had brought with him.

He played songs for us that he was learning and even shared some he was writing himself. We listened in awe as his fingers moved skillfully over the strings, and his voice filled the room with warmth. "This one's a work in progress," he said, strumming a few chords.

When Richard played a song, I didn't know the words to, I started whistling along with the tune. Richard grinned and stopped playing for a moment. "Hey, remember when I taught you to whistle?" he asked, chuckling.

"And how you got us both in trouble at church?" Richard laughed, adding, "Yeah, you were whistling during the prayer! Momma was furious."

I grinned, feeling a surge of happiness from the memory. "I thought I was saving Momma's soul!"

Richard laughed heartily, shaking his head. "Well, you definitely saved us from boredom that day," he joked, his eyes twinkling with amusement.

We all laughed together, that church incident feeling like a lifetime ago. The laughter brought us closer, bridging the gap that had grown between us over time and distance. Afterward, we played games together. Richard had us giggling with his antics, lying on the floor, pretending to be asleep, while we sneaked around him, trying not to wake him. Suddenly, he would spring to life, grabbing us amid squeals of laughter. "Gotcha!" he shouted, tickling us until we couldn't breathe from laughing so hard.

It felt like old times, a reminder of the love and joy that once filled our family.

When Momma got home, she was surprised to see him.

"Well, look who finally decided to show up," she remarked in an unwelcoming tone. She didn't hug him, and the warmth of the day quickly cooled.

"Hey, Momma," Richard said, trying to keep his tone light. "Thought I'd surprise everyone."

But the atmosphere turned tense when Richard noticed the near-empty pantry.

"Momma why isn't there any food in the house?" he asked, a hint of concern in his voice.

She sighed, dismissing his worry. "I'm working my tail off, Richard. You could stay and help us if you're so worried."

An argument ensued, their voices rising in frustration and hurt.

"I've got my life, Momma! I can't just drop everything!" Richard snapped back; his face flushed with anger.

"You think I wanted to be here alone? With all these mouths to feed?" Momma shot back, her exhaustion finally boiling over into full-blown anger.

Richard shook his head, hurt and anger etched across his face. "I'll never come back if this is how it's going to be," he said, storming out of the house.

As the door slammed shut behind him, a heavy silence settled in. Karen and I sat on the floor, tears streaming down our faces. We clung to each other, heartbroken at the thought that we might never see our happy and loving brother again.

"I miss him already," Karen whispered, her voice cracking.

"Me too," I replied, feeling the loss of his presence acutely. The joy he brought with him seemed to vanish as quickly as he had come, leaving us to wonder if he might be gone forever.

Chapter 11

LOCATION, LOCATION, LOCATION

The school year ended, and summer began with a mix of relief and uncertainty, leaving behind the stability and regular meals that came with school days. Karen and I faced the long, hot months ahead with trepidation, knowing that summer usually meant more time without Momma around.

It seemed like just another ordinary day when Momma came home with news that would once again shift the course of our lives. She announced, "We got to move, now!" That night was a flurry of packing, a hectic yet familiar routine for us. Cardboard boxes quickly filled with our belongings, the sounds of tape ripping and dishes clinking filled the air as we hurriedly prepared to leave.

By the next day, we found ourselves relocating to yet another mobile home park, this one closer to the heart of town and noticeably larger than the last. The new park buzzed with life; there were children playing in the streets and neighbors chatting on their porches. The hum of distant traffic and the laughter of kids in the background made this place feel more alive, yet it was intimidating to face an unfamiliar environment.

Our mobile home sat at the end of a long row, its faded blue paint peeling in the sunlight. Despite its worn appearance,

I couldn't help but notice the small garden out front, overgrown with weeds but brimming with potential.

"Looks like it could use some love," Karen commented, trying to lighten the mood.

I nodded, feeling a mix of anticipation and anxiety as we took it all in. "Maybe we could plant some flowers," I suggested, trying to imagine the garden in full bloom.

As we settled in, Momma explained the move with resignation in her voice, mentioning something about rent troubles. "It's not easy, kids," she said, rubbing her temples as if trying to ward off a headache. "But we're starting fresh. It's a new chapter."

Karen and I exchanged a skeptical glance, knowing all too well how often we had heard those words before. Still, there was a new spark in Momma that we hadn't seen before. She spoke of starting afresh and finally introduced us to the reason for her newfound happiness—a man named Howard.

We learned that Momma had met Howard while working at The Kettle.

"He's been coming in for breakfast for weeks," she told us with a shy smile. "Owns his own construction company and everything."

We met Howard a few days later. He pulled up in his shiny pickup truck, his presence both imposing and comforting. He was a tall man with kind eyes and a gentle smile that put us at ease.

"Hey there, I've heard a lot about you all," he said, extending a hand. His voice was warm, filled with a kind of sincerity that was rare in our world.

Howard's presence was pleasant; he was genuinely kind and seemed to bring out the best in Momma. He took the time to get to know us, bringing little gifts or helping with repairs around the house.

"This place could use a little fixing up," he said with a chuckle, looking around.

"Yeah, like the roof that leaks," I added, pointing to the spot where rainwater often seeped through.

He grinned. "I'll see what I can do about that."

Howard even mentioned that he might have a job for Richard if he ever wanted to move back home. "I could use a strong, young guy like him on my crew," he said one evening over dinner.

I felt a glimmer of hope at the thought.

"Do you think Richard would come back?" I asked Momma later, excitement and apprehension in my voice.

She shrugged, a faint smile on her lips. "Maybe. He'd be a fool to pass up a good opportunity like that."

Life felt almost normal for a while. We laughed more, ate better, and there was a sense of peace in the air. I found myself daring to hope that things might stay this way. However, the harmony was short-lived. One rainy day, a couple of months later, an intense argument ensued between Momma and Howard outside in his pickup truck. The bass sound of their raised voices cut through the downpour, tension hanging thick.

"Why can't you understand?" Momma yelled, her voice breaking.

Howard's reply was firm but pleading. "I'm just trying to help, Patsy. This isn't easy for any of us."

Their words blurred together, carried away by the rain, until finally, Momma's tears seemed to silence the storm itself. Howard drove off, the roar of his engine fading into the distance, leaving a void we all felt deeply.

With Howard's departure, Momma reverted to being the angry, distant person she had been before. It became evident that she soon yearned to forget by socializing, drinking, and dancing, often leaving us for days at a time. The absence of regular meals and a steady adult presence was hard on us, but Momma's sporadic returns with food were always a relief, especially when our supplies dwindled dangerously low.

As the days dragged on, the absence of Howard became more pronounced.

"I liked him," Karen admitted one night as we lay in bed, staring at the ceiling. "He made things better, even if it was just for a little while."

"Me too," I whispered back, wishing things could have been different.

As summer waned, the prospect of returning to school brought a sense of relief. School meant stability, regular meals, and the normalcy of adult supervision—a stark contrast to the unpredictability of our home life. As Karen and I prepared for the new school year, packing our bags and laying out our clothes, we couldn't help but wish for a sense of belonging and security that seemed just out of reach.

"Do you think things will ever be normal?" I asked Karen one night.

She sighed, hugging her knees to her chest. "I don't know, but we have to keep hoping," she replied, her words both a comfort and a challenge. "Besides, what is normal, anyway?"

As autumn approached, bringing with it the promise of a new school year, Momma gathered us together to announce yet another move. This time, we were heading to a place she referred to as 'The Projects'—government-subsidized housing meant for families in need of assistance.

With her characteristic optimism, she painted a rosy picture of our new home, describing it as a beautiful place with a fenced backyard where we could play.

"It'll be nice to have some space for you kids to run around," she said, trying to reassure us with a smile. Despite her upbeat tone, I couldn't help but feel apprehensive about another upheaval in our lives.

The day before our move, Momma took us shopping for school supplies. There was a certain excitement in preparing for the first day of school, an activity that momentarily distracted us from the thought of moving again. We filled our cart with notebooks, pencils, and a few new clothes. I remember holding a bright red backpack, hoping it would somehow bring me good luck in the new school.

"Do you think they'll like me here?" I asked Karen as we browsed the aisles.

"Maybe," she shrugged, eyeing a pair of sneakers. "But if they don't, who cares? We've got each other."

We shared a smile, trying to mask our worries with bravado. But the reality of our new neighborhood quickly set in upon our arrival.

The Projects stood in stark contrast to Momma's descriptions. The houses were brick, as she had promised, but they were gray and run-down, with peeling paint and broken windows. The grass in the yards was patchy and overgrown, littered with trash that danced in the wind. As we unloaded our belongings, I noticed the crowds of people watching us from the sidewalks and balconies, their expressions a mix of curiosity and disdain.

"Looks like we're not welcome," Karen whispered as she helped me carry a box inside.

I nodded, feeling the weight of every gaze on us. The stares and unwelcoming glances from our new neighbors were unmistakable. "Just keep your head down and mind your business," Momma advised, sensing our unease.

Our first day taking the bus to school was a harsh introduction to what life in this new place would be like. The morning was crisp, with leaves turning shades of orange and brown, but the air felt heavy with tension. As we approached the bus stop, I noticed the other kids huddled in groups, their eyes narrowing as we drew closer.

The bus was packed, and the noise was deafening. Karen and I tried to sit near the front, hoping to avoid trouble, but the jostling and shoving were unavoidable. I felt a sharp elbow jab into my side as we squeezed into a seat, the hostile whispers already reaching our ears.

"What are you doing here?" a boy sneered from across the aisle, his eyes cold and unwelcoming.

"Yeah, you don't belong here," another chimed in, his voice dripping with contempt.

The bus driver, an older man with a weary face, seemed oblivious to the brewing hostility. I wondered silently why it seemed so easy for others to hate us without even knowing who we were.

When we finally reached school, I felt a momentary relief, hoping that the atmosphere might be different within its walls. School was just the glimmer of hope I needed, I thought. The prospect of endless books in the school library was thrilling, and I cherished the new outfit Momma made for me from scraps she collected from her new job. After years of waitressing at The Kettle, she finally found a new position downtown working as a seamstress, something she truly enjoyed. Her work provided a sense of stability, allowing her to be home in the evenings and spend more time with us.

I thought I looked pretty in the mismatched fabrics of the dress, and the colors reminded me of a quilt we had back home. However, as I walked into Mrs. Watson's classroom, my excitement quickly turned to uncertainty. I noticed how different my clothes were from those of my classmates. While they wore crisp, store-bought outfits, I stood out in my patchwork dress. The feeling of being different, something I had often felt in the past, returned with a vengeance. I had assumed homemade clothes were normal, but here, they seemed to set me apart.

Despite my nervousness, my spirits lifted when I saw a desk with my name on it. I hesitated before sitting down, my eyes scanning the room. Beside me sat a girl with the biggest brown eyes I had ever seen. She turned to me with an infectious smile, her energy radiating across the room.

"Hi! My name is Jill. What's yours?" she asked cheerfully. Her friendly demeanor was mesmerizing, and the warmth in her voice was genuine.

"I'm PJ," I replied, a bit shyly.

She grinned even wider, leaning in conspiratorially. "I think your dress is beautiful. My grandma used to make me clothes just like that."

I felt a wave of relief wash over me. Jill's acceptance and easy friendship made me feel safe and happy. We talked throughout the day, sharing stories and laughing at our teacher's funny expressions. Her kindness transformed what could have been an overwhelming first day into one filled once again with possibility.

Mrs. Watson, our teacher, was an older woman with a kind face, and she encouraged us to be curious and explore innovative ideas. The classroom was filled with books and colorful posters, creating an environment that invited learning and creativity.

I could hardly wait to explore the library and immerse myself in the stories that awaited me.

As the day progressed, I found myself smiling more often, reassured by Jill's presence and the comforting routine of school. Living in the Projects was different, yes, but maybe different could be good. Amid change and uncertainty, I had found a friend, and with her friendship, the world seemed a little less daunting.

After school, the bus ride home was no better. The same kids from the morning continued their taunts, making sure we knew we weren't welcome. I clutched my new backpack tightly, feeling as if I were holding onto a lifejacket.

Once home, the sense of isolation lingered. Our neighborhood was a maze of similar-looking buildings, each one housing families with their own struggles and stories. The streets echoed with the sounds of shouting and laughter, but it felt like a different world from the one we had known.

At night, I lay awake, listening to the unfamiliar sounds of our unfamiliar environment, wondering if we would ever feel like we truly belonged. The challenges ahead seemed overwhelming, but as I drifted off to sleep, I held onto Karen's words—at least we had each other.

Chapter 12

A GLIMPSE OF ANOTHER LIFE

I will never forget the first time Jill invited me over to her house for a sleepover. I was ecstatic, practically bouncing with excitement. Momma packed my few belongings into our old suitcase, and off we went to Jill's house—a place with no trailers in sight, vastly different from anywhere I'd lived. Jill's house was like a fairy tale, with a long driveway and flowers blooming in the garden. Her one-story house looked cozy and inviting, with bright windows and a well-kept lawn.

When we arrived, Jill's older sisters, Jodie and Jane, were lounging in the living room, their laughter echoing through the house.

"Hey, PJ!" Jodie greeted me, flashing a smile that made me feel at ease. "We've heard so much about you."

"Yeah," Jane chimed in, winking. "Jill never stops talking about her new best friend!"

Jill tugged my arm excitedly, pulling me toward her room. "Come on! I want to show you my room!"

Inside, Jill's room was like something out of a dream. She had a white dresser with a large mirror and a cushioned stool that looked fit for a princess.

"This is where I do my homework and play dress-up," she said, opening a drawer filled with colorful scarves and trinkets.

"Wow! It's beautiful," I whispered, running my fingers over the soft fabrics.

Mrs. Kinney called us for dinner, and we sat at a beautifully set table with Mr. and Mrs. Kinney at each end. Her daddy was so jolly, laughing and chatting, clearly enjoying being surrounded by his family. Jill and I sat across from Jodie and Jane, who were teasing each other and sharing stories from their day. Pretty plates with matching napkins and silverware were set for each person, and colorful glasses sparkled in the soft light.

I had never seen anything like it. At home, we always ate in the living room, watching TV with frozen dinners. Sometimes, when Momma was home, we'd come back from school to find the windows open, the house clean, and something baking in the oven while country music played on the radio. Those days were rare, but they felt magical.

Mr. Kinney said grace, his voice gentle and full of gratitude. "Thank you, Lord, for this meal and for PJ joining us tonight," he prayed. The prayer was so sweet and hearing him thank God for me touched my heart in a way I couldn't explain.

After dinner, Jill and I retreated to her room, where we played games and laughed until our sides hurt. But as we unpacked my suitcase, tiny roaches crawled out, shattering the magic of the evening. Jill started screaming and stomping on the roaches. My face burned with embarrassment, and I started to pack my things to leave.

Mrs. Kinney came into the room, and I braced myself for the worst. Instead, she knelt beside me, her expression gentle.

"Sweetie," she said, brushing a stray tear from my cheek, "never let things on the outside dictate your worth. It's your heart that matters." Her words, so full of kindness and wisdom, left an impression on me. "You have a light in your eyes that shines bright, and I can't wait to see what amazing things you will do. Now, go with Jill and get ready for bed!"

Jill started brushing her teeth and I had no idea what she was doing. As I stood in the brightly lit bathroom, my reflection stared back at me, a mix of curiosity and uncertainty in my eyes. The Kinney's bathroom was pristine, with shiny tiles and the clean scent of soap in the air. It was a stark contrast to the worn-out bathroom at home, where I had never been taught the importance of this nightly ritual.

Mrs. Kinney handed me a brand-new toothbrush, her voice gentle and encouraging.

"Here you go, PJ," she said with a warm smile. "A toothbrush just for you. Now, I'll show you how to use it, okay?"

I nodded, clutching the toothbrush tightly as if it were a precious treasure. The bristles were soft and inviting, and I felt a strange mix of excitement and nervousness.

"I've never done this before," I admitted, my voice barely above a whisper.

"That's alright," Mrs. Kinney reassured me, her eyes kind and understanding. "We all have to start somewhere. Just put a little toothpaste on the brush like this," she demonstrated, squeezing a small amount onto the bristles, "and then gently brush your teeth in circles."

As I followed her instructions, I felt a tingling sensation in my mouth. The minty freshness was new and unfamiliar, but it brought a sense of cleanliness and care that I had never known. With each stroke of the toothbrush, a layer of shame and neglect begins to peel away, replaced by a feeling of newfound self-worth. Mrs. Kinney watched me with a smile, her presence comforting.

"You're doing great, PJ," she praised, handing me a cup to rinse with. "See? Easy peasy."

I rinsed my mouth, feeling the cool water wash away the foamy toothpaste.

"It feels... nice," I said, surprised by how refreshing the experience was.

"Brushing your teeth is important," Mrs. Kinney explained. "It's one of those little things that helps take care of you. You deserve to feel good and be healthy."

She then handed me one of Jill's nightgowns, its fabric soft and comforting against my skin. I marveled at its softness, at the sense of care it embodied. Wearing it felt like a hug, enveloping me in warmth and love.

As Jill and I climbed into her big, soft bed, I felt a wave of safety and security wash over me. We giggled and whispered in the dark, sharing secrets and dreams.

"I'm so glad you're here, PJ," Jill said, her voice filled with sincerity. "You're my best friend."

I smiled in the darkness, my heart full.

"I'm glad I'm here too," I whispered back, feeling for the first time that I belonged somewhere.

That night, I slept like a baby, surrounded in warmth and safety. The simple act of brushing my teeth became a profound moment of transformation, a small step toward a future where I could begin to take care of myself and believe in my own worth. It was a night of firsts, of discovering kindness and care in a world that had often felt cold and unkind. And as I drifted off to sleep, I held onto the hope that these small moments of love and acceptance could change everything.

The next morning, as I packed my suitcase, I felt a pang of dread on returning home. For the first time, I began to question why my life was so different from Jill's.

"Why can't my family be more like the Kinney's?" I wondered aloud as Momma drove us back.

"What do you mean?" Momma asked, a hint of defensiveness in her voice.

"I don't know," I said, hugging my knees to my chest. "I just wish things were different sometimes."

Momma sighed, focusing on the road. "We do the best we can, PJ. Life ain't always fair."

Her words didn't comfort me as they once might have. That sleepover opened my eyes to a different way of living and planted seeds of questioning and unrest in my mind. I began to doubt the teachings of Sunday School and the unconditional love of God I had been taught about when we lived in Nacogdoches. The disparity between my life and Jill's led me to question my worth. What was so wrong with me? Why was I given this life? The pain and fear in my heart grew, overshadowing the faint glimmer of hope Mrs. Kinney had sparked with her acceptance, and friendship that made me feel safe and happy… for a moment.

Jill's request to spend the night at my place filled me with a sense of dread. Every time she brought it up, I found an excuse to delay it.

"Next weekend, Jill. My mom's busy right now," I'd say, hoping she wouldn't press further. The truth was, I couldn't bear the thought of her seeing the conditions we lived in. The shame of our living situation was a heavy burden, one I wasn't ready to share with her.

Our home was nothing like Jill's. At our house, the tiny roaches were a constant presence. Opening a cabinet meant risking them falling on your head, lying in bed meant feeling them crawl in your hair, and every time we opened the fridge, we had to check for dead roaches in our food. Cat urine was everywhere, and usually on the beds we slept in. The thought of Jill encountering this reality was terrifying. I feared it would scare her away and reveal the truth about my life that I wasn't ready to face.

"If she sees how we live, she'll never want to be my friend again," I confided to Karen one evening, my voice filled with anxiety.

Karen nodded, understanding the weight of my fears. "It's not fair," she replied softly. "But she's your friend, PJ. She won't care."

I shook my head, unconvinced. In my mind, bringing Jill into my home would mean revealing a part of myself I was deeply ashamed of. I couldn't shake off the feeling that it would confirm my deepest fears about myself—that I was filthy and unworthy, not just of her friendship but of anyone's. This fear of being judged and rejected was paralyzing.

I wanted to maintain the image of myself that I had managed to portray at school—just another kid, no different from the rest. The prospect of Jill discovering the truth was something I couldn't face. So I kept making excuses, hoping to preserve the friendship we had, a friendship that meant the world to me, untainted by the harsh realities of my life.

As the school year ended, Jill and I were inseparable, eagerly planning how we would spend the summer together.

"We'll ride our bikes every day!" Jill exclaimed excitedly.

"Yeah, we'll have so much fun!" I agreed, my heart heavy with the knowledge of what I was hiding from her.

Then, something unexpected happened. Momma came into a bit of money and bought us a brand-new mobile home. I wasn't sure where the money came from, but the excitement of moving into a new place, especially one located in Big 'C' trailer park just blocks from Jill's neighborhood, was overwhelming.

"Guess what, girls?" Momma announced one evening, a rare smile on her face. "We're moving to a brand-new home, just a few blocks from your friend Jill's!"

Karen and I could hardly contain our excitement.

"Really, Momma? That's amazing!" I exclaimed, feeling a sense of hope I hadn't felt in a long time. Finally free from the shame I had felt about our old home, I was thrilled to have Jill over.

"You can come over anytime now, Jill!" I said with genuine excitement.

We spent the summer riding our bikes between our houses, enjoying a freedom and happiness that had been rare in my life. Our days were filled with trips to the nearby park's swimming pool, accessed by a trail through the woods, where we'd swim and laugh endlessly. For the first time, I felt like a normal kid, and the burden of shame slowly began to lift.

Back at my place, Jill and I were busy baking teacakes, and the kitchen was filled with laughter. Jill giggled as she surveyed the flour-dusted counters and scattered baking supplies.

"We're such a great team, even though we make the biggest mess!" she exclaimed, brushing flour from her cheek.

I grinned back at her, wiping my hands on my apron. "Who cares about the mess? It just means we're having fun!" I replied, watching the teacakes rise in the oven, filling the kitchen with a warm, sweet aroma.

On a particularly sweltering night, the air conditioner broke. Jill and I sat in the living room, trying to escape the oppressive heat. Jill fanned herself with a magazine, her face flushed.

"It's like a sauna in here!" she said, rolling her eyes dramatically. I laughed, tossing her a damp washcloth.

"Who needs air conditioning when we have each other?" I joked, draping the cloth over my forehead.

Despite the discomfort, those moments together solidified our bond—we were BOBFFs, Best of Best Friends Forever even though Jill's world was so different from mine.

One afternoon, as we lay on the grass in the backyard, she turned to me with a dreamy look in her eyes.

"You should see the redwoods in California," she said. "They're magical!"

I could only imagine the beauty of California's redwoods until that summer when Jill's family invited me to join them on their annual trip.

"Really? I get to come?" I asked, my eyes wide with excitement.

Jill nodded eagerly. "Yes! It'll be amazing, PJ. You'll see a whole new world!"

That trip was a revelation, exposing me to life and experiences far beyond the confines of our trailer park and the small world I had known. As we drove along the winding roads, peering out of the sunroof, I marveled at the sight of the towering trees.

"It's like another world," I whispered, acknowledging the truth she had told me. I was utterly captivated.

The trip to California with Jill and her family was not just a revelation to the world's vast beauty, but also a time for Jill and me to bond in ways we never had before. As we journeyed through the breathtaking landscapes, our friendship deepened in the shared experiences and simple joys of that adventure, like learning to French braid each other's hair. We would sit for hours in the backseat, fingers clumsily weaving through strands, laughing at our initial attempts.

"Oops, I think I made a knot!" Jill giggled, trying to untangle the braid on which she was working.

"We'll get it eventually," I assured her, concentrating on getting the braid exactly right.

Gradually, we improved until we could weave each other's hair into intricate patterns. It became our little ritual, a way of bonding that was uniquely ours.

Another memorable experience was picking peaches. We stopped at Jill's Aunt Tessie's house, where the backyard was heavy with ripe, juicy peaches. The thrill of plucking the fruit directly from the branches, feeling the soft fuzz against our palms, and tasting the sun-warmed sweetness was unlike anything I had experienced before. I bit into a peach, juice running down my chin. "This is amazing!" I exclaimed, savoring the fresh taste.

Jill nodded; her own peach half-eaten. "It's like eating sunshine!" she echoed, grinning.

Those endless stretches of road and the time we spent together riding in the backseat were the perfect backdrop for endless conversations, shared secrets, silly handshakes, and lots of laughter. We talked about everything and nothing, from our hopes and dreams to the silly and mundane.

"Do you think we'll be friends forever?" Jill asked one evening, her voice soft as we watched the sunset paint the sky in hues of orange and pink.

I nodded, feeling a warmth in my chest. "Of course, Jill. We're BOBFFs, remember?" I said, reaching over to squeeze her hand.

That time in the car brought us even closer, forging a connection that was more like sisters than friends. The California trip was a kaleidoscope of new experiences, and more than anything, it was a time that cemented my friendship with Jill. We returned home not just with memories of redwoods, mountains, and peaches, but with a friendship that had grown stronger and deeper through the shared adventures and the quiet moments of connection.

Chapter 13

BOBFF (Best of Best Friends Forever)

After summer and the move to Big 'C' trailer park, Jill and I started a new school year together, and our friendship only grew stronger. Despite the rough start to my school years, having Jill by my side made a world of difference. Jill's unwavering belief in me often led to experiences I would have never imagined on my own.

When my birthday came around that year, Jill insisted that I should have a party at my trailer.

"You've got to have one, PJ," she said one day at lunch. "I get invited to parties all the time, and it's about time everyone knows how amazing you are!"

I hesitated, feeling unsure about inviting people over, but her enthusiasm was contagious.

"Alright, let's do it!" I agreed, my heart racing with a mix of excitement and dread.

We sent out invitations to all the kids in our class, and to my surprise, they showed up! The living room was decked out with decorations Momma had put up, and Karen added colorful balloons to make the space feel festive. Momma even baked a homemade chocolate cake, complete with candles.

As the party got underway, I overheard a few of the kids whispering to each other.

"I thought she lived in a house, not a trailer," one of them said, looking around with thinly veiled judgment.

Trying to brush off the comments, I led everyone outside to show them around the trailer park. "This is where we pick blackberries," I said, pointing toward a patch of bushes near the railroad tracks.

The group walked with me, but I could tell they weren't impressed. As we made our way back, the awkwardness hung in the air, and I felt a pang of disappointment when they seemed relieved as their parents arrived to pick them up.

Jill stayed behind, her expression full of concern.

"I'm sorry, PJ. I thought it would be fun," she said softly, unsure of what else to say.

"It's okay, Jill. At least we tried," I replied, grateful for her support even when things didn't go as planned.

Jill and I shared countless memories that shaped our childhood, and with each new school year, we embarked on new adventures. One year, we decided to join the school choir together. Jill's voice was like an angel's, clear and beautiful, and though I was hesitant about singing in front of others, she had a way of making me feel brave enough to try.

"Come on, PJ," she'd say with that bright smile of hers, nudging me with her elbow. "It's just for fun. You've got a good voice, too, you know?"

I wasn't so sure about that, but with her by my side, I gave it a shot. We also joined a softball team together, and those games became a special part of our routine. My favorite part, though, wasn't the game itself—it was what came afterward. We'd head over to the concession stand, grabbing blue bubble-gum sno-cones, the syrup staining our tongues as we laughed and recapped the game. "Best part of the day," I'd say, holding up my sno-cone as we sat on the bleachers, our legs swinging freely.

"Agreed," Jill would laugh, slurping hers before it melted in the Texas heat. Mrs. Kinney always gave me a ride home after those games, and we'd sing songs in the car, windows down, the air rushing in, making us feel free. Those moments, the ones where life felt simple and carefree, stayed with me, nestled in the corners of my mind.

As we drove down the familiar road toward my house one evening, Jill turned to me. "Hey, PJ, we should try something new next year, something different."

I glanced at her, unsure of what she had in mind but excited by the idea. "Like what?"

She grinned mischievously. "I have a few ideas."

I smiled back, knowing whatever came next would be an adventure—just like everything else we did together. Little did I know the next chapter of our lives was going to bring changes we hadn't anticipated, shifts that would test our friendship and the world around us.

As I waved goodbye to Jill that night, I couldn't help but feel that we were on the edge of something new, something bigger than the two of us. And I had no idea how much I would need the strength of those memories for what was coming next.

Journal Entry September 4, 1992

I've always known what was right and what was wrong. Growing up, it was drilled into us. Stealing and lying were sins you just didn't commit. But what do you do when that's the only way to keep your brother and sister from going hungry? What do you do when you've got nothing, and no one, and those "sins" feel like your only way out? I've had to learn how to manipulate people just to survive. And yeah, it kept me and my siblings from starving, but it also came with a cost. A cost I wasn't prepared to pay. Every time I had to lie, every time I had to take something that wasn't mine, I felt a piece of myself breaking. Now, I'm left with this heavy, sinking feeling in my gut that I'll never be good enough. Never be worthy of anything better than this constant struggle. Therapy rips those old wounds wide open. I sit there, pouring my heart out, and all I feel is shame. It's like I've been stamped with this label "poor white trash." I know people can smell failure in me. It feels like I'm unworthy of trust, destined to screw things up. I wonder, does God even look at me anymore? Does He see anything worth saving? I don't even know if I can see it. All I can see is the mess I've made of things, the mistakes that follow me around like shadows. Sometimes I don't even know who I am beyond guilt and shame. The weight of it is suffocating, I'll never be able to dig myself out from under it. But then there's this small part of me, this tiny, stubborn part, that refuses to give up. I want to believe I can be more than the broken pieces of my past. I want to believe that, somehow, I'll find a way to heal. I'm holding onto the hope that maybe, just maybe, there's something better waiting for me out there. I don't know how I'll get there, but I have to try. I have to believe that one day I'll be free from shame. That I'll become someone worthy of love, someone who isn't defined by my past. Someone who can finally stand up and say, "I am enough."

Chapter 14

HUNGER

I remember the summer before my sixth-grade year vividly; it was a season of both innocence and responsibilities that would soon shape my adolescence. Those days seemed simpler, filled with easy friendships and challenges that felt less complicated. Back in sixth grade, life's demands hadn't yet shown up in full force, but the seeds of hardship had already been planted. My friendship with Jill was beginning to change as she started moving into other friendships with girls who lived lifestyles more like hers. The vast differences between our lives became more apparent, creating a subtle distance between us.

In the sweltering heat of that summer, hunger began to creep into our lives, transforming from a fleeting discomfort to a constant, gnawing presence. Our trailer park, with its rows of worn-out homes and dusty roads, held secrets of families struggling quietly behind closed doors. I remember the pangs of hunger, not just for food, but for normalcy, for a life that didn't feel perpetually on the brink of disaster.

It was one of those sweltering summer days when the poignancy of our situation hit me. I stood in our tiny kitchen, staring into cupboards that were empty, save for a few cans of beans and a half-empty box of crackers. Momma was nowhere to be found, having disappeared for weeks at a time as she often did, leaving us to fend for ourselves. When she finally returned, she claimed she had been working but never had enough money for groceries. Kent and Cherrie sat at the table, their eyes wide and hopeful, waiting for a meal that I wasn't sure how to provide.

"PJ, is there anything to eat?" Kent asked, his voice small and tinged with worry.

"I'll find something, don't worry," I promised, forcing a smile while panic rose in my chest. I rummaged through the cupboards, my heart sinking with each bare shelf I encountered.

During these desperate times, the lines between right and wrong began to blur. Hunger was a powerful force, capable of transforming innocence into desperation. One day, Karen came home with a bag of groceries which she hadn't left. She placed it on the table, avoiding my questioning gaze.

"Where'd you get this?" I asked, eyeing the bread and canned goods inside.

Karen was guarded. "A friend from a few trailers down," she replied. "They had extra." Her voice betrayed the truth we both knew. She spent a lot of time with a family nearby, and I suspected her visits had less to do with the boy she claimed to like and more to do with the meals she received there.

In those moments, hunger made thieves and liars out of the innocent. It became more than just a physical sensation—it was a constant reminder of our struggle to survive. During the school year, we relied on school lunches, often sneaking extra food into our pockets to stave off hunger later. But summer brought with it an emptiness—both in our bellies and in our days—that we couldn't easily fill.

Momma, in one of her more lucid moments, applied for government aid that she called 'food stamps', expressing hope that they would be approved soon. "This will help us get by," she assured us, though her words were often met with skepticism.

As I sat at the table, dividing the food Karen brought home, I felt the weight of our reality pressing down on me. In the depths of our hardship, we learned to live in a world where every choice was a balancing act between survival and morality, where the innocence of childhood was tinged with the harsh lessons of life. Her demeanor had changed; she was increasingly indifferent and quick to anger, mirroring Momma's own detachment. The dynamic between Karen and me had always been a rollercoaster of emotions, often marked by arguments and fights over the most trivial things. The pressures of our home life and personal struggles strained our relationship, and it finally reached a boiling point one day. It is a memory that still resonates with a mix of regret and disbelief.

The start of our dispute was something as mundane as laundry. Karen left her clothes on top of the dryer, and in my frustration, I ended up folding them and putting them away. But my irritation didn't end there. The cramped laundry room felt suffocating as I hastily shoved her clothes into a drawer.

"Can't you ever just do your own laundry?" I muttered under my breath, the heat of anger rising.

Karen leaned against the doorway with her arms crossed. "I was going to do it. You didn't have to touch my stuff."

I shot back, words escaping my mouth before I could stop them. "You're so fat, you have to wear 'fat lady' pants!"

My childish words hung in the air, laced with spite and pettiness. Karen's reaction was not what I expected. There were no angry retorts, no fiery comebacks. Instead, she looked at me, her eyes brimming with tears.

With her voice barely above a whisper, she said, "I'm not fat. I'm pregnant."

Her confession hit me like I had jumped off the roof and slammed into the ground, the breath knocked out of me, leaving me stunned and gasping for air. All my anger dissipated, replaced by shock and a sudden sense of concern. Pregnant? How? When? A million questions raced through my mind, but in that moment, all I could see was the hurt in my sister's eyes—hurt that I had just added to.

I stood there, speechless, the gravity of the situation sinking in. "Karen, I... I didn't know," I stammered, guilt washing over me. "I'm sorry. I didn't mean it."

She shrugged, wiping away her tears with the back of her hand. "It's fine. I haven't told anyone."

"But who's the father?" I asked, my voice still shaking.

She hesitated, glancing toward the window. "It's complicated," she admitted. "I don't even know if I can keep it."

The realization of my thoughtless remark and its impact on her in such a vulnerable moment filled me with remorse. This was more than just a sibling spat; it was a life-changing revelation for Karen, and by extension, for our entire family.

As I processed her words, I remembered how Karen had found solace in her friendship with a strange girl named Susan in the trailer park. She was always in her own world, moving slowly, her eyes often half-closed as if lost in a dream. Karen spent a lot of time with her, and I wondered if she had confided in her friend about the pregnancy.

"Does Susan know?" I asked, gesturing vaguely in the direction of the trailer park.

Karen shook her head. "No. I haven't told anyone, not even Momma." Her voice faltered, fear and uncertainty etched across her face.

"Do you want me to come with you when you tell her?" I offered, trying to bridge the gap I had created with my earlier outburst.

She managed a small smile, a glimmer of hope in her eyes. "Yeah, I'd like that."

We stood in the silence of the laundry room, the weight of Karen's secret hanging between us. It was a moment of vulnerability and raw emotion, one that would change everything. The thought of her navigating such a huge challenge alone filled me with determination to support her, no matter what.

In this world, where hunger was a relentless companion, we each found our own ways to survive. Karen sought escape in the company of others, while I grappled with the responsibility of feeding Kent and Cherrie. It was a life that forced us to grow up too fast, to learn the harsh realities of the world while still clinging to the remnants of our childhood. Hunger, in all its forms, was a teacher of hard lessons, ones that we learned day by day along the precarious path of our youth.

Whenever we asked why Momma was gone so long, she would say that she spent her nights watching sick people, disappearing for weeks at a time. The nights were long and lonely without her presence, and the gaps in our food supplies grew as empty as the rooms she left behind. When she finally returned, she looked weary and worn out, often brushing off our concerns with vague assurances. "I'm doing what I can, kids," she would say, exhaustion clear in her eyes. "You have to be strong."

I remember the day Karen and I decided she had to tell Momma about her pregnancy. We sat in the living room, the dim light casting long shadows across the worn carpet as we waited for Momma to come home from her shift. The silence between us was thick with anticipation and fear.

When Momma finally walked through the door, exhaustion etched across her face, Karen took a deep breath and stood up. "Momma, I need to talk to you about something important," she said, her voice steady but laced with anxiety.

Momma sighed, setting her purse down on the counter. "What is it now, Karen?" she replied, her tone weary.

"I'm pregnant," Karen blurted out, her eyes locked on Momma's face, searching for any sign of understanding.

For a moment, time seemed to stop. Momma stared at Karen, an unreadable expression on her face. To our surprise, she didn't get angry. Instead, she simply said, "Well, you can do something about it, and I'll help you."

Karen's face fell, her eyes widening in disbelief. "You mean an abortion?" she asked, her voice barely above a whisper.

Momma nodded, a matter-of-factness in her voice. "We can't afford another mouth to feed, Karen."

The words hung in the air like a weight, pressing down on us. I couldn't believe she would say that! We both couldn't. Karen looked crushed, the hurt clear in her eyes.

"But Momma, I don't want to do that," Karen said, tears beginning to spill down her cheeks. "I want to keep my baby."

Momma shrugged, turning away. "Do what you want, then," she said dismissively. "Just remember what I said."

Karen and I sat in silence after she left the room, the weight of Momma's indifference settling heavily on us. I reached out and squeezed Karen's hand, trying to offer some comfort in the face of her pain.

In stark contrast to Momma's callousness, we experienced rare moments of kindness that renewed our faith in humanity. During Momma's prolonged absences, our food supplies would dwindle until the cupboards stood bare. That's when Karen and I would embark on our desperate missions to Mac's Super Stop, a convenient store about two miles down the road. We had a plan: she would steal the hotdog buns, and I would take the wieners, hiding them under our shirts. We hated stealing, the guilt weighing heavily on us, but our hunger and the need to feed Kent and Cherrie overshadowed our moral dilemmas.

We became adept at our thievery, maintaining normal expressions to avoid suspicion. But if stealing hotdogs seemed too risky, we'd resort to knocking on neighbors' doors with fabricated stories about needing eggs or milk for a cake Momma was supposedly baking. To make our limited supplies last, we learned tricks like compressing bread into balls, pretending they were apples we could nibble on for hours. It was a sad game of make-believe, born out of necessity.

One fateful day at Mac's, as we were about to leave with our stolen goods, Mac called out, "Stop!" Our hearts sank. We turned, expecting we would be arrested and rot in jail. But instead, he handed us a bottle of mustard, saying with a hint of kindness, "I've seen you take hotdogs, but never mustard. Do you like mustard on your hotdogs?"

Karen hesitated, unsure of how to respond. "Yeah, we like it," she admitted quietly.

Mac then offered us a deal that would change everything. "You can ask me for food, and I will help you, but never steal from me again. Deal?"

I quickly agreed, "Deal!" while Karen remained skeptical, warning me later that nothing in life was ever free. However, that summer, Mac proved to be a man of his word. He provided us with all the food we needed, asking for nothing in return.

When Momma eventually came home and discovered our new arrangement, she drove to Mac's to set up a monthly account. Despite her reluctance to owe anyone anything, I sensed a faint relief in her. Maybe she was glad that in her absence we wouldn't go hungry, and she didn't have to worry about it. Whether she worried about us or not, Mac's generosity lifted a burden off our shoulders, at least for a while.

Chapter 15

BETWEEN BOYS AND BURDENS

Summer faded again into memory, and the arrival of middle school brought a new world of experiences and curiosities waiting to unfold before me. As usual, the school year promised a reprieve from our struggles, with the lure of new friends, teachers, and the structure and meals that school offered. It was a world where we could momentarily forget our worries, a place where we could be children again, if only for a few hours each day.

Among the curiosities of my middle school years were boys, who seemed like a different species altogether. They were always competing to see who was stronger or faster, pushing and shoving each other in the hallways, their laughter echoing down the corridors. I watched them from a distance, intrigued yet baffled by their antics, wondering what it was about them that captivated the girls in my class so much.

I noticed how the other girls acted around boys. There was an unspoken transformation that occurred, a delicate, almost helpless demeanor adopted that was in stark contrast to the girls' usual selves. There seemed to be a silent, unspoken competition, girls waiting for a boy to show interest, to invite them to the movies or to hold hands at the roller rink.

The roller rink quickly became the social hub of our town, a place where the worlds of boys and girls collided in a kaleidoscope of flashing lights and disco music. The rink itself was a circular track surrounding a polished wooden floor, with big, round, hard acrylic fur-covered ottomans where we perched to put on our skates. I yearned for a pair of those white roller skates all the girls had, adorned with big, colorful pom-poms. Instead, I was stuck with the sweat-soaked rental skates, perfumed by their previous renters, with brown and broken laces fraying at the ends.

"Come on, PJ!" Jill called out, already gliding effortlessly across the floor. "Let's see you shoot the duck!"

I wobbled onto the rink, feeling the weight of the heavy skates pulling at my ankles. Shooting the duck, where you skated while squatting on one leg with the other leg extended forward, was a move I admired but had yet to master. I watched enviously as other girls, their pom-poms bouncing with each glide, executed the move with grace and ease.

"Watch out!" A boy zoomed past me, narrowly missing my outstretched arms as I flailed for balance. His friends laughed as he showed off, skating backward and spinning effortlessly.

"Show-off," I muttered under my breath, trying to regain my composure. There was always that one middle-aged guy, too, who had perfected his technique, gliding on his skates the entire time, weaving through the crowd like a seasoned pro. His presence was a reminder of the skill I lacked, but also a challenge to improve.

A world of its own, a place where friendships formed and rivalries played out under the glow of neon lights, it was here that I felt both the thrill of freedom and the sting of insecurity, a mix of emotions that became an ever-present part of my growing up.

At twelve years old, I was beginning to develop an hour-glass figure, a change that left me self-conscious and uncertain. I felt awkward in my own skin, hyper-aware of how my body was growing in ways I couldn't control. My thighs seemed so big to me, and I desperately needed a bra, but I knew Momma couldn't afford one. I envied Jill's tall and thin frame, her straight lines unburdened by the curves that made me feel so conspicuous.

"I wish I had your boobs," Jill confessed one day as we sat side by side, lacing up our skates.

"Trust me, you don't," I replied, adjusting my shirt to hide what felt like an endless expanse of fabric struggling to contain my changing shape. "They're just... annoying."

Jill laughed, nudging me with her elbow. "Better than being flat as a board! My mom says they'll come in when they're ready, but I'm tired of waiting."

Her words brought a smile to my face, though inwardly I still grappled with my body image. Despite Jill's longing for curves, I couldn't help but wish for the simplicity of her figure, free from the scrutiny and self-doubt that came with developing early.

One Saturday night, as the disco ball cast shimmering reflections across the rink, a boy approached me while I was fumbling with the stubborn laces of my rental skates. His name was Danny, a boy from my class with sandy blonde hair and an easy smile that seemed to light up his face.

"Need some help?" he offered, nodding toward my tangled laces.

"Uh, sure. Thanks," I replied, feeling my cheeks warm with embarrassment.

As he knelt to help me, I noticed the worn state of his own skates, the laces frayed and patched in places. It was a small comfort to see someone else not conforming to the polished image everyone else seemed to strive for.

"You come here often?" he asked, tying the laces with practiced ease.

"Yeah, sometimes," I replied, trying to sound casual. "I like watching people skate."

He grinned, standing up and extending a hand to help me to my feet. "Well, maybe we can skate together sometime."

The unexpected invitation caught me off guard, a mix of excitement and nervousness swirling in my chest. "Yeah, I'd like that," I said.

As the night went on, we skated together, falling into an easy rhythm despite the noise and chaos around us. Danny's presence was a welcome distraction from the insecurities I experienced, a reminder that among the uncertainty of adolescence, there were moments of connection and understanding that made it all worthwhile.

Later, as I sat with Jill, sipping on soda and watching the crowd, she nudged me with a knowing smile. "Looks like someone's got a crush…"

I rolled my eyes playfully. "Oh, please. We're just friends."

Jill raised an eyebrow, a mischievous glint in her eyes. "Sure, just friends. That's how it starts."

Her teasing was light-hearted, but it made me think about the subtle shifts happening around us. The roller rink wasn't just a place for fun and games; it was a stage for the unfolding drama of growing up, where friendships deepened, and the first stirrings of romance took root.

As I watched the colorful pom-poms bounce to the beat of the music and felt the cool breeze of the air conditioning against my skin, I realized that these were the moments that made life vibrant and meaningful. The roller rink was more than just a place to skate; it was a sanctuary of memories, a place where the worries of the world faded into the background, leaving only the joy of the present moment.

As the evening ended and we exchanged goodbyes, I left the rink with a lighter heart, knowing that in between the challenges of life were pockets of happiness and belonging waiting to be discovered. It was a lesson I carried with me as I stepped into the unknown territory of adolescence, ready to face whatever came next with newfound courage and resilience.

These experiences at the rink and beyond taught me that while life could be difficult and unpredictable, it was also filled with beauty and connection that made every hardship worth enduring. And as I lay in bed that night, worn out from tracing countless circles in skates, the echoes of laughter and music still ringing in my ears, I felt grateful for the small, precious moments that made the journey worthwhile.

Social dynamics, in general, were puzzling yet fascinating. Like the TWIRP (The Woman Is Required to Pay) game season, a unique tradition where the roles were reversed, and girls got the chance to ask boys to a football game. My eyes were set on Billy, a boy whose cuteness hadn't gone unnoticed by me.

"I'm thinking of asking Billy to the TWIRP game," I confessed to Jill one afternoon as we sat on the swings at the playground.

Jill was now tall and lean, with a natural tan, shoulder-length brown hair, and beautiful brown eyes. She was always so joyful and smiling, her presence like a warm ray of sunshine. But as I spoke, her face fell, and she hesitated before speaking. "Oh, I was thinking about asking him too," she admitted, her voice barely above a whisper.

A knot formed in my stomach, my insecurities flaring up. Jill was pretty and confident, and I worried that Billy would surely choose her over me. Determined not to lose this opportunity, I seized the moment one day during a break at school. Boys and girls lined up on opposite sides of the sidewalk, and I mustered all my courage to cross that divide and ask Billy to the TWIRP game.

My heart pounded as I approached him, my mouth dry with nervousness. "Hey, Billy," I said, trying to keep my voice steady. "Would you like to go to the TWIRP game with me?"

Billy looked surprised but nodded casually. "Sure, sounds fun," he replied, glancing at his friends who were snickering in the background. I was over the moon, barely noticing the giggles from his friends or Jill's disappointed look.

That evening, I called Billy to arrange the details, my mind already racing about what I would wear. "So, what time should I pick you up?" I asked eagerly.

"Uh, let's meet there," Billy suggested, sounding less enthusiastic than I had hoped. "My mom will drop me off."

After our conversation, I went to Momma, hoping she could spare some money for a new outfit. However, Momma's tight finances meant shopping for a new outfit was out of the question.

"I'll make you something special," Momma offered, smiling as she pulled out a roll of lace fabric.

The result was a blouse that looked uncannily like our old white lace kitchen curtains—see-through lace with puffy sleeves and ruffles around the chest. I felt ridiculous in it, like a white cloud drifting awkwardly through the football game crowd.

"I'm sure you'll look beautiful," Momma reassured me, but I wasn't so sure.

My hopes of covering it with my green school jacket were dashed by the impractical design of the blouse. As I sat next to Billy at the game, his reaction was a mix of shock and discomfort.

"Nice blouse," he commented awkwardly, shifting in his seat.

"Thanks," I mumbled, wishing I could disappear into the stands. The evening ended abruptly when he left early, claiming his mom was waiting for him.

"I'll see you around," he said quickly before darting off, leaving me feeling exposed and humiliated.

That night, I lay in bed questioning everything. How could I, a 'poor white trash girl from the trailer park,' ever hope for a boy like Billy to like me? I was dressed in a curtain, after all. I resigned myself to the idea that Jill could have him. Billy never spoke to me again, avoiding even a glance in my direction.

Jill tried to comfort me the next day at school. "He's not worth it," she said gently, squeezing my hand.

But the experience at the TWIRP game was more than just an awkward social encounter; it was a painful lesson highlighting differences between my world and that of my peers, a daily reminder of where I stood in the social hierarchy of school life. I vowed never to let myself feel that way again.

As I was trying to feel comfortable in my own skin, Karen had her baby at just fifteen. She named him Eric, and he was the cutest little boy I had ever seen, with a tuft of blonde curly hair and bright, curious eyes. I remember the first time I held him, his tiny fingers wrapped around my own, and how his innocent gaze momentarily dissolved the heavy weight of our family struggles.

Karen's relationship with Momma had always been strained, but Eric's arrival brought about an unexpected change in her. Oddly enough, Momma started staying home more, finding genuine happiness in caring for her grandson. She would cradle Eric in her arms, humming softly to him, her eyes filled with a warmth and joy I hadn't seen in a long time.

"Look at him, PJ," Momma said one day, her voice tinged with wonder as she gently rocked Eric to sleep. "He's a blessing, don't you think?"

I nodded, watching the peaceful rise and fall of Eric's chest as he slept. "He really is, Momma," I agreed, feeling a flicker of hope amid the chaos of our lives.

Karen, on the other hand, was caught in a whirlwind of change. Determined to create a better future for herself and Eric, she worked tirelessly. She earned her GED, enrolled in nursing school, and took a job at a pizza delivery place to make ends meet. Her days were long and exhausting, leaving her with little time to spend with Eric.

"Thanks, Momma," Karen said one evening, dropping Eric off before rushing out the door. Her words were hurried, her face a mask of fatigue. "I don't know what I'd do without you watching him."

Momma smiled, waving her off. "Go on, get to work. Eric and I will be just fine," she assured Karen, her attention already focused on Eric, who gurgled happily in her arms.

With Karen constantly busy, our relationship grew more distant. We barely saw each other, and when we did, she seemed so angry at the world. Her frustration with our circumstances often bubbled over, and I found myself avoiding her to escape the tension.

"Why's she so mad all the time?" I confided in Jill one afternoon as we sat in my room, trying to study but too distracted by the thoughts swirling in my head.

Jill shrugged, twirling a strand of her brown hair around her finger. "She's just overwhelmed. I mean, being a mom and trying to do everything she's doing? It's a lot, PJ."

I sighed, staring out the window. "I guess. I just wish things could be different; you know?"

As much as I understood Karen's struggles, the gap between our lives seemed insurmountable. Her world was filled with adult responsibilities and challenges, while I was still navigating the awkward maze of school. The rare moments we spent together felt strained, a reminder of how much our paths had diverged.

Despite the distance, I couldn't help but admire Karen's determination. She was fighting for a future for herself and Eric, and in some small way, it inspired me to face my own challenges head-on. Yet, the shadow of our family's past loomed large, a constant reminder of the hurdles we all had to overcome.

Still, little Eric was a beacon of hope, a symbol of innocence and possibility in our often-tumultuous world. His presence brought a glimmer of light into our lives, a reminder that even in the darkest of times, there was still room for joy and love.

Chapter 16

OUTSIDE LOOKING IN

As I journeyed through middle school, my friendship with Jill began to show signs of strain. We had always been close, but teenage social pressures began to create cracks in our bond. Jill was always joyful, smiling, and full of life, drawing people in effortlessly. I admired her ease in social situations but also envied it. While I felt clumsy and awkward, Jill seemed to thrive in the social maze of middle school with an ease of which I could only dream.

Our choir competitions were a source of joy for both of us, yet I often felt the sting of embarrassment creeping in. Jill's mom, who was incredibly kind, would pack extra pillows and lunches for the long bus rides to make sure I had enough to eat and even gave me extra money for snacks and souvenirs. Her generosity was heartwarming, but I could see how it embarrassed Jill, who worried that her friends might notice the special treatment. One day, as she handed me a lunch bag, Jill whispered, "You don't have to tell anyone, okay?" Her eyes pleaded for discretion, and I nodded, feeling the weight of her embarrassment mixed with my gratitude.

The cheerleader tryouts were another turning point for us. We practiced together for weeks, perfecting our routines in her backyard. Jill's natural athleticism shone, while I struggled to keep up. On the day of the tryouts, we stood side by side, nervously awaiting our turn. Jill squeezed my hand, whispering, "We've got this." Her confidence bolstered my spirits, but when the results came in, Jill made the team, and I didn't.

"You were amazing," she told me, trying to soften the blow, but the disappointment was sharp and heavy in my chest. I managed to smile, congratulating her even though I felt like a failure.

At lunch, Jill often sat with the popular kids, and though she sometimes invited me to join them, I always felt out of place. Their conversations revolved around weekend plans and fashion trends I knew nothing about. One afternoon, as I approached their table, Jill shifted uncomfortably, unsure whether to wave me over. I sat at the edge, trying to blend in, but the whispers and sideways glances from her friends made it clear I didn't belong.

"Hey, we're going to the movies this weekend," one of the girls announced. Jill just gave me an apologetic look, knowing I wouldn't be included.

Then came the tryouts for school officers. Eager to carve out a space for myself, I decided to run for a position. I poured my heart into my speech, focusing on the importance of kindness and inclusivity. Standing in front of my classmates, I spoke with a voice trembling with passion. Jill sat in the audience, giving me a thumbs up, and for a moment, I felt confident. But when the results were announced, only the popular kids made the cut, leaving me disheartened and feeling more isolated than ever.

Despite my efforts to fit in, I felt increasingly alienated. Jill's life was filled with social activities and friendships that seemed out of reach for me. I missed the easy camaraderie we once shared, but I couldn't shake the feeling that maybe she was embarrassed by me.

One afternoon, as we walked outside, I finally asked her, "Are we still best friends?"

She hesitated, then said, "Of course we are," but her tone was uncertain, and I couldn't help but wonder if she truly meant it.

Throughout these experiences, I grappled with the complexities of our friendship and my place in the social landscape of middle school. While I cherished the moments of joy and connection with Jill, the growing divide between us was a constant reminder of the challenges that lay ahead.

As I stumbled through the blur of sixth and seventh grades, eighth grade arrived with its own set of challenges and expectations. Looming on the horizon was a significant milestone—the transition to high school. Our school had planned a graduation ceremony, followed by a dance on Friday night. It was an event everyone looked forward to, a rite of passage into the next phase of our lives.

So, when Jill and her friends invited me to the eighth-grade dance, my heart leapt with excitement. I was thrilled, yet anxious, knowing the other girls would be wearing beautiful dresses and makeup. I approached Momma with a mix of hope and dread. As expected, she said she could sew a dress more beautiful than anything from a store.

"Momma, I don't want to stand out," I said hesitantly, remembering the TWIRP game shirt fiasco. "It needs to look like everyone else's dress."

"Don't you worry, sweetheart," Momma replied with a smile, her eyes twinkling with determination. "I'll make you a dress that will shine, just like you."

The result was a dress that took my breath away—a soft white cotton A-line dress with baby blue lace and tiny pearl buttons.

Momma held it up with pride. "See? I told you it would be beautiful," she said, brushing a tear from my cheek.

"It's perfect, Momma," I whispered, overwhelmed with gratitude. Her suggestion to braid my hair with a matching ribbon and baby's breath brought tears to my eyes. For once, I felt like I could stand alongside the other girls and feel equal.

The night of the dance, I dressed at Jill's house. We helped each other with hair and makeup, and I reveled in the feeling of being just another girl getting ready for a dance. Jill glanced at me with a smile as she adjusted her dress. "You look amazing, PJ!" she said, her eyes shining with excitement. "We're going to have so much fun tonight!"

The school gym was transformed into a dazzling wonderland, decked out in our school colors—green, yellow, black, and white. Brightly colored balloon archways framed every corner, creating perfect spots for photo opportunities, while upbeat music filled the air with energy and excitement.

Typical punch and snack tables were set up, offering refreshments to the guests, and adult chaperones stood at strategic points, ensuring everything ran smoothly. While the adults watched couples dancing too close or searched for anyone lingering too close to the punchbowl to exclude from the party, I took it all in; I had never felt so included, and it was wonderful! A sense of belonging, new and exhilarating, washed over me.

Later in the evening, as the DJ played a slow song, the boy from the skating rink approached me, his cheeks flushed with nervousness. "Would you like to dance?" he asked, his voice barely audible over the music.

I nodded, feeling my heart race as we moved to the dance floor. As we swayed to the music, I couldn't help but smile. "I never imagined I'd be dancing with you tonight," I admitted, glancing up at him.

He grinned, his eyes twinkling. "Me neither, but I'm glad I am."

As the night went on, the feeling of acceptance and joy enveloped me. High school suddenly seemed full of possibilities, and with Jill by my side, I felt ready to face it.

The summer returned along with constant reminders of the differences between my friends and me. They had their own skates for the rink, Gloria Vanderbilt and Jordache jeans, and money for movies—things I couldn't afford. My longing for these things grew, and when Momma made me a pair of jeans that looked like the popular brands, I was torn.

The jeans were perfect in every way except for the missing designer label. I couldn't bring myself to wear them, and Momma's hurt was evident.

"Don't they fit right?" she asked, her voice filled with hope and just a touch of vulnerability.

"They're fine, Momma. I just... I just don't like them," I mumbled, avoiding her eyes.

"PJ, I spent a lot of time making these for you," she said, her eyes searching mine for understanding. The disappointment in her voice was hard to ignore, and it made my chest tighten with guilt.

Clothing and comparing myself to my peers was just one issue I faced navigating the stormy waters of adolescence; our house was filthy, and the roaches were out of control. Every night, I could hear them skittering across the countertops and scurrying into dark corners. The sheer number of them was overwhelming. Opening a cabinet meant risking roaches falling on your head, and I would feel them crawling in my hair as

I lay in bed. All food had to be kept in the refrigerator because roaches would get into anything left out.

We had too many cats and dogs, and the litter box for the cats was so full of dried poop and urine that the whole house smelled awful. The stench was suffocating, a mix of cat urine and stale air clung to everything. I smelled awful, too; my hair and clothes carried the odor of our home wherever I went.

The shower floor had worn through the particle board of the trailer, leaving gaping holes where you could see the ground outside. I watched in disbelief as cats used the holes to sashay in and out, like our trailer was one giant, disgusting pet door.

My bitterness about our financial situation grew and I didn't realize then how much my attitude was hurting Momma, who was trying her best with the little resources she had. It was a time of conflicting emotions—a desire to fit in clashing with the reality of our life, and a growing resentment that I struggled to keep at bay.

Momma was a proud woman, determined to provide for us even as she juggled multiple jobs. Working as a seamstress downtown, she often stayed up late to finish orders. "I watch sick folks at night, too," she'd tell us, exhaustion lining her face. "It's honest work, and it helps us get by."

When she came home after a long day, the toll of her struggles was visible. Yet, even when she was tired, she tried to maintain some semblance of normalcy for us, especially with baby Eric. She'd hum softly while making dinner, her voice a gentle comfort against the backdrop of our worries. "We'll be alright, babies," she'd say, and I wanted so desperately to believe her.

Chapter 17

FROM HUNGER TO HOPE

As occupied as Momma was, I couldn't count on her to help me with anything, not even to prepare me for the most normal of life's events. It was Jill's sister who came to my aid when Jill and I found ourselves on the cusp of a new, daunting chapter of womanhood: our first menstrual cycles. It was a time marked by confusion, fear, and the kind of camaraderie that only comes when you're navigating the unknown with your best friend.

Armed with a box of tampons, Jill's older sister decided to give us a crash course. "It's easy," she assured us, with the confidence of someone who had clearly forgotten her own first time.

Jill, always a bit braver than me, took the first plunge. After a few minutes in the bathroom, she emerged, her face a comical mix of triumph and discomfort. "I did it," she whispered, as if she'd just defused a bomb. "Your turn."

Armed with determination, I locked myself in the bathroom. One by one, the tampons met their fate—each attempt was a little more frustrating than the last. By the time I was down to the last soldier in the box, it was do or die. After a final, desperate attempt, I managed to insert the tampon. Ouch! How uncomfortable! I emerged from the bathroom, trying to walk normally but feeling like I was part cowboy, part robot. "I did it," I declared, trying to match Jill's earlier bravado.

The rest of the summer, we avoided tampons like they were cursed relics. We found other ways to enjoy our time, deciding that swimming could wait. "Next year, we'll be pros," Jill joked, but we both knew we weren't in any rush to revisit that adventure.

As the summer faded and the new school year approached, Jill and I were filled with a mix of excitement and apprehension. High school, with its new challenges and opportunities, was a far cry from the simpler days of grade school or even middle school.

From the very start, Jill and I were on parallel but diverging paths. She quickly found her place among the popular crowd—the cheerleaders, the student council members, and the dancers. Her outgoing personality and vibrant energy drew people to her naturally. I, on the other hand, felt like an outsider. High school's complex social hierarchy was daunting, and I often found myself on the fringes. My experiences over the summer, while enriching, also deepened my sense of not fitting in.

The disparity in our circumstances, which seemed smaller when we were younger, now loomed larger than ever. During these changes, our shared interests, like being in the marching band and chorale, kept our friendship anchored.

"Hey, ready for band practice?" Jill would ask, her enthusiasm undimmed.

"Yeah, let's do this," I'd respond, grateful for the familiarity of our friendship in this new environment.

Despite our diverging social circles, Jill never wavered in her support for me. "I brought an extra lunch bag for you," she'd say, her thoughtfulness a comfort with the chaos of high school life. Her gestures, though kind, were constrained, a constant reminder of our different lives. They fueled my resolve to be more independent, to find my own place in this new world.

High school brought a world of new challenges and a heightened sense of the social hierarchy, and popularity seemed like the key to a smoother experience. I found myself constantly striving to fit in. I continued to audition for cheerleading and various clubs, but each attempt ended in rejection. Jill, who had once been my closest confidant, drifted away, caught up in her own high school journey. I couldn't really blame her; our lives diverged more with each passing day.

"If only I had nicer clothes or didn't live in a rundown trailer plagued by roaches," I lamented to Jill one afternoon. She listened; her face sympathetic. "You're great just the way you are," she said, trying to reassure me.

But my sense of not belonging at school was overwhelming, and with Jill no longer part of my daily life, I felt even more isolated. Determined to change my circumstances, I set my sights on getting a job. The obstacle was my age—no one seemed willing to hire a fifteen-year-old. But necessity is the mother of invention, and in a moment of desperation, I decided to stretch the truth. I convinced myself that if I claimed to be sixteen, doors would open for me.

After school, I would hastily swap the school bus for my worn-out bike, pedaling as fast as I could to Fred's Hickory Stick, a nearby barbecue restaurant. My heart pounded the first time I told the lie about my age, but to my surprise and relief, it worked. I was hired! Working at Fred's Hickory Stick was a new and exciting experience. I quickly learned the ropes of waiting tables—serving food promptly, refilling drinks, and always wearing a smile.

The job was more than just a means to earn money; it was a place where I felt a sense of accomplishment and independence.

The tips I earned were a bonus, providing me with the financial means to buy some of the things I longed for. I thought that this was the first step towards blending in at school, towards feeling a little less like an outsider. I found a new confidence budding within me inside the bustling environment of the restaurant. The job taught me valuable skills and gave me a glimpse of a world beyond the confines of school and the trailer park. It was a world where my age, my background, or the clothes I wore didn't define me—a world where I could be just another hardworking individual making her way.

One particularly rainy day, as I prepared myself for the wet ride with trash bags taped around me, an unexpected savior appeared. Mrs. Kinney's car pulled into the driveway, and she called out to me, "Get in! You're going to catch a cold out there."

I gratefully climbed into the car, relieved to avoid the rain. "Thank you, Mrs. Kinney," I said, my voice filled with appreciation.

"It's nothing, dear. Just remember to focus on your schoolwork too, alright?" she replied, her tone gentle yet firm.

Working under Fred while in high school was a valuable experience. I managed my responsibilities enough to join the high school marching band, which reconnected me with Jill. We lived close enough that I could catch a ride home with her after games, although our interactions were often awkward. Our conversations mostly centered around her experiences with boys and felt distant to my own life.

While I didn't have a relationship to discuss in return with Jill, I harbored a secret crush on an upperclassman from my Geometry class who sat directly behind me. His name was John—he had dark curly hair, charming dimples, and a smile that could light up a room. He had this habit of twirling my hair during class, a gesture that left me completely distracted.

"Your hair is so soft," John would tease, twirling a strand around his finger.

"Stop it!" I giggled, my cheeks turning crimson.

As a result, I flunked Geometry, too caught up in the warmth of his attention to focus on the lessons. John's interest in me was baffling. It stirred new emotions, a mix of excitement and disbelief. Why would someone like him be interested in me?

Besides John, there were two other boys at school who seemed to like me, but my self-doubt was a barrier too high to overcome. In my mind, I was still that beaten-down girl from my father's house, unworthy of anyone's affection. This yearning for love and acceptance began to overshadow everything else. I found myself seeking validation in all the wrong places, trying to fill the void left by a life of hardships.

"Why can't my life be as easy as yours?" I complained to Jill one afternoon after school.

She shrugged, looking uncomfortable. "You know, things aren't always as perfect as they seem."

The hunger for belonging and security drove me to make choices I later regretted. I couldn't help but wonder why my life was so fraught with challenges while others, like Jill, seemed to have it all.

Mrs. Kinney's presence in my life was a constant reminder of what kind and considerate behavior looked like. She often spoke highly of my mother's strength as a single parent, not knowing the full extent of our struggles. "Your momma works so hard for you all," she'd say with a smile, her words well-meaning but missing the mark. If only she knew the reality of our situation, her perception might change. But in her kindness, Mrs. Kinney offered a glimpse of the love and stability I so desperately craved.

As high school progressed, I grappled with these conflict-ing feelings—the hunger for a normal teenage life, the desire for love and acceptance, and the lingering effects of my past. It was a complex mix of emotions, one that I traversed with caution, always wary of the shadows of my earlier life looming over me.

As the summer after my first year in high school ended, Mrs. Kinney, the ever-present angel in my life, extended an invitation that would open a new chapter for me. She invited me to attend church with her family, including the youth group where Jill was a member. This invitation marked my first return to church since leaving Nacogdoches years before.

"Come with us this Sunday," Mrs. Kinney suggested kindly. "I think you'll enjoy it."

"I'd love to," I replied, grateful for the invitation and the chance to be included.

Walking into the church felt like stepping into a different world, one that was both familiar and foreign. My memories of church were distant and hazy, but there was a comforting familiarity in the hymns and the warm smiles of the congrega-tion. My initial motivation for attending youth group wasn't spiritual; it was more about being with my peers, trying to find a place where I might fit in.

To my surprise, I discovered a gift I didn't know I had—a talent for singing. Encouraged by the youth director, I sang a few specials during the church services. Each note I sang felt like a release, a way to express the emotions I couldn't put into words. The positive response from the congregation was over-whelming. People appreciated my voice, and for the first time in a long time, I felt like I had something valuable to offer.

The youth director took me aside one day and said, "Your voice is a gift, a beautiful instrument given by God. It's something you should share with others, not just because you can, but because it can touch and heal hearts."

Singing in church became more than just a way to show-case my talent; it became a means of connecting with something larger than myself. It was a balm for my soul, a way to find peace transcending the chaos of my life. Though my focus in attending church initially wasn't on God, these experiences began to shift my perspective, opening me up to the possibility of finding solace in faith.

This was a turning point for me—from the struggles with hunger and belonging to discovering a sense of purpose and a glimpse of hope in unexpected places.

Journal Entry September 10, 1992

Today, exhaustion washes over me like a heavy blanket after my therapy session with Barbara. She keeps pushing me to confront and reevaluate my emotions surrounding my Daddy and the men who have crossed my path. I have what they call "Daddy issues." As I dig deep, I start to realize something; there's a thread that connects my anger towards God and my anger towards my Daddy. Why didn't Daddy protect me during that awful year we lived with him? He had to have known something was wrong. But instead of choosing us, he chose a new family. The pain of that abandonment still cuts deep. But as I reflect on the time, I spent with him, a new understanding begins to surface. He loved me, in the only way he knew how, even if it was flawed and imperfect. It's a realization that shakes me, stirring up all sorts of conflicting emotions. I still feel the anger and the hurt, but I'm starting to see the love too—the kind of love that's limited by who he was and what he was capable of. In this process of discovery, I'm also reminded of the love God has for me. It's a love so boundless that He sent His own Son to sacrifice Himself for our sake. I sit here, grappling with the enormity of that sacrifice, and I can't wrap my head around it. As a mother, I can't even imagine making that kind of choice for Kyle. Yet God did it for all of us. Today's session has left me emotionally drained, but I feel more aware of the complexities of love, forgiveness, and the strange, delicate balance of the human heart. Healing isn't simple, and neither is understanding love, whether it's the love of a father who failed me or the love of a God who has never stopped loving me. It's all a process of growth, of peeling back the layers and finding peace in the only love that's truly unconditional.

Chapter 18

A FATHER'S LOVE

I hadn't seen my Daddy since we left his house in Lufkin years before to move to Huntsville. The holidays always served as a poignant reminder of the choice we had to make between spending time with Momma or Daddy, and we invariably chose Momma. The memories of our time with Dorothy and our stepsiblings were too painful, and we avoided returning to that house whenever possible.

However, my sudden need for a vehicle drove me to reconnect with my father. When I called Daddy about helping me get a truck, he was surprisingly responsive.

"Well, I reckon we can find you something decent," he said over the phone, his voice a mix of surprise and curiosity. "I work at a used car lot now, and they have good deals at the auctions. Might just find you a gem!"

The thought of seeing him again filled me with both excitement and apprehension. I wondered how much he might have changed over the years. After about a week, he called with the news that he had found a truck for me. I was overjoyed but puzzled about how I would get to Lufkin.

"Don't you worry about that, PJ," Daddy assured me. "I'll come up there and pick you up myself."

I was astonished by his offer, and the day he arrived, I watched as his old pickup pulled into our driveway. I took a deep breath, my heart racing with a blend of nostalgia and anxiety. As he stepped out, I saw that Dorothy was with him, along with their son, Jed.

Dorothy hadn't changed much, still smoking and in possession of the same old demeanor that I remembered. Daddy, on the other hand, was as tall and lean as ever, though his once black hair was now streaked with silver. He looked different, but his presence still had the same commanding air.

"Look at you, PJ," he said with a smile as he hugged me, his voice a low rumble. "You've grown up real nice. Taller than your Momma, that's for sure."

"Thanks, Daddy," I replied, a mix of pride and unresolved resentment swirling inside me. It was strange to feel this connection after so many years apart. I wondered if he was thinking about the time we had spent together back then, the struggles we faced—the chaos.

Momma stood a bit awkwardly at the doorway, arms crossed, watching the reunion. Her gaze flickered between Daddy and me, a silent acknowledgment of the complicated history we all shared.

"You've got yourself a real looker of a daughter, Fate," she said playfully, her Southern drawl lacing each word.

Daddy grinned, a hint of flirtation in his eyes. "Well, she takes after you, Patsy. It's not my fault she got all the good genes."

Dorothy, observing the banter, rolled her eyes and exhaled a cloud of smoke. "Are we going to stand around all day or hit the road?"

As we piled into the car, I realized how strange it was to see my parents interact like this; it was both lighthearted and oddly familiar, a reminder of their shared history that had led to our family of seven. Standing next to them, I noticed how much I resembled Momma—her curvy figure, auburn hair, and hazel eyes, although thankfully, I was taller, with ever-present freckles dotting my cheeks.

The drive to Lufkin was mostly quiet, the air between us filled with the hum of the truck's engine and the occasional rustle of Dorothy's cigarette pack. Daddy glanced over at me a few times, as if trying to bridge the gap that time had carved between us.

We stopped at a small café along the way, a place he frequented. As we walked in, the smell of fresh coffee and frying bacon enveloped us. Daddy introduced me to a few of his buddies, locals who were regulars at the café.

"This here's my daughter, PJ," he announced with a touch of pride.

"Nice to meet you," one of the men said, tipping his hat. "Fate told us about you. You've got yourself a good Daddy here."

I nodded, feeling both awkward and strangely validated. Could it be that he actually cared for me? I wondered what he had said about me to these people and whether he had thought of me often over the years.

Over breakfast, Daddy tried to fill the silence with questions about my life, asking about school and how I was doing in Huntsville. It was a bit stiff at first, but there was a genuine interest in his eyes.

"You ever think about coming back to Lufkin?" he asked, his tone casual but probing.

I hesitated, choosing my words carefully. "I like it in Huntsville, Daddy. It's different, but it feels like home now."

He nodded, accepting my answer with a slight sigh. "Well, you know you're always welcome back here. We'd love to see you more."

As we finished our meal and got back on the road, I realized that this trip was more than getting a truck. It was a chance to reconnect, to understand the complexities of our family ties, and even to heal some old wounds. Despite everything, I found myself hoping that this time, things might be different, that, just maybe, my Daddy had changed, too.

But being with my father also brought back a flood of horrid memories, each one like a sharp sting. The long-forgotten feelings of fear, neglect, and helplessness resurfaced, overwhelming me with their intensity. Memories of being bullied and tormented by my stepsiblings, the indifference and sometimes outright hostility from Dorothy, and the crushing sense of abandonment when Daddy chose his new family over us were all too vivid.

That year in Lufkin was the darkest of my childhood, my stepsiblings cornering me, threatening, taunting.

"You'll never be one of us," Tanya sneered, her eyes cold and mocking.

Bobby, laughing at my discomfort, chimed in, "Yeah, you're just white trash." During the visit, those memories lingered just beneath the surface, threatening to pull me under. They were a constant shadow in my life, shaping my perception of love, trust, and family.

As we drove to Lufkin, the silence between Daddy and me was only broken by the occasional question.

"How's school?" Daddy asked, his eyes on the road.

"It's fine," I replied, not wanting to delve into the details of my life that felt so separate from his.

"I heard you're working at a restaurant," he said, trying to make conversation.

"Yeah, Fred's Hickory Stick," I confirmed, my voice flat.

The journey with him was a stark reminder of the resilience I had developed in the face of adversity, a testament to my determination to rise above the circumstances that had once defined me. It was difficult to reconcile the man sitting next to me with the one who had allowed such pain to enter my life, but as I sat there, I realized I was no longer that helpless child.

As Daddy's car pulled into the driveway of that house in Lufkin, I was transported back in time. The sight of the old hollowed-out tree in the yard, where Karen and I used to hide, was a reminder of the desperate measures we had taken to escape our reality. It represented a place of refuge in a world where we felt constantly under threat.

The car idled as Daddy noticed my face turning pale and my hands clenching tightly in my lap. He gave me a sidelong glance, eyes narrowing as he studied my reaction. "PJ, you all right?" he asked, his voice gruff yet somehow soft around the edges.

"I can't go in there, Daddy," I admitted, my voice trembling as memories of past horrors swirled in my mind. "Please, can we just go?"

He hesitated, his gaze shifting from me to the house, as if seeing it anew through my eyes. "You know, I always thought you were tougher than the rest," he muttered. It was not exactly an apology but at least it was an acknowledgment of sorts.

I nodded, tears pricking my eyes as I struggled to hold onto my composure. "I had to be," I whispered.

With a grunt, he threw the car into reverse, backing out of the driveway. His jaw was set, the lines of his face deep with unspoken thoughts. "We'll go to the lot," he said shortly. "No need to dwell on what's done."

Relief washed over me as we drove away from the house, the distance putting a small buffer between me and the pain it represented. I watched the tree fade from view, feeling a knot of tension begin to unwind inside me.

We arrived at the used car lot, and there it was—my truck, a 1972 Chevrolet in blue and white. Its paint glinted in the afternoon sun, a bright spot amid the lingering shadows of my past. I stared at it, feeling a swell of emotions.

"This here's yours if you want it," Daddy said, nodding toward the truck. "Four payments of $66.75, and it's all yours. Thought you might need a fresh start."

"Thank you, Daddy," I replied, my voice steadier.

He nodded again; his gaze fixed on the truck. "You're a tough kid, PJ. You'll make it."

As I drove back to Huntsville, each mile put between me and Lufkin felt like a step toward reclaiming my life. This new-found independence led me to leave my job at Fred's Hickory Stick, a place that had provided financial support but also held uncomfortable memories. Fred, the owner, was a big, jolly man, always with a smile, but his jovial nature masked a darker side.

Whenever he took me into the walk-in cooler, his hands would roam over my body, and I would just wait silently for him to finish, then go back to work as if nothing had happened. I had learned to endure it, convinced that being used like that was all I was worth, a belief ingrained from being labeled poor white trash. Working there felt like yet another cycle of shame I was trapped inside.

The owners of the convenience store, a kindly older couple named Mr. and Mrs. Miller, had put up a Help Wanted sign. I hesitated in front of the store, nerves dancing in my stomach, before taking a deep breath and walking inside.

"Can I help you?" Mrs. Miller asked from behind the counter, her gray hair pulled back in a neat bun. She had a warm smile that made me feel welcome.

"Hi, I'm PJ," I said, trying to keep my voice steady. "I saw your sign outside, and I'd like to apply for the job."

Mrs. Miller's eyes brightened as she looked me over. "Of course! We could use some extra hands. Do you have any experience working in a store?"

I nodded, recalling my time at Fred's. "Yes, I've worked at a restaurant before, handling customers and cash."

Mr. Miller emerged from the back, wiping his hands with a towel. "What's this about a job?" he asked, his voice deep and gravelly.

"PJ here is interested in the position," Mrs. Miller explained, gesturing toward me. "She's got experience in customer service."

Mr. Miller gave me an appraising look. "You a hard worker, PJ?"

"Yes, sir," I replied, meeting his gaze. "I'm willing to learn and do whatever's needed."

He nodded slowly, considering my words. "We're a small operation here, but we treat everyone like family. We'll need you to stock shelves, work the register, and help keep the place tidy. Think you can manage that?"

"I can manage it," I assured him, feeling more confident. "I really want this job."

Mrs. Miller smiled again, glancing at her husband. "Well, I think you'd be a great fit, PJ. What do you think, Harold?"

Mr. Miller scratched his chin. "She seems like a good kid. I say we give her a shot. You can start next week if you're available."

Relief washed over me, and I grinned widely. "Thank you so much! I won't let you down."

As I left the store, a sense of accomplishment filled me. I had a vehicle and had secured a job on my own, steps toward independence and proving to myself that I could shape my own destiny. The prospect of working at the convenience store brought a renewed sense of hope, a chance that maybe, just maybe, I could build something better for myself.

Chapter 19

WHEN IGNORANCE MEETS INNOCENCE

On the first day at the store, I quickly adapted to the tasks. I found a rhythm in the routine of stocking shelves, ringing up customers, and cleaning. Not only was I away from Fred's groping hands, but the Millers treated me kindly, offering advice and guidance in addition to employment, and I felt a sense of belonging I hadn't experienced in a long time.

Each shift brought a sense of pride and confidence, though my father's absence still lingered in my mind. Since driving the truck off the lot, Daddy hadn't called to check on me or the truck. I had sent off my first payment and was left wondering if he had even received it. Deep down, I couldn't shake the feeling that his gesture of giving me the truck was fleeting, perhaps a momentary act of kindness or simply a way to make a sale.

One afternoon, while I was behind the counter restocking the gum and candy, I sighed and said to myself, "Why hasn't he called? He must have gotten the payment by now."

My co-worker Jenny looked over at me, raising an eyebrow. "Still nothing from your dad, huh?"

I shook my head. "Not a word. It's like he forgot I exist again. You'd think after giving me the truck, he'd at least want to know how I'm doing."

Jenny leaned against the counter with her arms crossed. "You should call him, PJ. Sometimes you've got to remind people you're here."

I shrugged. "I don't know, Jen. He just... doesn't care as much as I hoped."

Interrupting my thoughts was a new distraction, suddenly appearing in the form of Todd, a young college student who often stopped by the store for gas. One afternoon, as I rang up his purchase, he flashed me a charming smile and said, "Hey, PJ—what are you doing Saturday night?"

My heart skipped a beat. "Uh, nothing much, I guess. Why?"

"Well," he said, leaning casually against the counter, "I was thinking maybe we could catch a movie. What do you say?"

I was taken aback, a mix of disbelief and excitement flooding my senses. "You want to go to the movies... with me?"

"Why not?" Todd grinned. His confidence was infectious. "I think it'll be fun."

After a moment of hesitation, I nodded, smiling despite myself. "Yeah, sure. I'd like that."

The idea of a college guy being interested in me, a high school girl, was thrilling. Being a college town, Huntsville had its share of young, attractive students, but I never imagined one would notice me.

Saturday night arrived, and our date was simple yet exciting. After dinner and a movie at the local theater, I expected Todd to take me back to my truck at the store. Instead, he drove us to his place, a small but tidy travel trailer.

As he parked and turned off the engine, I glanced over at him, uncertain. "Your place?"

"Yeah," he said, hopping out of the car and opening my door for me, "I figured we could hang out here for a bit. I promise it's not a mess."

I hesitated for a moment but then followed him inside. The trailer, though cluttered, was far cleaner and better organized than my home. As I looked around, taking in the unfamiliar surroundings, a mix of emotions swirled within me. I was flattered by his attention yet uneasy about being in such an intimate setting with someone I barely knew.

The excitement of the date mingled with a nagging sense of apprehension. I was stepping into uncharted territory, both exhilarated and nervous about what this new experience might bring. I couldn't help but feel a little hesitant. No one ever told me not to go into a young man's home alone. I sat down in his tidy tiny home and looked up at him as he stood over me with a strange look on his face.

"So," Todd said, leaning against the counter, "what do you think?"

"It's nice," I replied, trying to keep my tone casual. "A lot neater than I expected."

He laughed, sitting beside me. "Yeah, I try to keep it clean. It's not much, but it's home."

I sat down in Todd's tidy tiny home, feeling the mix of anticipation and nerves twist in my stomach. Todd stood over me with a strange look on his face, one I couldn't quite read. After a moment, he reached out and gestured for my hand.

"Come on," he said softly.

I hesitated but then took his hand. He led me to the back where a bed was pushed against the wall. The room felt even smaller with both of us in it, and my heart raced as I realized what was about to happen.

Todd didn't say anything as he gently pushed me down onto the bed. I lay back, trying to steady my breathing. He slid my jeans down to my ankles, not bothering to remove my boots.

"I heard it can hurt," I said nervously, trying to break the tension.

Todd shrugged, "It won't be that bad. Just relax," he said.

I had heard the girls at school talk about what sex was like for the first time—the awkwardness, the pain—so I was nervous about what was coming. My mind raced with thoughts, but they all came crashing down to the moment I found myself in, giving a stranger something so precious as my virginity.

Surprisingly, the thing I noticed most was it didn't hurt like I had expected. Todd made a lot of noise on top of me, and then, just as quickly as it started, he stood up and pulled his pants back on.

I lay there for a moment, confused. Finally, I sat up and pulled my jeans back on. "Why didn't it hurt?" I wondered silently, recalling how even using a tampon had been more uncomfortable than my first sexual encounter.

On the way back to the convenience store, we didn't exchange a single word. As we pulled into the parking lot, I looked over at him, searching for something—reassurance, acknowledgment, anything.

Todd pointed to the passenger door and said, "Thanks, I'll call you later."

"Sure," I replied, trying to mask the confusion and disappointment in my voice.

I got out and watched as he drove off, leaving me standing alone in the dim light of the parking lot. I climbed into my truck, my mind a tangled mess of emotions. Everything had happened so fast, and I couldn't shake the feeling of shame that clung to me.

Sitting alone in my truck, I felt a wave of regret wash over me. It all felt so jumbled up and I couldn't help but feel bad about myself. At school, everyone gossiped about girls who hung out with older guys, and now I was one of them. I didn't want to be talked about like that, but it seemed like it was already too late.

"I promise myself I won't do something like that again," I whispered to the empty cab of my truck, trying to make sense of it all.

My thoughts drifted to my dad, how he never really showed he cared. The way he was absent from my life made me feel like that's just how things are with guys. You have to give something to get a little bit of love or even just attention. I knew it wasn't the best idea, but part of me felt like it was the only way to feel noticed.

I sat there for a long time, grappling with the weight of what had just happened, the reality settling heavily on my shoulders. It was a lesson learned the hard way, and as I drove home that night, I couldn't shake the feeling that I needed to find a different way to navigate this world.

Journal Entry, September 26, 1992

Today's my birthday, and there's a small spark of happiness, like a single candle flickering in the dark. But even as I try to hold onto that happiness, my mind keeps drifting back to Lenny. Does he ever think about our son? Does he ever think about the life we used to share?

So many questions swirl around in my head, all of them left unanswered. It feels like the man I married just disappeared one day, leaving this huge, empty space behind. I find myself thinking about who he used to be—the guy who was so much fun, so honest, and always trying to make everyone happy. He was my best friend. And now... now it feels like he's a stranger.

As much as it hurts, I know I'll start feeling better with time. But the sadness lingers, especially when I think about how Kyle won't ever get to know his dad the way I did. One day, I'll have to explain to Kyle why his father doesn't love us like he once did, why he's not around. The thought weighs heavy on me, but I know it's something I'll have to face sooner or later. When the sadness feels too overwhelming, I find myself praying. It's a small comfort, but it helps. Gives me a little hope. I keep reminding myself that I need to be strong for Kyle, to be the best mom I can be. I want him to feel loved every single day, no matter what. Every day, I'm trying to pick up the shattered pieces of my heart and put them back together. I'm hoping that, eventually, I'll figure out the answers to all these questions that haunt me, learn how to forgive, and create a future where Kyle feels safe and loved; despite everything we've been through. One day, I'll find peace in all of this. But for now, I just take it one day at a time, holding onto the belief that love, in the end, will be enough to carry us through.

Chapter 20

FIRST TRUE LOVE

Working at the convenience store, I saw all sorts of people come and go, each one a fleeting presence in my day. But one afternoon, as the sun cast long shadows across the pavement, I noticed a young man in a shiny red Jeep. He was tall and athletic, with curly blonde hair framing a face lit up by a larger-than-life smile. His blue-gray eyes had a playful sparkle, and his skin boasted a deep tan that suggested he spent plenty of time outdoors.

He came into the store to pay for his gas, offering me a casual nod and a friendly smile as he handed over the money. Something about him seemed familiar, like someone I might have passed in the halls at school, but I didn't think much of it at the time. He left, but then returned a few minutes later to buy a soda, explaining with a sheepish grin that he had forgotten it earlier.

Still, I didn't think too much of it until he came back a third time. This visit was different. He lingered near the counter, looking a bit uncertain, before finally speaking up.

"Hey," he said, his voice tinged with a nervous charm. "I know this might sound crazy, but my friends dared me to ask you out on a date."

I blinked in surprise, taken aback by his straightforward-ness. "Really?" I replied, curiosity piqued. "Do you go to our high school?"

"Yeah, I'm a senior," he said, nodding with that same daz-zling smile. "I graduate this year."

I couldn't believe it. He was charming, had that infectious charisma, and drove a Jeep—all major points in his favor. My heart fluttered with excitement and nervousness. This encoun-ter, unexpected as it was, felt like the beginning of something new and thrilling.

But then a nagging thought crossed my mind. What if he and his friends knew about my awkward date with the college guy? I tried to push aside my doubts as I considered Lenny's offer.

"You sure you want to go out with me?" I asked, half-jok-ing, trying to gauge if there was any hint of mockery in his eyes.

"Of course I do," Lenny replied earnestly, his blue-gray eyes meeting mine. "Why wouldn't I?"

"Okay, let's do it," I said, smiling despite myself. We agreed to meet after work on Saturday night, and I suggested the store as our meeting point because I was embarrassed about him see-ing my home.

Lenny had a way of keeping me on my toes—one minute he was silly, making me laugh with his goofy antics, and the next, he was intense, affectionate, and took my breath away. That duality was part of what drew me to him. When he showed up for our first date with a giant teddy bear and a bouquet of flow-ers, I couldn't help but grin.

"Wow, you're really pulling out all the stops, huh?" I teased, accepting the gifts with a smile.

He winked at me. "Just wanted to make sure you know how special you are."

The evening was unexpectedly delightful. We hit up a local arcade, where Lenny's competitive streak came out in full force. He was all about winning, but in the most playful way.

"You're going down, PJ!" he declared, a mischievous glint in his eye as we squared off over a game of Pac-Man.

"In your dreams, Lenny," I shot back, laughing as I tried to keep up with him.

Later, we grabbed pizza, and watching Lenny devour an entire pie by himself was both astonishing and hilarious.

"Do you ever stop eating?" I asked, raising an eyebrow at him.

"Not when there's pizza," he replied with a grin. "It's like a personal challenge."

For the first time in what felt like forever, I genuinely enjoyed a date. Lenny was a gentleman through and through—he held my hand, put his arm around me, and even opened the Jeep door for me.

As we drove, I couldn't help but express my gratitude. "Thanks for making tonight so fun."

"No problem," he said, glancing over at me with a smile. "I'm glad you had a good time."

He shared that he didn't live with his parents anymore but was rooming with a friend in a small trailer. I could see a flicker of something in his eyes when he mentioned his home life, so I asked him about it.

"I used to live with my dad after my parents split up," Lenny began, his tone growing more serious. "But when he remarried, things went south. My stepmom... she's a real piece of work. She'd get drunk and beat me up for little things—like not cleaning my room or tracking mud in the house after hunting."

I looked at him, my heart aching at the thought. "That's awful, Lenny. How did you handle it?"

He sighed, his playful demeanor fading as he continued. "One day, I just had enough. I stood up to her, told her I wasn't gonna take it anymore. She threw all my stuff out on the lawn and told me to leave. The worst part? My dad just sat there, didn't say a word. He just watched."

I felt a pang of understanding hit me deep. "I'm sorry, Lenny. I know how it feels to have a dad who doesn't seem to care."

He nodded, his expression softening as he looked at me. "That's why we get along so well, PJ. We both know what it's like to be let down by the people who are supposed to protect us."

By the time we arrived at his place, I was hesitant about going inside. The memory of my last experience in a guy's home flashed through my mind, but Lenny's sincerity and the connection we were building made me feel safe. When we walked in, his roommate was there, which helped ease my nerves.

"Hey, I'm Mike," his roommate said, offering a handshake. "Nice to meet you. Lenny's talked about you."

"Oh—has he?" I asked, glancing at Lenny with a smirk.

"All good things, I swear," Lenny said, grinning as he clapped Mike on the back.

Mike grabbed his keys and headed for the door. "I'm out for the night, but we should all hang out sometime."

After Mike left, Lenny and I were alone in the trailer. I felt a mix of excitement and nervousness, but Lenny's warmth and the way he'd shared his story with me put me at ease.

"So, what do you think of the place?" Lenny asked as he sat down on the sofa, patting the cushion beside him.

"It's nice," I replied, taking a seat next to him. "It feels cozy."

"I'm glad you think so," he said, leaning in closer. "Can I ask you something?"

"Sure," I said, my heart starting to race.

"Can I kiss you?" Lenny asked, his voice gentle and sincere.

"Yes," I whispered, and before I knew it, his lips were on mine, soft and sweet.

The kiss was tender at first, but as it deepened, I felt a warmth spreading through me. There was something about Lenny that made me feel wanted, safe even. When we finally pulled apart, he looked into my eyes, his expression serious but kind.

"You're special, PJ," he said softly, his thumb brushing lightly across my cheek. "Don't ever forget that."

"Thanks," I replied, feeling a little breathless. "I needed to hear that."

As I sat there with Lenny, I realized this was more than just a date. It was the beginning of something new, something that might help heal the parts of me that had been so badly hurt.

It was different from before. He sat me up and removed my blouse and then my bra. He looked at me for the longest time and then kissed my neck. He whispered in my ear. "You are so beautiful." He removed his shirt, and we were skin on skin, exploring each other. I had never felt this way and thought to myself this must be what love feels like. He finished undressing me and we went to his bed. As we both laid there under the covers, he asked me if I have ever been with someone sexually and I answered, "Once." We quickly became one and this time it was painful. He apologized and noticed the blood all over his sheets. Lenny said, "I thought you weren't a virgin!" I'm not, but it did not feel this way before." I explained what had happened the last time, and he laughed uncontrollably. He said, "That guy must have had a pencil-dick!" I told him I didn't remember seeing his penis and Lenny laughed even more.

The night had been a blur of new feelings and experiences, leaving me questioning my choices. I couldn't help but worry about whether Lenny would want to see me again or if he had just gotten what he wanted from me. Waking up the next morning, the wave of emotions washing over me including guilt, I knew I had to hurry back home to change before school, but the thought of facing Momma after being gone a whole night filled me with dread. She had her own set of struggles, and I often felt like an additional burden to her. I worried about her reaction, fearing her disappointment or anger.

As Lenny drove me home, his dark blonde curls blowing in the wind from the open window, he tried to make small talk to lighten the mood. "So, how was your first Jeep ride?" he asked, glancing at me with a playful smile. The way his tan skin caught the light made him look so striking, I could hardly keep my eyes off him.

I managed to smile in return. "It was good. I mean, it was fun," I replied, my mind elsewhere, lost in the whirlwind of emotions from the night before and the apprehension of the upcoming confrontation with Momma.

"Hey, don't worry too much," Lenny said, sensing my unease. "I'll call you later, okay?"

I nodded, offering him a quick smile before stepping out of the car.

Once I reached home, I braced myself for Momma's reaction. To my surprise, she seemed more concerned than angry. As soon as I walked through the door, she was there waiting for me. "Where have you been? I was worried sick!" she said, her voice tinged with relief rather than anger.

I mumbled, "I stayed over at a friend's house," not wanting to divulge the whole truth.

Momma looked at me for a long moment, as if trying to read my thoughts, and then simply nodded. "Well, next time, call me, alright? Let me know where you are," she said, letting the matter drop. I was grateful for her unspoken understanding, or it was her own preoccupations that kept her from probing further.

As I prepared for school, a part of me wished for something I never thought I'd want—discipline from Momma. The absence of guidance and structure in my life brought about this odd longing. While most teens might have delighted in a lack of rules, I found myself feeling set adrift in my own life, like a sailor lost at sea without a compass. This freedom, instead of being liberating, felt disorienting, leaving me unsure of which path to follow. I often observed how Jill's parents were with her, setting boundaries and enforcing rules. It wasn't just about punishment; it was a sign of their involvement and concern in her life. They disciplined her by taking away privileges when necessary, teaching her about consequences and responsibility.

I sighed, glancing over at Momma, who was busy with her morning routine. "Momma," I hesitated, "do you ever think about, I don't know, giving me more rules or something?"

Momma paused and looked at me with a raised eyebrow. "You want more rules, PJ? What's gotten into you?"

I shrugged, unsure how to explain what I was feeling. "I just see how Jill's parents are, and sometimes it seems like... I don't know, like it shows they care."

Momma sighed, a hint of weariness in her eyes. "PJ, I've always wanted you to have freedom, to figure things out for yourself. I don't always know the best way, but I'm trying."

I nodded, appreciating her honesty, yet still wishing for a little more guidance.

I realized that Momma's hands-off approach was her way of coping with her own struggles, and perhaps it was also her way of giving me room to grow. But part of me still longed for her to set limits, to show me that she cared enough to teach me about accountability. It would have been a sign that she was paying attention, and that my actions mattered to her.

Chapter 21

WITHOUT BOUNDARIES

As Momma set off for her new job at the college dining hall, where she would be working as a cook, I watched her prepare for the day. "Are you sure you don't need anything for school?" she asked, adjusting her apron.

"I'm fine, Momma," I replied, hoping for a hint of concern in her voice.

Her new job brought her joy, and for my siblings and me, the added benefit of free meals during our after-school visits was certainly a treat. However, to my hidden dismay, Momma's reaction to my late return the night before was devoid of any anger. She simply asked, "Did you have a good time last night?" adding before I had the chance to answer, "Just don't be late for school again, okay? I don't have time to deal with them."

"Yeah, it was alright, and don't worry about the school, I wrote a note and signed your name last time." I answered, waiting for something more from her.

Her casual demeanor left me with a sense of longing for some indication that she cared, that my actions mattered enough to warrant her attention and guidance. I hesitated before leaving the house, wanting to say something that might spark a deeper conversation, but the words wouldn't come.

As I drove to school, these thoughts weighed heavily on me. The night with Lenny had been a step into a world I knew little about, a world where I had to make my own choices without much guidance. It was both exhilarating and terrifying.

At school, with all the chatter and laughter of my classmates, I couldn't help but feel a bit disconnected. During lunch, a friend of mine noticed my distraction. "Hey, PJ—you, okay? You seem a bit out of it," she commented, concern in her eyes.

"I'm just... thinking about a lot of things," I said, trying to brush it off with a smile.

"They'll work themselves out," she assured me, her voice kind and supportive.

Her words were comforting, but I still felt like I was grappling with questions about love, desire, and the need for guidance—all while trying to find my place in this ever-changing world. The certainty that defined my friends' lives was something I longed for, even as I navigated my way through the complexities of growing up.

Each morning, I would make a stop at the laundromat on my way to school. In the bathroom sink, I would wash my hair thoroughly, making sure it was clean and fresh. While I did that, my clothes tumbled in the dryer with scented sheets to rid them of the awful smell of cat urine and cigarette smoke from home.

The conditions at home had worsened, with roaches running rampant and the stench of cat urine and feces permeating everything. Despite the situation, I didn't want to hurt Momma's feelings by complaining about it, so my routine at the laundromat became my secret solution.

As I exited the laundromat each morning, I'd often run into the owner.

He'd smile and say, "You're the only customer who shows up just to use the sink."

I'd laugh and reply, "The bathroom has the best water pressure."

This little ritual gave me a sense of control, allowing me to face the world, and my classmates, my peers, without feeling ashamed.

Lenny and I became inseparable quickly after that first date, both of us desperately seeking a connection with our troubled family backgrounds. Lenny's home life was filled with challenges, too; the tense relationship with his stepmother, who was always finding fault with him, continued and his father was often absent. After one particularly nasty argument with her about mud he had tracked into the house after hunting, she snapped.

"Clean this up, now!" she yelled, her face twisted in anger.

Lenny, tired of her constant berating, stood his ground. "It's just a little dirt. I'll clean it up," he said, trying to stay calm.

But she wasn't having it. "You're just like your father—useless!" she spat. Without warning, she began throwing his clothes out of the closet and into the front yard. "Get out!" she screamed.

His father, sitting in his usual chair, just watched silently as Lenny's things were tossed outside. That silence, more than anything else, cut Lenny deeply.

"I'll go," Lenny said, his voice hollow as he started gathering his belongings.

One evening, after an intense argument with his roommate about the rent he couldn't pay, I found myself saying the words before I even thought them through. "Why don't you stay at my place?" I suggested, hoping to offer him some comfort.

Lenny looked at me, surprised. "You sure? I mean, you told me your place isn't exactly..." he trailed off, trying to find the right words.

I nodded, brushing off his concerns. "Yeah, it's not much, but it's better than dealing with your roommate. Besides, I want you there."

"Alright," he agreed, his eyes softening. "If it means being with you, I don't care where we live."

My feelings for Lenny were deep and all-consuming. I was truly in love, willing to do anything for him. We settled into a routine, finding solace in each other's company despite the state of my home. Lenny's presence made everything feel more bearable, even though the whispers started not long after he moved in.

One day, as I was walking down the hallway at school, I overheard a conversation between two girls from my class. They were standing by the lockers, their voices hushed but not enough to avoid my ears.

"Did you hear PJ moved her boyfriend into her house?" one girl whispered, her tone dripping with judgment.

The other girl snickered. "Yeah. What kind of girl does that? She's practically living with him. I bet she dropped out already."

I felt a flush of embarrassment and anger. The comments stung, but I didn't let on that I had heard them. Instead, I just walked faster, pretending their words didn't bother me, but inside, they echoed, making me question everything.

A few days later, Lenny got a call on the house phone from his biological mother in Florida. We were sitting in the small living room when the phone rang. He picked up the receiver, his expression shifting from curiosity to surprise, then to excitement.

"Hey, Mom," he said, holding the phone to his ear. I could hear her faint voice on the other end, but not enough to make out the words. Lenny listened intently, nodding along.

"Yeah, I'm here with PJ," he replied, glancing at me with wide eyes. "What's up?"

As the conversation continued, I watched as his eyes lit up with excitement. "Really? A franchise business?" he repeated, his voice rising with enthusiasm.

He looked at me with a grin, "Mom, that sounds amazing. I'd love to, but...I'm with PJ now."

There was a pause as his mother spoke, and I could see the wheels turning in Lenny's mind. Finally, he nodded. "I'll talk to her."

He hung up the phone and turned to me, barely containing his excitement. "PJ, she wants me to come to Florida. It's a huge opportunity! She's got this company that sells franchises, and there's a chance I could own part of it one day."

I tried to process what he was saying, feeling a mix of excitement and fear. "That's incredible, Lenny," I said slowly. "But...Florida?"

"Yeah," he nodded eagerly. "And I want you to come with me. We can start fresh, just the two of us. What do you think?"

At fifteen, I didn't hesitate. The idea of escaping to a new place, far from the judgmental whispers and the suffocating environment of home, was too appealing. "Let's do it," I agreed, a thrill running through me at the thought of such a bold move.

We packed our belongings into black trash bags, the few things we had, and I made a stop to tell Momma I was leaving. She was sitting on the porch, smoking a cigarette, when I approached her.

"Momma," I began, trying to keep my voice steady. "I'm going to Florida with Lenny."

She looked at me, her expression unreadable for a moment. Then she exhaled a cloud of smoke and nodded. "Be careful, PJ. Call me when you get there," she said, her voice calm, almost nonchalant.

A part of me longed for her to object, to insist that I stay, but she didn't. "Are you sure you want to do this?" she asked, but her tone lacked urgency, as if she already knew my answer.

"Yeah, Momma. I need to do this," I replied, searching her face for any sign that she might try to stop me.

"Alright then," she said, standing up and giving me a quick hug. "Take care of yourself."

Even the school principal didn't object when I told him about my move. As I walked into his office, clutching the paperwork in my hand, I could feel my heart pounding. The principal, a tall man with graying hair and a stern expression, looked up from his desk as I entered.

"What can I do for you, PJ?" he asked, his voice sounding tired.

I swallowed hard, trying to keep my voice steady. "I'm here to drop out, sir. I'm moving to Florida," I said, holding out the papers for him to sign.

He took the papers from me, his brow furrowing as he read them. "Florida? You're leaving school?" he asked, glancing up at me over the rim of his glasses.

"Yes, sir," I replied, nodding. "I'm going with my boyfriend."

He studied me for a moment, then gave another weary sigh. "Alright," he said, picking up his pen. "But you need to understand what you're giving up. This isn't something you can easily undo."

"I know," I whispered, watching as he signed the paperwork.

Once he finished, he handed the papers back to me. "You'll need to clean out your locker and turn in all your school books," he instructed, his voice carrying a note of finality.

I nodded, taking the papers. "Thank you, sir," I said softly.

He gave me a long, thoughtful look. "Good luck, PJ. I hope you find what you're looking for," he said, his tone more resigned than hopeful.

I forced a smile, trying to hide the mix of emotions swirling inside me. "Thanks," I mumbled before turning and heading out of his office.

As I walked down the hallway to my locker, the reality of what I was doing began to sink in. I started to pull out my books, stacking them on the floor next to me. Each book felt heavier than the last, a physical reminder of the life I was leaving behind.

Finally, I closed my locker door for the last time and made my way back to the office to return the books. The secretary barely glanced at me as I handed them over, and as I walked out of the school, I couldn't help but feel a strange mix of freedom and fear. I was leaving everything I knew behind, but for the first time, the future was entirely up to me.

Chapter 22

FROM SHADOWS TO STABLE

So off we went, driving my truck all the way to Jacksonville—an eighteen-hour journey that felt like a lifetime. Upon arriving late at night, we stayed with Lenny's sister, Lori, and her husband, Jerry. Their two large red Dobermans were intimidating, but they eventually warmed up to us.

However, it didn't take long for me to realize that Lori didn't approve of me. I overheard her talking to Jerry one evening, not bothering to lower her voice.

"I don't know what Lenny's thinking, bringing that girl here," Lori said, her tone filled with disdain.

"She's just a kid," Jerry replied, not as harsh but not defending me either.

Lori scoffed. "Exactly. What kind of future does she think they'll have together? Lenny's got so much potential, and he's wasting it on some girl he barely knows."

The words stung, but I didn't let on that I had heard them. Instead, I tried to focus on the opportunity ahead, hoping that once we got settled, things would get better. But deep down, I knew that no matter where we went, the shadows of our pasts and what we came from would follow us. Lenny and I were connected by the scars left by our fathers, and that connection was both our strength and our weakness.

The atmosphere at Lenny's sister Lori's house was thick with tension, the kind that hung in the air like a storm cloud, ready to burst at any moment. From the day we arrived, it was clear that Lori didn't like me. She had a sharp, disapproving look that she never bothered to hide, and her husband, Jerry, was even worse—a man with a dangerous edge, always teetering on the brink of violence.

One night, that tension exploded into something much darker. Lenny and I were working at the pizza restaurant Lori owned when a fight broke out at the bar next door. We heard shouting, the crash of breaking glass, and then a gunshot that cut through the night like a blade. We rushed outside to see Jerry standing over one of the brawlers, a gun in his hand, his face twisted with anger.

"Jerry, what are you doing?" Lenny shouted, fear lacing his voice as he grabbed Jerry's arm.

Jerry barely glanced at him; his eyes wild with fury. "This bastard had it coming!" he snarled, shaking Lenny off.

Within minutes, the police were there, lights flashing as they swarmed the scene. Jerry was arrested on the spot, and we were all dragged into the chaos, our names added to the list of witnesses. The image of Jerry with that gun, his face contorted in rage, stayed with me long after the police took him away. But what terrified me even more was the realization that we'd have to testify in court.

We were subpoenaed to give depositions, and in the months leading up to that day, Jerry's presence loomed over us like a dark shadow. He was released on bail, and he came back home more dangerous than ever. His drinking escalated, and the drugs only made him more unpredictable. Every day felt like walking on eggshells, never knowing when Jerry would snap.

One night, the fear reached a boiling point. Jerry, drunk and high, stormed into the small room Lenny and I shared, the door slamming against the wall. He had a gun in his hand, the same one from the bar fight, and he was pointing it right at Lenny.

"You think you can rat me out and get away with it?" Jerry slurred, his voice dripping with menace. "I'll kill you both before you get the chance."

"Put the gun down, Jerry," Lenny said, his voice calm but firm, even as his hands trembled. "You don't want to do this."

Jerry's eyes flicked to me; his face twisted into a sneer. "You shut your mouth," he spat. "You're just as guilty."

I was frozen in fear, my mind racing. I wanted to scream, to run, but I couldn't move. The only thing I could think of was that we needed to get out of there before it was too late.

Lori suddenly appeared in the doorway, her face pale. "Jerry, stop this!" she yelled, her voice shaking. "You're going to get yourself locked up for good."

For a moment, Jerry hesitated, the gun wavering in his hand. Lenny took the opportunity to grab my arm and pull me towards the window. "Go, PJ, now!" he urged.

We didn't waste a second. I scrambled out of the window, my heart pounding in my chest. The night air hit me like a shock as I landed on the grass outside, but I didn't stop to catch my breath. Lenny was right behind me, and we ran until we were sure Jerry wasn't following.

We found refuge in a small, dingy hotel, checking in under fake names. The room was cold and impersonal, but it felt like a sanctuary compared to what we had just escaped. We knew we couldn't stay there forever, but at least we were safe for the night.

"We have to get out of Florida," I whispered, sitting on the edge of the bed, my hands still shaking. "We can't live like this."

Lenny, grim-faced, nodded. "You're right. But we have to give those depositions first, or the police will come after us. As soon as we testify, we'll leave. We'll go back to Texas."

The weeks leading up to the depositions were a blur of fear and anxiety. Every time we left the hotel, I was terrified we'd run into Jerry. But we kept our heads down and stayed as far away from Lori's house as possible.

The day we gave our depositions was one of the hardest days of my life. We walked into that courtroom with our heads held high, but inside I was shaking. I recounted everything I saw that night, every terrifying detail, while Jerry glared at us from across the room. The weight of his stare was like a physical force, but I kept going, determined to get through it.

When it was finally over, Lenny and I walked out of the courthouse without looking back. We knew we couldn't stay in Florida a minute longer. We packed up the little we had left, stuffing everything into black trash bags, and hit the road.

The drive back to Texas was long and quiet. We didn't talk much, both of us lost in our thoughts. But as the miles between us and Florida grew, I started to feel something I hadn't felt in a long time—relief. We were finally free from Jerry's threats, free from the fear that had hung over us like a dark cloud.

When we reached Huntsville, it felt like we were finally able to breathe again. The familiar sights and sounds of Texas were a balm to our frayed nerves. We were safe, and that was all that mattered.

Not long after we returned, Lenny and I made the decision to get married. Our wedding was simple—a courthouse ceremony with just a few close friends and family. There were no grand celebrations, but there was love, and that was enough.

Momma did her best to make the day special. She baked a beautiful cake and hosted a small reception at her house. It wasn't the wedding I had dreamed of as a little girl, but it was ours, and that made it perfect.

Our time in Florida was behind us, but it had left its mark. We were different people after—stronger, more resilient, and determined to create a life for ourselves that was free from the chaos we had left behind. As we moved forward, I reflected on Momma's life and the challenges she had faced. Becoming a mother at an early age, losing her father early on, and raising us alone after Daddy left had taken its toll. But through it all, her love for us never wavered, even if it wasn't always easy to see, she loved us the best she knew how.

Lenny and I had come through the fire, and now, as husband and wife, we were ready to face whatever the future held. We had survived the worst, and that was something no one could ever take away from us.

However, the harsh reality of our situation soon set in. Lenny struggled to find steady work in Texas, and our financial woes seemed to deepen. The excitement of being newlyweds was overshadowed by the constant stress of our precarious living situation. Living at Momma's house was far from ideal—it was even worse than before with more roaches, more dogs, and more cats. The house reeked of pet odor, and the roaches scurried across the floor and walls, making it hard to feel at home.

One evening, as we sat on the worn-out couch in the dimly lit living room, I sighed, "Lenny, we can't stay here forever. We need to find our own place."

He nodded; his face etched with determination. "I know, PJ. I'll find work, and we'll get out of here. I promise."

The very next day, we found an opportunity at Charlie's Training Stables, a renowned Arabian horse training barn. The job was demanding, requiring us to wake up before the first light of dawn. The truck had broken down for the last time and without the means to afford a car, we rode bikes we managed to buy from a pawn shop each morning, covering the five miles to the stables under the Texas sky.

Our daily bike rides to Charlie's Training Stables were an integral part of our routine. They were moments of tranquility, a chance to witness the awakening of the world around us. However, one morning brought an adventure we hadn't anticipated, turning our tranquil commute into a scene straight out of a slapstick comedy.

As we pedaled down the familiar road, the first rays of the sun peeking over the horizon, an unexpected chorus of barking shattered the morning calm. From a nearby house, a gang of dogs, varying in size but united in mischief, burst forth. Their barks were a mix of enthusiasm and what seemed like a canine version of "Hey, look! Two-wheel intruders!"

Before we knew it, they were on our heels, their barks echoing in the early morning air. The scene must have looked comical—Lenny and I pedaling furiously, a motley crew of dogs in hot pursuit, nipping playfully at our feet. I risked a glance back and couldn't help but laugh at the sight of a tiny Chihuahua, its legs a blur, trying to keep up with its larger companions.

Lenny, ever the problem-solver, decided we needed a plan to avoid a repeat performance the next day. His solution? A squirt gun filled with bleach water. "It's non-harmful but should give them a surprise," he said with a mischievous grin.

The next morning, armed with our new 'defense system,' we set off. Sure enough, our canine friends were lying in wait, ready for their morning chase. As they started their enthusiastic pursuit, Lenny turned and squirted a gentle mist of bleach water towards them. The dogs, taken aback by this unexpected turn of events, stopped in their tracks. The expressions on their faces were priceless—a mix of confusion and surprise, as if saying, "What in the doggone world was that?"

From that day on, our morning rides were peaceful once again. Occasionally, we'd see the dogs lounging on their porch, eyeing us with a newfound respect mixed with a hint of playful wariness. It was as if they had a silent agreement with Lenny: "We won't chase you, but we're keeping our eyes on you, two-wheelers." This humorous episode became one of our cherished stories, a reminder of the small, unexpected adventures that peppered our life in those days.

Interspersed between hard work and daily challenges were moments like these, bringing laughter and lightness, making our journey memorable. Our situation at Momma's house had pushed us to seek something better, and finding a small efficiency out in the country for unbelievably cheap was our first step towards building a life of our own. It wasn't much, but it was ours, and it felt like a fresh start away from the chaos we had both known.

Chapter 23

REINS AND REGRETS

Our time at Charlie's Training Stables was more than just a job; it was a chapter in our lives where we discovered the depth of our resilience, the joy of hard work, and the unspoken language of love and understanding that we shared. In the company of each other and the noble Arabian horses, we found a sense of purpose and a glimpse into a future filled with hope and possibilities. Even though we made mistakes, the lessons we learned were invaluable, shaping us into the people we were becoming.

Charlie, the owner of the stables, was a man of few words but full of knowledge. His quiet authority and expertise with Arabian horses were evident in everything he did. Under his guidance, Lenny and I learned the intricacies of caring for these majestic creatures. Our days started early, at 5 a.m., when the sky was still dark, and the world was silent except for the soft nickers of the horses as we made our rounds.

"Morning, Proud," I'd whisper as I approached his stall. The stallion would nicker softly, his breath visible in the crisp morning air as he nudged my hand for attention. Proud was a magnificent creature, all muscle and grace, and collaborating with him was both an honor and a challenge.

Lenny and I would muck out the stalls, toss fresh shavings, and ensure everything was clean and in order. "You think they know how good they've got it?" Lenny joked one morning, tossing a pile of shavings into a stall.

"They'd better appreciate it," I replied, laughing as I worked alongside him.

Charlie would often oversee our work, occasionally offering quiet advice. "Remember, it's not just about feeding and cleaning," he said one day. "These horses need exercise too. You two take a couple of mares out for a ride later."

"Really?" I asked, surprised but excited.

"Really," he nodded. "Just keep it to a walk and a light trot."

The idea of riding the horses, even if just for exercise, thrilled me. Lenny and I saddled up a couple of the mares and took them out on the trails. Riding through the sprawling fields, the wind in our hair and the world opening around us felt like pure freedom.

"Race you to the tree line," Lenny challenged, a mischievous grin on his face.

"You're on," I replied, laughing as we urged the horses forward, the thrill of the moment pushing us to go faster.

In the evenings, we'd ride our bikes back home, exhausted but content. The setting sun cast long shadows on the road, and the cool evening breeze soothed our tired muscles. Those rides were our time to reflect on the day, to dream about the future, and to appreciate the simple yet profound joy of our life together.

Charlie was known for taking his prize horses to horse shows, where they were always the center of attention. Usually, Lenny would accompany him as the groomer, but one day, Charlie approached me with a proposition.

"PJ, I need Lenny to stay behind for the upcoming show," Charlie said, his eyes assessing me. "Think you can manage it on your own?"

"Me?" I asked, my heart skipping a beat. "Are you sure?"

Charlie nodded. "You've got what it takes. Just need someone to keep the horses looking their best."

I wanted to be confident, but the thought of going without Lenny made my stomach twist. I didn't want to be away from him, not even for a few days. So, I did what I thought was my only option—I pretended to faint the day before the trip, right by a big pile of shavings.

Charlie, of course, saw right through my act. "Ain't no time for naps, PJ," he said, nudging me with the toe of his boot. "You'll be fine. Now get up."

I couldn't fool him, and in the end, I found myself on the road to the show without Lenny. It was intimidating, but I was determined to prove I could manage it.

When we arrived at the horse show, Charlie set up a cot for me right next to Proud's stall. Proud was worth millions of dollars, and someone had to be with him 24/7. I tried to stay awake, listening to the sounds of the arena, but eventually, exhaustion took over, and I fell asleep.

I was jolted awake by shouts echoing through the barn. "Stallion loose! Stallion loose!"

My heart raced as I investigated Proud's stall, only to find it empty. Panic set in; I scrambled to my feet, searching for the runaway stallion that was my responsibility. I found him at a stall with a mare who was ready for breeding—the scent must have driven him insane.

"Proud! No!" I shouted, rushing to grab his lead rope, my hands trembling with a mix of fear and embarrassment.

The scene was chaotic, with other handlers rushing to help me. We finally managed to get Proud back into his stall, but the damage was done. I was mortified, certain that word would get back to Charlie.

When I returned to the stables, Charlie didn't say a word about the incident, but I had no doubt he knew. The silence was almost worse than a reprimand. I learned a valuable lesson that day about the responsibilities that come with handling such valuable animals.

Bathing the horses after a long day of work was one of our regular tasks. Proud was always a handful. He was feisty and had a habit of trying to bite me whenever I got too close.

"Lenny, you better take Proud today," I said, holding up my hands in surrender. "He's got it out for me."

Lenny laughed, shaking his head. "You just gotta show him who's boss, PJ."

"Yeah, well, he seems to think he's the boss," I retorted, remembering the narrow escape when he escaped his stall and watching as Lenny expertly managed the priceless, unruly stallion.

Aside from bathing the horses, we were responsible for keeping all the tack clean and conditioned. It was meticulous work, rubbing oil into the leather until it was supple and shining. My hands were always calloused and slick with oil, but there was something satisfying about it.

Lenny thrived in this environment. He had a natural way with the horses, a calm confidence that they responded to. Watching him work, I couldn't help but think maybe we could have our own stables one day. The thought of it filled me with hope, a dream that seemed within reach as we worked side by side. But life has a way of teaching us lessons, some harder than others.

Lenny and I learned one such lesson in a way we never expected.

One Friday evening, we decided to join a few old school friends from town at a local gathering, thinking it would be a harmless night of fun. The night was a whirlwind of laughter, stories, and more drinks than we were used to.

"Come on, just one more!" someone urged, and we laughed, caught up in the moment.

The next day, our heads heavy and our spirits low, we faced the literal harsh light of reality. The thought of facing the stables in our condition seemed impossible.

"I can't do it today, PJ," Lenny groaned, burying his face in his hands.

"Me neither," I admitted, feeling the weight of our mistake settle in.

We made the regrettable decision not to go in, not realizing the full impact of our absence. When we finally mustered the courage to face Charlie, his disappointment was obvious.

"You should've come in and worked it off," he said, his voice heavy with disappointment. "You let me down, but worse, you let the horses down."

"We're sorry, Charlie," I said, my voice barely above a whisper.

He shook his head, his eyes filled with a sadness that cut deeper than any reprimand. "I expected better from you both," he said, his words echoing in our minds long after we left.

The ride home was somber, the loss of our jobs a blow, but the realization that we had betrayed Charlie's trust and our own standards was a heavier burden to bear.

"We really messed up," Lenny said quietly, his voice tinged with regret.

"Yeah," I agreed, the weight of our mistake pressing down on us.

That evening, as we sat in the quiet of our little home, we made a promise to each other. "We'll never let this happen again," Lenny said, his eyes locked with mine.

I nodded, feeling a sense of determination rise within me. "We'll do better. We have to."

It was a painful lesson, but one that was necessary for our growth. We vowed to uphold a standard of responsibility and integrity in all that we did; we knew we'd remember this experience and it would shape the decisions we made moving forward.

Chapter 24

THE SECOND RETURN

The days that followed were filled with job searches and endless reflection. We missed the stables, the horses, and even those early morning rides that had once been a chore but now felt like a lost luxury. Lenny and I often talked about how much we missed it, but we knew that chapter had closed. It was time to look ahead, to new opportunities, and to live up to the promise we made to each other.

"We'll find something better," Lenny assured me one evening as we sat at the kitchen table, scanning the classifieds. His voice was steady, but I could hear the uncertainty lurking beneath his words.

"I hope so," I replied, trying to muster the same confidence. "But where do we even start?"

Faced with limited options, we made the difficult decision to move back to Florida. The idea felt like a retreat, a concession to the circumstances we couldn't control.

"Are we really doing this?" I asked Lenny as we packed our meager belongings into the back of the old used truck we bought a week ago.

"We don't have much choice, PJ," he sighed. "We tried here, but maybe we'll have better luck back in Florida. I heard that Jerry was sent to prison for a while, so we don't have to worry about him."

Returning to Florida was a humbling experience. We settled in St. Augustine, a town that was supposed to represent a fresh start, but it wasn't long before the romantic image of a quaint coastal town clashed with the reality of our daily struggles.

Lenny's mother, surprisingly, seemed more receptive to us now that we were married. When we arrived at her doorstep, she greeted us with a faint smile and a lukewarm welcome.

"So, you two finally tied the knot, huh?" she said, looking at Lenny with a mix of skepticism and mild approval.

"Yeah, Mom," Lenny replied, trying to keep the conversation light. "We're just trying to make it work."

Despite her apparent change in attitude, Lenny remained resolute in his decision not to work for her again. "I can't go back to that," he told me one night, his voice filled with stubborn pride. "We need to do this on our own."

"Maybe we should consider it," I suggested hesitantly. "It might make things easier, at least for a little while."

But Lenny shook his head. "No. We're better off finding our own way, PJ."

Life in St. Augustine didn't unravel all at once; it was a slow, creeping change that began to seep into the corners of our marriage. At first, everything seemed hopeful, like we could make it work, but the excitement of being together quickly started to fade under the weight of our struggles.

It all started with trivial things. Lenny found a job at a boat refinishing company working with fiberglass. He began spending more time pier fishing with his friends from work. "I'm heading out with the guys, you want to come?" he'd ask, glancing at me as he grabbed his fishing gear.

I tried to keep the disappointment out of my voice. "No, you go ahead," I'd say, forcing a smile. "I think I'll just stay home."

At first, I didn't mind it. I told myself that Lenny needed some time to unwind, that he deserved a break after everything we'd been through. But as the days turned into weeks, his trips became more frequent, and the hours he spent away grew longer. It wasn't just fishing—it was an escape from the reality we were both struggling to face.

One afternoon, as he was getting ready to leave again, I couldn't hold back any longer. "Lenny, do you have to go every day after work?" I asked, trying to keep my tone light but failing to hide the frustration that had been building inside me.

He looked at me, surprised by the question. "It's just fishing, PJ. I need some time to clear my head."

"I know," I said, my voice softer. "But I feel like you're drifting away. We barely spend any time together anymore."

Lenny sighed, running a hand through his hair. "I didn't realize you felt that way. It's just... everything's so heavy right now. I need to get out and feel like I can breathe."

"I get that," I replied, my heart aching at the distance growing between us. "But I need you too, Lenny. We're supposed to be in this together."

He hesitated, then nodded. "Okay, I'll try to cut back. We can do something together tomorrow?"

But tomorrow never seemed to come. Lenny's promise to cut back on his fishing trips quickly faded, replaced by the same pattern of leaving early and returning late. I found myself sitting alone often, staring at the walls of our small apartment, the silence pressing in on me. The loneliness I felt was suffocating, and no matter how many times I tried to reach out to him, it seemed like he was slipping further away.

The moments when he was home were different too. He wasn't the same playful, affectionate Lenny I had fallen in love with. Instead, he was distant, his mind always elsewhere. Even when we were together, it felt like there was a wall between us that I couldn't break through.

One night, after another long day of feeling like a ghost in my own home, I decided to confront him again. He had just come back from fishing, his clothes smelling of salt and seaweed.

"Lenny, we need to talk," I said, my voice trembling slightly.

He looked up from where he was unlacing his boots. "What's up?"

"I can't do this anymore," I blurted out, tears welling up in my eyes. "I feel like I'm losing you, like you're not here with me at all."

He frowned, standing up and crossing the room to sit next to me on the couch. "PJ, what do you mean? I'm right here."

"No, you're not," I said, shaking my head. "You're always out, and when you're home, it's like you're somewhere else. I don't know how to reach you."

Lenny sighed heavily, leaning back against the couch. "I didn't realize it was that bad. I'm just trying to cope, you know? Everything has been so overwhelming, and I guess I've been running away from it."

"I need you here with me, not just physically but emotionally too," I said, reaching for his hand. "We're supposed to be a team, but it feels like I'm doing this alone."

He squeezed my hand but didn't say anything for a long moment. Finally, he nodded. "I'm sorry, PJ. I'll try to do better."

But things didn't change. If anything, they got worse. Lenny's time away from home only increased, and when he was there, he was even more withdrawn. The closeness we once had was slipping through my fingers, and I felt powerless to stop it.

I noticed it in other ways too. Lenny's affection, which used to be so genuine and tender, became more distant. Our moments of intimacy were reduced to quick, emotionless encounters that left me feeling more alone than ever. I missed the way he used to hold me, the way we used to laugh and make love like nothing else in the world mattered.

One night, as we lay in bed after another one of those brief, unsatisfying encounters, I turned to him, hoping for some sign that he still cared. "Lenny, do you still love me?"

He didn't answer right away, and when he finally did, his voice was so quiet I almost didn't hear him. "Of course I do, PJ. Why would you ask that?"

"Because it doesn't feel like it," I whispered, my voice breaking. "I miss you... I miss us."

Lenny turned over, pulling me close, but it felt more like a habit than an expression of love. "I'm here," he murmured, but his words felt hollow as he shared his dream of becoming a police officer. "It's what I really want to do, PJ," he said, his eyes bright with hope. "But I need two years of college for it."

"Can't we figure something out?" I asked, desperate to see him happy.

Lenny shook his head, frustration creeping into his voice. "We can't afford it. There's a private academy that offers training, but it costs too much. We can barely make rent as it is."

His dream of a stable career seemed further out of reach with each passing day, and I could see the toll it was taking on him. He felt trapped, and so did I. The romantic notion of starting a new life in a picturesque coastal town had faded, replaced by the constancy of financial struggle and unfulfilled aspirations.

As I lay there in the dark, listening to the sound of his breathing, I realized that the man I loved was slipping away from me, and I didn't know how to bring him back. The life we had envisioned together was crumbling, and no matter how hard I tried to hold on, it felt like we were destined to fall apart.

Chapter 25

KYLE'S HELLO, MOMMA'S GOODBYE

The fatigue was constant, accompanied by a sense of weariness that I couldn't shake. At first, I chalked it up to stress and the weight of our everyday struggles, but when the flu-like symptoms began to linger, I started to worry. One afternoon, while out running errands, I found myself standing in the pharmacy aisle, staring at the pregnancy tests. My heart raced as I reached for one, telling myself it was just to rule out the possibility. There could be lots of reasons my period was late.

Back home, I held the test in my hand, the seconds ticking by like hours. When the result appeared, my breath caught in my throat. It was positive. I was going to be a mother.

Stunned, I sat down on the edge of the bed, the realization washing over me in waves. "Lenny," I whispered to myself, knowing I had to tell him right away. My mind was a whirlwind of thoughts—how would we manage this? Could we afford it? But beneath the worry was a flicker of excitement, a tiny spark of hope that, just maybe, this was the start of something beautiful.

When Lenny came home that evening, I could hardly contain myself. As he walked through the door, I blurted out, "Lenny, I'm pregnant!"

For a moment, he just stared at me, his expression unreadable. Then, a slow, wide grin spread across his face. "You're pregnant?" he repeated, as if needing to hear the words again to believe them.

I nodded, tears welling up in my eyes. "Yes, we're going to have a baby."

Without warning, Lenny swooped me up into his arms and twirled me around the room. "We're going to be a mommy and daddy!" he exclaimed, his voice filled with a mix of disbelief and joy. He set me down gently, cupping my face in his hands. "This is amazing, PJ! I can't believe it!"

In that moment, the weight of our financial troubles, the stress of our unstable situation—they all seemed to melt away. For the first time in what felt like forever, there was nothing but pure, unfiltered happiness between us. We laughed, cried, and talked late into the night, our minds racing with dreams and plans for our future.

As the days passed, reality began to settle in. We knew we were on a tough road ahead, especially with me being pregnant without any insurance. The thought of navigating this new chapter without proper medical care was terrifying. But Lenny, always the optimist, refused to let the fear take over. "We'll figure it out," he reassured me one evening as we sat on the couch, his hand resting protectively on my still-flat stomach. "Whatever it takes, we'll do it."

After some searching, we found a clinic downtown that provided care for expectant mothers in our situation. The building was old and a bit run-down, but the staff were kind and welcoming. They didn't judge us for our circumstances; instead, they offered support and guidance. "You'll be in good hands here," the nurse said, giving me a reassuring smile during our first visit. "We're going to make sure you and your baby are healthy."

As we left the clinic that day, Lenny squeezed my hand. "See? We're going to be okay," he said, his voice filled with determination. "We're going to make this work."

And as I looked at him, my heart swelled with a mixture of love and hope. We didn't have much, but we had each other. And now, we had something even more precious—a little life growing inside me. Despite the challenges ahead, I knew we were about to embark on the most incredible journey of our lives.

The early days of my pregnancy were far from easy. The nausea hit hard, and it seemed like nothing would stay down— except for Taco Bell's Taco Supreme. It became my go-to meal, ironically the only thing that settled my uneasy stomach. Lenny and I took long walks on the beach near our place, the salty air helping to soothe my nausea. The sound of the waves was calming, and it was during these walks that we began to talk about names for our baby.

One evening, as we strolled along the shoreline, Lenny turned to me with a thoughtful expression. "What do you think about Kyle for a boy?" he asked, kicking at the sand.

I smiled, feeling the name roll around in my mind. "Kyle Anthony," I said, trying it aloud.

Lenny nodded but then tilted his head, as if considering something. "What about Kyle Austin?" he suggested. "It just has a nice ring to it."

We stopped walking, and I bent down to write the names in the sand, watching as the waves inched closer. "Kyle Austin," I repeated, liking how it sounded. "Our son, Kyle Austin."

Lenny grinned, his hand resting on my growing belly. "Our son," he echoed, a touch of wonder in his voice. It was surreal to say those words, to imagine the little boy we'd soon hold in our arms.

As the months passed, the excitement of expecting our first child grew. We tried thinking of girl names, too, but nothing ever felt right. It was as if deep down, we already knew. Then, during a routine checkup, our intuition was confirmed—we were having a boy. The doctor smiled as she pointed to the tiny, grainy image on the ultrasound screen. "There he is, your little man," she said, and tears sprang to my eyes.

Lenny squeezed my hand, his voice thick with emotion. "Kyle Austin," he whispered, and it felt more real than ever.

Month nine of my pregnancy approached; I felt enormous and increasingly uncomfortable. Every movement was a struggle, and I spent most of my days resting, trying to find a position that didn't hurt. Lenny was a constant source of support, but I could see the worry in his eyes. We were both first-time parents, navigating uncharted waters, and the closer we got to the due date, the more anxious we became.

Then, to my surprise and relief, my brother Kent drove Momma all the way from Texas to Florida to be with me during those last few weeks. It was a gesture I hadn't expected, and when they arrived with baby essentials—clothes, bottles, and even a bassinet—I felt a wave of gratitude that nearly overwhelmed me.

"Momma, you didn't have to do all this!" I exclaimed as she unpacked the bags.

"Nonsense," she replied, brushing off my words. "I'm your mother, PJ. I want to be here for you."

Momma's attentiveness was something I hadn't experienced much as a child, and her support during this critical time was incredibly meaningful to me. We spent the days preparing for the baby, folding tiny clothes and setting up the bassinet.

Momma sat with me, rubbing my swollen feet and telling me stories about when she was pregnant with us kids.

But my due date approached and then passed with no sign of the baby. I could see the concern etched on her face. "You're overdue, sweetheart," she said one evening, her voice soft with worry. "You need to take it easy."

I nodded, trying to hide my own anxiety. The days dragged on, each one more uncomfortable than the last. Every night, I hoped that it would be the night, that I'd wake up to labor pains and know that it was time. But the days kept passing, and still, there was no sign of our little Kyle Austin.

Eventually, Momma's stay would have to end. She needed to return to Texas to care for her brother, who was living with her and needed her assistance due to his declining health. As much as I wanted her to stay, I knew she had her own responsibilities back home. But as the days continued to drag on without any sign of labor, I couldn't help but feel a growing sense of unease. I was ready for our son to arrive, ready to hold him in my arms and finally start our new life together as a family.

Despite Momma's anxiousness to get back to Texas for her brother, I found myself praying for my baby to hurry up and come so she could spend some time with me and her grandchild. I knew how important it was for her to be there, not just for me, but to hold her new grandson. As the days stretched on, I could see the worry in her eyes, but she stayed, determined to see this through with me.

During this waiting, my mother-in-law, Enid, and sister-in-law, Lori, organized a baby shower for me. It was a thoughtful gesture, even though most of the guests were people I didn't know very well. The shower was a welcome distraction, a chance to celebrate the new life that was about to join our family. But the tension between Momma and Enid was evident.

Enid, with her cold and controlling demeanor, made me feel like I was constantly walking on eggshells. I was always trying to meet her expectations, yet it felt like I could never quite get it right. My nature as a pleaser clashed with her domineering attitude, and I could sense Momma's protective instincts bristling every time Enid made a sharp comment or gave a disapproving look.

"She's just got a different way about her," Momma whispered to me when she caught me flinching after one of Enid's remarks. "But don't let her get to you, PJ. You're doing just fine."

I nodded, trying to focus on the joy of the occasion. Despite the underlying tensions, I did my best to enjoy the shower. It was heartwarming to receive so many gifts for our unborn child, and for a moment, I allowed myself to bask in the excitement of the motherhood that lay ahead.

After enduring several false alarms and making three separate trips to the hospital, the day finally arrived. My labor was progressing slowly, and I was suddenly, keenly aware of the small, rural hospital and its staff's lack of experience. The venue didn't inspire much confidence, and the thought of something going wrong filled me with dread.

The hospital's policy of allowing only one visitor at a time in the labor room meant that Momma had to wait outside in the hallway. I could see the frustration on her face when she peeked in through the door, her hands gripping the edges as if she could will herself to be in the room with me.

"Are you okay, PJ?" she asked every time she switched places with Lenny.

"Yeah, Momma, I'm okay," I replied, forcing a smile. "It's just taking longer than I thought."

Lenny tried his best to comfort me, but I could see the worry etched into his features. He wasn't used to seeing me in pain, and the slow progress of the labor was wearing on both of us.

My labor dragged on, and the doctor advised that I needed to relax to help the baby out. "We're going to give you something through the IV," he said, his voice calm and reassuring. "It'll help you relax, and things should move along more quickly after that."

I nodded, too exhausted to argue. As soon as the medication entered my system, I felt my body start to relax, the tension easing out of my muscles. It was remarkable how quickly it took effect, and soon, things started moving more rapidly. The pain intensified, but so did the urgency, and before I knew it, the room was a flurry of activity.

Then, in what felt like both an eternity and a fleeting moment, our son was born. The doctor held him up, and the world stopped. Lenny and I stared at the tiny, squirming life we had created together, overwhelmed by a love so deep and profound that it was unlike anything I'd ever felt.

"Kyle Austin," I whispered, feeling the name settle finally where it belonged—into my heart.

Lenny, tears streaming down his face, leaned over and kissed my forehead. "Thank you, PJ," he said, his voice thick with emotion. "Thank you for our son."

It was a touching moment, seeing such vulnerability and gratitude in his eyes. The exhaustion of the labor faded into the background, replaced by the overwhelming joy of holding our son for the first time. His tiny fingers wrapped around mine, and I felt a fierce protective love surge through me. This little life was now the center of my world, and I knew I would do anything to protect and nurture him.

Unfortunately, our joy was short-lived. Kyle was born with slight jaundice, a common yet unsettling condition. The nurses assured me it was nothing serious, but when they took him away to treat it, I felt a pang of anxiety. The separation, even though it was for his well-being, was unbearably difficult.

"I'm going to take your mom back home so she can get some sleep and then I'll be back." Lenny said with tired look-ing eyes. Hours stretched by without Kyle being brought back to me, and my anxiety deepened into an all-consuming need to see him. "Where is my baby?" I asked every nurse who passed by, my voice trembling with fear. "Why hasn't he been brought back yet?"

"They're just treating the jaundice, ma'am," one nurse replied, her tone gentle but firm. "He'll be back soon, I promise."

But I couldn't wait any longer. My need to see Kyle pro-pelled me out of my hospital bed, despite the exhaustion and pain that still gripped my body. I remember the cold hospital floor under my feet, the stark hallways stretching before me, each step fueled by a single thought—to lay eyes on Kyle and ensure he was safe.

I tip-toed through the maze-like corridors of the hospital toward the nursery and a sharp pain shot through me. I realized blood was trickling down my legs; it was too soon for me to be walking, too soon after the ordeal my body had just endured.

"PJ, you need to get back to bed," a nurse said as she caught sight of me, her eyes wide with concern.

"But my baby…" I protested, my voice shaking.

"I'll bring him to you, I promise," she said, guiding me back toward my room. "You need to rest, or you won't be any good to him when he comes back."

Reluctantly, I allowed her to help me back to bed. The worry still gnawed at me, but exhaustion finally won out, and I closed my eyes, trusting that Kyle would be brought to me soon.

And he was. A few hours later, they brought Kyle back, his tiny face swaddled in a soft blanket. The relief I felt was indescribable as I held him close, feeling his warmth against my chest.

Lenny returned showered and rested, bringing Momma with him, who had been pacing the hallway and they finally came in. Momma's face softened as she looked at her grandchild. "Oh, PJ, he's beautiful," she whispered, tears glistening in her eyes.

"I'm so glad you're here, Momma," I said, my voice thick with emotion. "I couldn't have done this without you."

She smiled, brushing a strand of hair away from my face. "I wouldn't have missed this for the world, honey. But I'm afraid I'll have to leave soon. Your uncle needs me back in Texas."

I nodded, understanding but still wishing she could stay just a little longer. "I know but thank you for staying as long as you did."

She kissed my forehead, her touch gentle. "You're going to be a wonderful mother, PJ. Kyle is lucky to have you."

Bringing Kyle home was a surreal experience, a mix of overwhelming joy and the daunting realization that we were now responsible for this tiny, fragile life. As we carefully placed him in the bassinet that Momma had brought from Texas, I felt a wave of emotions. The drive from the hospital had been nerve-wracking; every bump in the road made me glance back to check on him, half expecting something to go wrong. But in the quiet of our home, everything felt still, peaceful.

Momma, with her years of experience, immediately took charge, guiding me through the first hours of caring for Kyle. She was gentle but firm, showing me how to swaddle him tightly so he'd feel secure, how to check if he was too warm or too cold. But the biggest challenge was breastfeeding. I had read about it, heard about it, but nothing could have prepared me for reality.

"Here, honey, let me help you," Momma said, as she adjusted the pillows around me, making sure I was comfortable. Kyle was fussing, his tiny face scrunched up, his little fists waving in the air.

"I don't know if I'm doing this right," I confessed, feeling a mix of anxiety and frustration as I tried to position him correctly.

"You're doing fine," she reassured me. "It takes time for both of you to learn. Just relax, and he'll sense that."

I took a deep breath, trying to calm the nerves that were threatening to spill over. Momma helped guide Kyle's mouth to the right spot, and after a few tries, he latched on. The sensation was strange at first, a mix of discomfort and relief as he began to nurse.

"There you go," Momma smiled, brushing a stray tear from my cheek. "See? You're already getting the hang of it."

As I watched Kyle nurse, I felt a deep connection to him, a bond that was growing stronger with each passing moment. The worries of whether I would be a good mother, whether I could handle the responsibility, began to fade away, replaced by a fierce determination to do everything I could for him.

Over the next few days, Momma was by my side, introducing me to the new world of motherhood. She taught me how to burp Kyle after feeding, how to soothe him when he was fussy, and most importantly, how to trust my instincts.

"You'll be fine, PJ," she said, one afternoon as we sat together in the living room, Kyle sleeping soundly in his bassinet. "Just take it one day at a time."

Her presence was a comfort, a reminder that I wasn't alone on this journey. Even Lenny, who had been hesitant and unsure at first, was starting to find his footing as a father. I watched as he held Kyle, his large hands cradling our son with such tenderness that it brought tears to my eyes.

All too soon, the time came for Momma to leave. As she packed her things, a deep sense of gratitude welled up inside me. "Thank you, Momma, for everything," I said, my voice trembling with emotion.

She hugged me tightly. "You're going to be a wonderful mother, PJ. Just remember, you can always call me if you need anything."

Lenny and I watched as Momma and Kent drove away, their car disappearing down the road. "We've got this," Lenny said, wrapping his arm around me as we stood in the doorway, Kyle sleeping peacefully in my arms.

"Yeah, we've got this," I echoed, feeling a new sense of strength and resolve. This was the beginning of our journey as parents, and despite the challenges that lay ahead, I knew we would face them together.

Journal entry, October 10, 1992

In the quiet reflection of my therapy sessions, I've unearthed an important truth about love—it's rooted in selflessness and acceptance. The idea of love I held previously was wrong; I believed it was about loving others the way I desired to be loved. However, I've come to understand that true love is about meeting the needs of the loved one, not the lover. This realization has reshaped my approach to love, especially in my role as a mother to Kyle. As I watch Kyle grow and develop his own personality, complete with unique preferences and behaviors, I am learning the art of grace. My role is not to mold him into a version of what I think he should be but to nurture his true self. I want him to feel cherished for who he is, ensuring he never feels the need to put on a mask or hide his genuine self to gain approval or love.

Kyle's second birthday is a reminder of how swiftly time passes and how significant my influence is in his early years. He entered this world enveloped in love, with two parents filled with hope and dreams for his future. It's vital for Kyle to never doubt his importance in our lives or question his existence as anything less than a cherished blessing. Reflecting on the journey with Lenny, his father, I see a love that was intended to be everlasting. Yet, life has a way of presenting challenges and temptations that can lead even the most loving hearts astray. The entrance of another woman into Lenny's life, at a moment when our bond seemed unbreakable, has left deep scars on my heart. Dealing with the aftermath of a fractured love is a daily struggle. There's a part of my heart that remains wounded, yet knowing Kyle was born from a union of genuine love brings a certain comfort. He is the embodiment of the beauty that our love once held and remains a testament to the fact that even during heartache, love can bring forth incredible joy and wonder. The journey with Lenny, though filled with pain, is not one I regret. From that love came Kyle, the most precious gift I could have ever received. He stands as a constant reminder that love, in all its complexity and despite the scars it may leave, is a powerful force capable of bringing forth beauty and joy. The memories of our time together as a family, however bittersweet, are treasured pieces of my life's journey.

Chapter 26

A VISIT HOME AND A STRAINED RETURN

Before my pregnancy and Kyle's birth, I had worked toward and achieved something I never thought possible—I completed my dental assistant training. It wasn't just a job; it was a milestone in my life that brought with it a sense of pride and accomplishment. One year of school and then graduating with honors was a testament to my hard work and determination. I remember the day I received my certificate, feeling a swell of pride that I hadn't felt in a long time. It was a new chapter, a fresh start, and it filled me with a sense of purpose and confidence.

Getting the job at a reputable dental practice in town was a stroke of luck, but it also felt like the universe was finally throwing me a bone after all the challenges I had faced. The office was a bright, welcoming place, with state-of-the-art equipment and a team of professionals who were supportive and encouraging. Dr. Meyers, the senior dentist, was a mentor to me from the start. He took the time to teach me, to explain the why behind every procedure, and to ensure that I felt confident in my role.

"PJ, you're a natural at this," Dr. Meyers would say after a particularly challenging procedure. His words meant the world to me, as they validated all the effort I put into this new career path.

Working at the dental office felt like stepping into a new world—one where I was valued and respected. The patients were kind, the work was fulfilling, and for the first time, I was on solid ground. So after, when I found out I was pregnant with Kyle, everything shifted.

The news of my pregnancy brought joy and excitement, but it also introduced a host of new challenges. With a baby, I had to start thinking about daycare, finances, and how I would balance my job with being a mother. The decision to place Kyle in daycare was one of the hardest choices I ever made. I dropped him off every morning, feeling my heart tug as I left him in someone else's care.

"You're doing this for him," I reminded myself as I walked out the door, fighting back tears. "You're working to give him a better life."

Breastfeeding while managing my work schedule was a daily battle. Determined to give Kyle the best start in life, I pumped during breaks at work and stored the milk in the office fridge. I had become obsessive about ensuring that he had the best nutrition possible. I made sure to pump and freeze as much as I could, labeling each bag with the date and time, ensuring everything was perfect for him.

In the evenings, the relief of finally being able to nurse him was mixed with the physical discomfort of engorged breasts. It was a painful reminder of the sacrifices I was making, but holding Kyle close made it all worth it. I knew he would be eating real food soon, so I was also determined to make my own baby food, pureeing fresh fruits and vegetables, convinced that homemade was always better than store-bought.

As if adjusting to life with a newborn wasn't enough, Lenny's decision to enroll in the police academy moved forward, adding another layer of stress to our little family. The academy was expensive, and the costs of the necessary gear—a gun, holster, and uniform—pushed our already strained budget to the limit. We were living paycheck to paycheck, and the pressure was mounting.

"Are you sure we can afford this?" I asked Lenny one night as we sat at the kitchen table, going over our bills.

"We don't have a choice," he replied, his tone resolute. "This is my ticket to a better life for us. I need to do this, PJ."

I nodded, understanding his drive but still feeling the weight of our financial burden. "I just want to make sure we're making the right decisions," I said softly, glancing over at Kyle sleeping peacefully in his bassinet.

"We are," Lenny assured me, reaching across the table to squeeze my hand. "We're going to get through this. We always do."

The days turned into a blur of work, daycare drop-offs, and trying to make ends meet. Every night, I collapsed into bed, exhausted but determined. My role as a dental assistant had given me confidence; being a mother had given me purpose. Despite the challenges, I knew I was doing everything I could for my family, and that gave me the strength to keep going.

Still, I couldn't shake the constant worry about how we would afford everything Kyle needed, on top of all our other bills. The financial stress was one thing, but what gnawed at me even more was how much Lenny, and I had changed. Our relationship, once filled with affection and laughter, seemed to be crumbling under the weight of our new responsibilities.

One evening, as we sat at the kitchen table, I hesitated before bringing up my concerns. "Lenny, I'm worried about how we're going to manage. The bills, Kyle's needs... it's all piling up."

Lenny barely looked up from the newspaper he was pretending to read. "We'll figure it out, PJ," he muttered, his tone flat and distant.

"Will we?" I pressed gently, trying to reach the man I used to know. "It feels like we're drifting apart, Lenny. You're always so... moody. We don't talk like we used to."

He sighed, finally meeting my gaze, but his eyes held no warmth. "I'm just tired, okay? The academy, work, trying to make everything work... it's exhausting. I don't have the energy for... for everything else right now."

His words stung, and I fought back the tears that threatened to spill. "I miss us, Lenny," I whispered, more to myself than to him. But he just looked away, the silence between us heavier than any argument.

The joy that Kyle brought into our lives was undeniable, but the challenges of balancing work, motherhood, and a strained relationship with Lenny were taking their toll. I longed for the days when our love overcame any obstacle, but with each passing day, those times felt like a distant memory.

When Kyle was four months old, the weight of everything started to feel unbearable. Homesickness crept in, mingled with the fog of postpartum depression that seemed to cling to me no matter how hard I tried to shake it off. Lenny's increasing distance and his harsh demeanor only made me feel more isolated.

One afternoon, I couldn't hold it in any longer. "Lenny, I think I need to go home for a bit," I said, my voice trembling. "I'm not... I'm not okay here. I need to see my family."

He looked at me, his expression unreadable. "You want to leave?" he asked, a hint of something like anger in his voice.

"Not leave, just visit," I clarified, desperate for him to understand. "I'm struggling, Lenny. I feel so alone."

There was a long pause before he finally spoke. "Do what you need to do," he said, his tone cold. "But I can't go with you. I've got the academy."

My heart sank at his response, but I knew I couldn't stay, not in the state I was in. Just when things felt like they couldn't get any darker, Momma stepped in. She offered to help with the financial burden of Lenny's police academy expenses, a gesture that brought tears of relief to my eyes. And then, to my surprise and immense gratitude, she sent a round-trip flight for Kyle and me to visit Texas during the summer.

"Momma, I don't know what to say," I said over the phone, my voice breaking. "Thank you... I really need this."

"Honey, you and Kyle need to come home, even if it's just for a little while," she replied, her voice soft and understanding. "We'll take care of you. You don't have to go through this alone."

The prospect of going home, of being surrounded by familiar faces and places, and introducing our beautiful baby boy to the family, was like a beacon of hope in my fog of sadness. I knew Lenny couldn't join us on this trip, but for the first time in months, I felt like I could breathe again. I held onto the hope that this trip would give me the strength I needed to keep going, to keep fighting for my family.

Lenny took on a job as a security officer, in addition to his commitments at the police academy. I felt a bit relieved to have some time away from him, to escape the tension and unhappiness that had started to poison our marriage. Just as I was getting ready to leave, Lenny mentioned a woman named Ari from his job.

"Yeah, there's this woman, Ari," he said casually one evening as we were finishing dinner. "She's having a tough time with her marriage, so I bought her some flowers to cheer her up."

I froze, the fork halfway to my mouth. "You... bought her flowers?" I asked, trying to keep my voice steady.

"Yeah, just to lift her spirits," he replied, not seeming to think much of it.

I couldn't believe what I was hearing. "Lenny, do you really think it's appropriate to buy flowers for another woman? Especially when we're having our own issues?"

His face hardened, and his voice grew defensive. "What's the big deal? I was just trying to be nice. If you think I'm messing around with another woman, I might as well do it since you already think I have!" he snapped.

His words hit me like a slap in the face, leaving me shaken and confused. I could see the frustration in his eyes, and I couldn't help but wonder if it stemmed from his struggles with his career. The dream of becoming a police officer seemed to be slipping away from him, and maybe that was fueling his behavior toward me. Nevertheless, his reaction and the mention of another woman only deepened the strain on our already fragile relationship.

As I boarded the plane to Texas with Kyle, my mind was a whirlwind of emotions. I was eager to be home, to find solace in the company of my family, and to take a much-needed break from the growing complexities of my marriage. The journey to Texas felt like a temporary escape, a chance to breathe and gather my strength for whatever lay ahead with Lenny.

When I arrived in Texas with Kyle, Momma was at the airport waiting, her eyes lighting up the moment she saw us. She wrapped me in a tight hug, her embrace filled with a warmth I had been missing for far too long. She took one look at Kyle, her face softening with a tenderness I hadn't seen in years.

"Oh, PJ, he's just perfect," she whispered, her voice thick with emotion as she stroked Kyle's soft cheek. "I've missed you both so much."

We drove back to her house. I could feel the tension easing out of me. There was something about being back in Texas that brought a sense of peace. But I also knew that coming home meant facing the reality of my situation with Lenny, a reality that had become increasingly difficult to ignore.

That evening, after I put Kyle to bed, Momma and I sat down in the living room. She made us both a glass of sweet tea, and I could sense she had something on her mind.

"How's Lenny been treating you?" she asked, her tone casual but with an edge of concern that was hard to miss.

I hesitated, not wanting to worry her, but the look in her eyes told me she already knew something was wrong. "It's been... tough, Momma. He's been distant, moody, and... I just feel like we're not connecting the way we used to."

She set her glass down, her face hardening. "He's supposed to be your husband, PJ. He should be treating you with respect, not making you feel like you're not important. You deserve better than that."

"I know, Momma," I replied, feeling a lump in my throat. "He mentioned this woman from work, and he bought her flowers... well, it's just been hard. I don't know what to think."

Her eyes narrowed, and I could see the anger simmering beneath the surface. "What woman? And what the hell is he doing buying flowers for another woman? That's not right, PJ. If he's messing around, you don't need to put up with that."

"I don't know if he's doing anything," I said quickly, trying to calm her down. "He just mentioned it, but when I asked him about it, he got really defensive."

Momma shook her head, her frustration clear. "You and Kyle should come back home, PJ. You don't need to be dealing with this nonsense. Come back to Texas where you belong. We can figure something out."

Her words tugged at my heart, and for a moment, I imagined what it would be like to move back. But then the memories of growing up in that house— the roaches, the animals, the filth— flooded back. I couldn't raise Kyle in that environment. I couldn't subject him to the same things I had endured.

"I love you, Momma, and I appreciate everything you've done for us," I said softly, trying to find the right words. "But I can't move back here. Kyle deserves both a mom and a dad, and I need to give him a life where he's safe, healthy and happy."

Momma's eyes softened, and I could see the pain in them. "I just want you to be happy, PJ. I want you to be somewhere you're loved and cared for. If that's not with Lenny, then you need to think about what's best for you and Kyle."

Her words hung in the air, heavy with the truth I wasn't ready to face. I knew she was right, but I wasn't sure if I was ready to make that decision yet. All I knew was that I couldn't live the way I had grown up, and I wouldn't let Kyle go through that either.

"I'll figure it out, Momma," I promised, giving her a small smile. "I just need some time."

She nodded, pulling me into a hug. "Just remember, PJ, you've always got a place here. No matter what."

As I held her close, I felt a mix of emotions—love, guilt, determination—but most of all, a resolve to create a better life for Kyle. Even if it meant facing difficult truths and making tough decisions, I knew I had to do whatever it took to protect him and give him the life he deserved.

Despite the brief relief my trip to Texas brought to me, the distance between Lenny and me lingered like an unwanted guest. I tried to convince myself that his behavior was just due to exhaustion from the police academy and his job, always trying to give him the benefit of the doubt. But no matter how much I tried to rationalize it, the gap between us seemed to widen with each passing day.

As the months flew by, the holiday season arrived, bringing with it a mix of emotions. This was a special year—Lenny was finally graduating from the police academy, and it was Kyle's first Thanksgiving. I felt a glimmer of hope, a sense of gratitude that, just maybe, things were starting to align for our little family.

"Lenny, it's Kyle's first Thanksgiving, and your graduation, too. This is supposed to be a time to celebrate," I said one evening, trying to break through the wall that seemed to have built up between us.

"Yeah, I know," Lenny replied, but his voice lacked the enthusiasm for which I was hoping. He was distant, as if his mind was elsewhere.

I sighed, deciding to let it go for now. Maybe he just needed more time to adjust, I thought. But as the holiday approached, I couldn't shake the feeling of unease.

The challenge came with the visit to Lenny's mother for Thanksgiving. Every time we went there, it was the same story—tension simmered just beneath the surface. Enid's constant criticisms of my mothering skills, her thinly veiled comments about our financial struggles, wore me down.

"Maybe if you were a bit more careful with your spending, you wouldn't be in such a bind," she said, her tone as sharp as ever.

"I'm doing the best I can," I replied, trying to keep my voice steady, but inside, I was seething.

Lenny, as usual, said nothing, just sat there, letting the tension hang in the air. I shot him a glance, hoping for some support, but he remained silent, staring at his plate.

After dinner, I couldn't wait to leave. The weight of Enid's words, the silence from Lenny, it all felt too much to bear.

"Can we go now?" I whispered to Lenny, my patience fraying at the edges.

"Yeah, let's get out of here," he replied, finally seeming to come to life.

We bundled Kyle up and headed for the door. But the temporary relief from our departure was short-lived, replaced by a sinking feeling in my stomach. Something was coming, I could feel it. And I wasn't sure if we were ready for it.

Chapter 27

HE LOVES ME, HE LOVES ME NOT

Back at home, Lenny's mood was dark and distant. He didn't say much after we left his mother's house, and I could feel the tension tightening like a noose around my neck. As soon as we walked in the door, he made a beeline for the bathroom, muttering something about needing a hot bath. He didn't even glance at Kyle, who was fussing in my arms, tired from the long day. The silence that followed Lenny's retreat into the bathroom was deafening.

I tried to calm Kyle, rocking him gently, but my mind was racing. Lenny had been pulling away for months, and I had no idea why. The man I married, the one who used to make me laugh and hold me close, seemed like a stranger now. It was like he was slipping through my fingers, and I didn't know how to stop it.

I couldn't take it anymore. I needed answers. With Kyle finally settled in his crib, I walked into the bathroom, where Lenny was soaking in the tub, steam rising around him. His eyes were closed, and he looked peaceful, like the tension of the day had melted away. But I couldn't shake the feeling that something was deeply wrong.

"Lenny," I began, trying to keep my voice steady, "are you mad at me? What did I do?"

He didn't open his eyes. "Nothing," he muttered, his voice flat, emotionless.

I sat down on the edge of the tub, searching his face for any sign of the man I once knew. "Then why do you keep shutting me out? Why won't you talk to me?"

Finally, he opened his eyes and looked at me, but there was no warmth there, no love. Just a coldness that chilled me to the bone.

"I don't love you anymore," he said, his words hitting me like a punch to the gut.

For a moment, I couldn't breathe. It felt like the air had been sucked out of the room, leaving me gasping for something, anything to hold onto. My mind raced, flashing through every moment we'd shared – the good times, the bad, the promises we made to each other. How could it all come to this?

"Are you serious?" I whispered, my voice trembling. "After everything, you're just... done?"

Lenny didn't answer right away. He just stared at the water; his expression unreadable. "Yeah," he finally said. "I'm done."

The anger bubbled up inside me, hot and fierce. How dare he? After eight years of marriage, after everything we'd been through together, how could he just throw it all away like it meant nothing? I wanted to scream, to lash out, to make him feel the pain he was causing me. For a brief, terrifying moment, I even imagined grabbing his head and shoving it under the water, drowning him in the tub. The thought shocked me, and I pushed it away, horrified by the darkness that had flashed through my mind.

Instead, I forced myself to stay calm, to think rationally. I wasn't going to let him destroy me like this. If he wanted out, fine. But he was going to have to face the consequences.

"Fine then," I said, my voice hardening. "I'll take Kyle and move back to Texas. How about that?"

I expected him to react, to show some kind of emotion—shock, anger, regret, anything. But he just looked at me with the same cold, indifferent gaze.

"OK," he said, his voice so casual it made my blood run cold. "I'll help you pack."

His words cut through me like a knife, breaking something inside me that I didn't even know was still whole. He didn't care. He really didn't care if I left, if I took Kyle and walked out of his life forever. The realization hit me like a freight train, leaving me numb and shattered.

I got up from the edge of the tub, my legs shaking. "You're really going to let us go, just like that?" I asked, my voice barely above a whisper.

Lenny didn't even look at me. "Yeah," he said, closing his eyes again. "Just like that."

I left the bathroom, feeling like the ground had just fallen out from under me. The man I loved, the father of my child, was gone, replaced by someone I didn't recognize. And there was nothing I could do to bring him back.

In disbelief, I began to pack, my hands trembling as I folded Kyle's tiny clothes into his diaper bag. The room felt too quiet, the air thick with the weight of what was happening. My breath came in shallow gasps, and my vision blurred as tears welled up, threatening to spill over. I couldn't wrap my mind around it—how could Lenny, the man I had loved so deeply, just let us go like this?

I glanced over at him, hoping to catch a flicker of emotion, a sign that he would stop me, but he just stood there, arms crossed, his face a mask of indifference. My heart pounded in my chest as I tried one last time, my voice trembling. "Lenny, are you really going to let me leave? Let me take Kyle and just… go?"

He didn't meet my gaze, just stared at the floor, his silence more deafening than any words. The sound of Kyle's soft coos as I zipped up the diaper bag felt like a cruel contrast to the shattering of our family. I paused, clutching the edge of the crib for support, feeling the cool wood under my fingers as a tether to reality.

"Please, Lenny," I whispered, tears streaming down my face. "Don't let us go. Don't do this."

He finally looked up, but there was no warmth, no remorse in his eyes. "It's better this way," he said, his voice flat, void of the love that once filled our home.

I bit down on my lip, trying to keep myself from crying out, from letting the despair consume me. I focused on the mundane details—the pattern on the carpet, the ticking of the clock, anything to keep from falling apart. But as I placed Kyle's favorite blanket in the bag, reality hit me like a ton of bricks. He wasn't going to stop me. This wasn't a scary tactic. He was really letting us go.

When Lenny drove us to the bus station, the ride was silent, the tension thick. I stared out the window, the streets blurring past, feeling as though I was drifting through a nightmare. The station was cold and sterile, the harsh fluorescent lights buzzing overhead as I clutched Kyle close, my heart pounding with a mix of fear and disbelief.

I fumbled for change at the payphone, my fingers shaking as I dialed Momma's number. The phone rang, each chime echoing in the empty space between us, until finally, her voice answered at the other end.

"Momma, it's me," I choked out, tears spilling over as I tried to keep my voice steady. "I need money for a one-way ticket."

Her voice was soft, full of concern. "What happened, PJ? Are you alright?"

"No, Momma," I whispered, the words catching in my throat. "Lenny... he's letting us go. He's letting us leave, just like that."

I could hear her sigh, a mix of sadness and frustration. "I'll send you the money. You and Kyle just come home."

After hanging up, I turned to Lenny, my last shred of hope clinging desperately to the thought that he might change his mind. "Please, Lenny," I begged, my voice breaking. "Don't let us get on that bus. Don't let us go."

But he didn't say a word. He just turned and walked away, leaving me standing there, my heart shattering with each step he took. The sound of his retreating footsteps echoed in my mind, a painful reminder that this was really happening.

Sitting on the bus, holding Kyle close, I felt the full weight of what was happening. The engine roared to life, the vibrations running through my body as if to jolt me into accepting this new reality. I stared out the window, tears streaming down my face, hoping that Lenny would come running after us, that he would pull us back and say he'd made a mistake.

But as the bus pulled away, the station fading into the distance, a cold, sinking feeling settled in my chest. This wasn't just a temporary escape. This was the end of a chapter in my life, a chapter that I never thought would close so abruptly, so painfully.

The bus ride stretched out before us, each mile taking us further away from the life we once knew. I fed Kyle, his small, innocent face unaware of the turmoil around us, as I tried to stifle my sobs, the weight of our uncertain future pressing down on me like a heavy blanket.

Chapter 28

HEARTACHE TO REFUGE

After a grueling 24-hour bus journey, filled with the restless cries of Kyle and the ache of weariness that settled deep into my bones, we finally pulled into Huntsville, Texas. As the bus groaned to a stop, I looked out the window at the familiar sights that stirred a whirlwind of emotions within me—relief at having finally arrived, nostalgia for a time long past, and a gnawing apprehension about what lay ahead.

As I stepped off the bus, clutching Kyle close to my chest, I saw my brother-in-law, Melvin, and my youngest sister, Cherrie, waiting for us. The sight of them brought a fleeting sense of comfort, a small reprieve amid the chaos that had become my life.

"PJ, you made it," Cherrie said softly, her voice laced with both relief and fatigue. She looked so different from the sister I remembered—her once bright eyes now dull with the weight of too many hardships, her posture slumped as if the very air around her had grown too heavy to bear.

"Yeah," I replied, forcing a smile as I adjusted Kyle in my arms. "We're here."

Melvin helped with our bags, driving us to their mobile home on Momma's property. As we approached, the reality of where I had returned hit me with full force. The land was cluttered with trailers, a far cry from the dreams I had once harbored for myself and my son. This wasn't the life I had imagined—not for me, and certainly not for Kyle.

The moment we stepped out of the car, a series of barks and meows greeted us. At least fifty cats and twenty dogs swarmed the area, their presence overwhelming. I held Kyle tighter, his tiny head resting against my chest; as we parted the noisy throng, a surreal sense washed over me.

"This way," Melvin gestured towards the wooden steps leading up to Momma's trailer, which creaked ominously under our weight. Each step felt like a reminder of the decay and neglect that had taken hold of this place—of my life.

As I opened the door, the familiar yet dreaded scent of animal urine, feces, and cigarette smoke assaulted my senses. The air inside the trailer was thick with it, the stench clinging to everything it touched. I felt a wave of nausea rise, but I swallowed it down, forcing myself to move forward.

"This is where you'll be staying," Cherrie said, opening the door to my old bedroom in the back. "Momma set up the crib here for Kyle."

I nodded; my throat tight as I stepped inside. The room was cramped and cluttered, just like the rest of the trailer. It was very different from the home I had tried to create in Florida, the life I had worked so hard to build for Kyle. And now, here I was, bringing my innocent son into the very environment I swore he would never know.

As I laid Kyle in the old crib, I took a deep breath, trying to steady myself. The crib was a relic from my own childhood, and seeing it now filled me with a mix of sorrow and despair. I glanced around the room, my eyes landing on the familiar, worn-out furniture, the peeling wallpaper, the pervasive grime that seemed to coat every surface. This was the life I had left behind, and now I was back, trapped by circumstance.

"PJ," Cherrie's voice broke through my thoughts. "You, okay?"

I looked at her, seeing the concern in her eyes. "Yeah, I'm just… tired," I lied, giving her a weak smile. "It's been a long trip."

She nodded, understanding, but I could see the sadness in her gaze. "If you need anything, just let me know."

"Thanks," I replied, my voice barely above a whisper.

As the evening wore on, I tried to settle in, unpacking what little we had brought with us. Kyle's cries pierced through the quiet, and I hurried to pick him up, cradling him close as I walked him around the small room, trying to soothe him.

"It's okay, baby," I whispered, my heart aching with guilt. "Momma's here. Everything's going to be okay."

But as I looked around the trailer, at the filth and decay that surrounded us, I knew that wasn't true. The sense of hopelessness was suffocating, a weight that pressed down on my chest, making it hard to breathe.

Later that night, after Momma and Cherrie had gone to bed, I lay down on the small, lumpy mattress that now served as my bed. Kyle was in the crib beside me, finally asleep after what felt like hours of crying. Exhausted, I closed my eyes, trying to find some semblance of peace.

But it was short-lived. I was jolted awake by the sound of Kyle's cries, his wails cutting through the darkness. I switched on the lamp, and what I saw made my blood run cold—roaches. They were swarming over the room, over the crib, over my baby boy.

"No, no, no," I whispered, panic surging through me as I quickly picked Kyle up, brushing the roaches off him, my hands shaking with horror. I checked him frantically, making sure none had crept into his ears, his mouth, anywhere they could harm him.

"God, please help us," I whispered to myself, tears streaming down my face as I held Kyle close. "Please, I can't do this."

But there was no one to help. I was alone in this, and I had to protect my son. I laid him back down, and then climbed into bed beside him, determined to keep watch, to make sure nothing else happened to him.

As I lay there, staring up at the ceiling, the weight of the situation pressed down on me like a physical force. The life I had wanted for Kyle was slipping away, replaced by a nightmare I couldn't escape. But as I looked at my sleeping son, his tiny face peaceful in the dim light, I knew I had to find a way out. For him. For us.

"I'll get us out of here, Kyle," I whispered, my voice trembling with emotion. "I promise you that. I'll find a way to give you the life you deserve, no matter what it takes."

Dawn crept through the curtains, casting a soft glow over Kyle's peaceful face. I knew it was time to act. My heart tightened at the thought of what I had to do, but there was no other choice. I gently laid him down, careful not to wake him, though his brow furrowed slightly as if he sensed I was about to leave him. The ache in my chest deepened—leaving him, even for a moment, felt like tearing a piece of myself away.

I sat quietly beside him, the old mattress creaking beneath me, and reached for the phone on the nightstand. The dim light in the room made the screen glow like a beacon, stark against the darkness that seemed to fill every corner of this place. My fingers hovered over the keypad, trembling slightly under the weight of our situation. I knew that making this call meant exposing our vulnerabilities, admitting how desperate things had become. But for Kyle, I was ready to do whatever it took.

I took a deep breath and dialed Donna's number. Donna was Lenny's older sister, living just an hour away in College Station. Each beep of the keypad sounded unnervingly loud in the quiet room, my heart pounding as the phone rang. The sound echoed in my ears, amplifying my anxiety. I wasn't sure what to expect, but I knew I needed help, and she was the only one I could turn to.

Finally, Donna's familiar voice answered, warm and concerned. "Hello?"

"Hi, Donna, it's PJ," I whispered, trying to steady my voice. "I... I need to talk to you. It's important."

"PJ? What's going on?" Donna's voice immediately shifted to a tone of worry, and I could imagine the frown creasing her forehead.

I hesitated for a moment, gathering the strength to speak. "It's... it's a lot, Donna. Things have gotten bad, and I don't know what to do anymore."

As I poured out the whirlwind of events that had led me to this moment, my voice cracked with each word. The pain of recounting my story was almost unbearable, but I knew she needed to understand. I could almost feel Donna's sympathetic gaze through the phone, and I imagined Rich, her husband, listening in the background, his concern matching hers.

"PJ, we're here for you," Donna said softly after I finished. "We'll do whatever we can to help. You and Kyle deserve better than this."

"Thank you," I whispered, tears stinging my eyes. "I don't know what I would do without you."

As the call ended, the morning sun began to cast a harsh light on the dilapidated surroundings of my mother's house in Huntsville. The peeling wallpaper, the cluttered floor, the overwhelming stench—it all seemed so much clearer now, so much more unbearable in the daylight. I held Kyle close as I stood up, feeling a mix of determination and apprehension. We had to get out of here, away from this squalor, away from the life I had promised myself I would never let Kyle experience.

"Just a little longer, baby," I murmured to Kyle, who stirred slightly in his sleep. "We're going to be okay. I promise."

With that promise, I took a deep breath, knowing that the road ahead wouldn't be easy, but it was one I had to take. For Kyle. For us. And I would do whatever it took to give him the life he deserved, no matter how hard it would be.

Chapter 29

BOUND BY THE PAST, BROKEN BY LOVE

The house stood there, a stark reminder of the neglect and hardship that had marked my childhood. The peeling paint, the cluttered rooms, the pervasive odor of animals and decay—it all came rushing back, and with it, the realization that I couldn't bear for my baby to grow up in these conditions. As much as I loved my mother, the thought of Kyle being raised in this environment was unbearable.

Momma stood in the doorway, her expression a mix of hurt and confusion. She didn't understand why I was leaving, and I couldn't bring myself to explain. How could I tell her that the very home she provided, which I knew she struggled to keep, was now the source of my deepest fears? The words lodged in my throat, too painful to speak aloud, knowing they would only wound her further.

"Take care," she murmured, her voice barely above a whisper, laced with concern and sadness.

I nodded, unable to meet her eyes, the weight of our unspoken truths hanging heavily between us. I secured Kyle in his car seat, stealing a glance at his innocent face, blissfully unaware of the turmoil around him. The drive to College Station felt end-less, the silence between me and Kyle filled with a whirlwind of emotions. Kyle, with his chubby hands and bright eyes, played contentedly in the backseat, a stark contrast to the storm brewing in my mind.

When I finally pulled into Donna and Rich's driveway, a tentative sense of hope began to flicker. Their home was more than just a refuge—it was a potential turning point. Stepping out of the car, I felt the burden of my past and the uncertainty of my future pressing down on me, but there was a sliver of hope that things could change, that Donna could help.

As I sat at Donna and Rich's kitchen table, I recounted the whirlwind of events that had led me to their doorstep. My voice trembled as I spoke, the pain of my recent experiences cutting through each word. Donna listened intently, her sympathetic gaze and Rich's concerned frowns offering some comfort in my turmoil.

"I just... I just couldn't stay there, Donna. Not with Kyle. Not after everything," I said, my voice barely holding steady.

Donna reached across the table, taking my hand in hers. "You did the right thing, PJ. You're safe here, and we'll help you figure this out."

Her warmth and understanding were like a balm to my wounded heart. Donna and Rich graciously offered us ref-uge, and the thought of staying in their nurturing home, far removed from the chaos of Momma's, was a relief I hadn't real-ized I needed. The normalcy and stability of their suburban life, with its quiet neighborhood and friendly faces, seemed like a sanctuary for me and Kyle.

As we finished lunch, the phone rang, cutting through the moment of peace. Donna answered, her face growing serious as she listened. When she hung up, her expression was grave.

"What is it, Donna?" I asked, my stomach knotting with dread.

Donna hesitated, then sighed. "That was Lori. She said Lenny... well, he's already moved on, PJ. He's with someone else. Ari, the woman he mentioned before. She's living in your apartment now."

The news hit me like a punch in the gut. "What? How long—how long has this been going on?" My voice was barely a whisper, the shock rendering me numb.

Donna's eyes softened with sympathy. "I don't know, PJ. I'm going to talk to him. I'll try to get some answers."

But deep down, I knew there was no undoing the betrayal I felt. The thought of Ari in our home, living the life I had fought so hard to build, was more than I could bear. My mind spiraled with confusion and anger, the weight of everything crashing down around me.

As I sat there, the enormity of what I had lost, and the uncertainty of what lay ahead, became all too real. The pain was sharp and unrelenting, but in Donna's kitchen, surrounded by her warmth and compassion, I found the strength to face it. The road ahead was uncertain, but I wasn't alone. And for now, that was enough.

I lay in bed that night, in the room Donna and Rich had so generously offered, and I clung to Kyle, feeling the rise and fall of his small chest against mine. His steady breathing was a gentle reminder that innocence and purity still existed in my world, despite the chaos that had consumed my life. The realization crept over me slowly, like a cold tide washing in—I knew my life with Lenny was over. The man I had once loved, the man I had built a life with, had chosen a path that didn't include us.

It was a harsh truth to swallow, and as I stared into the dim light filtering through the curtains, I felt the weight of it pressing down on my chest. I had to be strong, not just for myself, but for Kyle. Our future was uncertain, but I vowed at once to build a new life for us—one filled with love, stability, and the happiness we both deserved. I took Kyle to the crib Rich had put up in the room next to mine and carefully laid him in it.

Tears streamed down my face, each one a testament to the pain and betrayal I felt. The news that Lenny was not only moving on but also starting a new family cut deeper than I could have imagined. It brought back memories of my own father, who had chosen another family over us, leaving my brothers, sisters, and me to fend for ourselves. The old wounds, which I thought had healed, were ripped open, and I was left grappling with the echoes of abandonment that seemed to be repeating themselves in my life.

Kyle's cries from the next room jolted me from my thoughts. I wiped my eyes and hurried to him, finding Donna and Rich already there, cradling him with such tenderness and love. Their warmth of affection for Kyle was the opposite of the cold abandonment I felt from Lenny. It was a small comfort to my turmoil, a reminder that not everyone in my life was willing to walk away.

Later, as I sat alone in the living room, the weight of everything crashed down on me. My body shook with sobs, and for a fleeting moment, the thought of ending it all crossed my mind—a desperate desire to escape the crushing rejection and loss. But then Donna's firm voice broke through the fog of despair.

"PJ," she said, her voice filled with both compassion and urgency, "you can't give up. You're all Kyle has. You must fight for him, for both of you."

Her words struck a chord deep within me. She was right. I couldn't let despair consume me. Kyle needed me, and I was his only hope. I wiped my tears, determined to find the strength I needed to move forward.

I returned to the bedroom as Donna's words echoed in my mind. I knew I had to muster the courage to keep going, not just for my sake but for Kyle's. He was my beacon in this darkness, the reason I had to rise above the hurt and betrayal. I lay in bed, silently praying for the strength and guidance to get through this. My faith had wavered in the past, especially during those dark moments in the closet years ago when it felt like my prayers had gone unanswered. But now, in this moment of utter despair, I reached out to God again, pleading for the strength to be the mother Kyle deserved.

Sleep finally claimed me, and a sense of determination began to take root. I would not let Lenny's actions define me or dictate Kyle's future. I promised myself, and I promised Kyle, that I would fight for a better life for us, no matter how daunting the path ahead seemed. It was a vow born of pain but fueled by the fierce love I had for my son.

The following morning, Donna, with her usual resourcefulness, pulled some strings and secured me a job interview at a customer support company. "You'll be great at this," she assured me, her confidence in me giving me the strength I needed to face the day.

The job offered regular hours and insurance benefits—a lifeline I desperately needed. As I sat in the waiting room, I couldn't help but think about how far I had come. Growing up, I had watched Momma in constant survival mode, taking on any job she could to keep us afloat. It wasn't just her story—it had become mine too, like a blueprint I had unknowingly followed. But as I sat there, I realized that I didn't have to follow that same path. I could carve out a new one, not just for me, but for Kyle as well. And with that thought, I stood a little taller, ready to face whatever came next.

Chapter 30

FIRST DAYS, NEW WAYS

The idea of breaking the cycle and stepping into a professional role seemed like a distant dream. My life, up until
that point, had been all about scraping by, surviving rather than
thriving. This job interview represented a departure from the
narrative I had always known. It was both thrilling and unsettling to imagine myself in a world I had never dared to aspire
to. The interview was more than just a potential job; it was a
seismic shift in how I viewed my place in the world. For the
first time, I was standing at a crossroads between the familiar
path of survival and an unknown road filled with potential and
growth.

On the morning of the interview, I found myself standing in front of the mirror, staring at my reflection in one of
Donna's business suits. It was unlike anything I had ever worn
before—an elegant, dark gray suit with a fitted jacket that
cinched at the waist, giving me a silhouette I barely recognized
as my own. The skirt fell just below my knees, and the fabric
felt luxurious against my skin. The blouse was crisp white, the
kind that looked like it belonged in a magazine rather than on
someone like me.

I fiddled with the sleeves, pulling at the cuffs, trying to adjust the jacket so it felt less like a costume. The outfit was clearly expensive, and for a moment, I felt like an imposter—like a child playing dress-up in her mother's clothes. But as I took a deep breath, something shifted inside me. Wearing that suit gave me a strange sense of empowerment. It was as if, by donning this armor, I could momentarily shed the weight of my past and step into a new identity, even if just for the duration of the interview.

"Donna, are you sure this looks, okay?" I asked, still tugging at the jacket, my voice betraying my nerves.

Donna walked over and gave me a once-over, her eyes softening with a mix of pride and encouragement. "You look perfect, PJ. Just be yourself. You've got this," she said, squeezing my hand.

I nodded, swallowing the lump in my throat. "Thanks, Donna. I'm just...I'm so nervous."

"That's normal. But remember, they're lucky to have you. Go in there and show them what you're made of," she said, her tone firm, as if she were willing her confidence into me.

The interview itself was a blur of questions and answers. I tried to project confidence, to articulate my eagerness to learn and contribute, even as self-doubt nagged at me with every word I spoke. The interviewer, a stern-looking woman with sharp eyes behind her glasses, nodded thoughtfully as I spoke, her expression inscrutable.

"Tell me about a time you faced a challenge and how you managed it," she asked, her pen poised over the notepad.

I hesitated for a second, then decided to be honest. "Well, I've faced a lot of challenges, but I've always found a way to keep going. I'm a quick learner, and I'm determined to make a better life for my son. I may not have all the experience you're looking for, but I have the drive and the willingness to do whatever it takes to succeed here," I said, my voice steady despite the butterflies in my stomach.

Each nod from the interviewer felt like a small victory, a sign that, just maybe, I was more than the sum of my past struggles.

As I walked out of the office, I couldn't shake the mix of hope and apprehension that clung to me. I desperately needed this job—not just for the financial security it would provide, but for the sense of normalcy and self-worth it represented. It was a chance to build a better life for Kyle, to show him a world beyond the limitations of our past.

Back at Donna and Rich's, I paced the living room, the phone clutched in my hand, replaying every word of the interview in my mind. "Do you think I did okay?" I asked Donna for the hundredth time.

Donna smiled reassuringly. "You did great, PJ. Now you just have to wait and see. They'd be crazy not to hire you."

Days passed in a blur of anxious waiting, each one stretching longer than the last. The phone mocked me with its silence, the doubts creeping in like shadows. Was I really qualified for this job? Could I truly fit into this new world? The fears of rejection and failure loomed large, threatening to overshadow the small spark of hope that the interview had ignited.

Then, one afternoon, the phone rang. My heart leaped into my throat as I grabbed it, my hands trembling.

"Hello?" I answered, my voice barely steady.

"Is this PJ? This is Susan from the customer support company. We're pleased to offer you the position," the voice on the other end of the line said.

Relief and gratitude flooded through me as I accepted the offer, my voice quivering with emotion. "Thank you, thank you so much," I managed to say, tears of relief streaming down my face as I hung up.

My first day at the company was a whirlwind of nervous excitement. I stepped into the office, greeted by a stack of paperwork—forms for insurance, health benefits, and other essentials. It felt surreal, like I was stepping into a new chapter of my life, one where stability and security were finally within reach.

"Welcome to the team, PJ," the office manager said, handing me a packet of documents. "We're glad to have you."

"Thank you, I'm really excited to be here," I replied, trying to keep the nervousness out of my voice.

I filled out each form, feeling a growing sense of belonging and responsibility. This was it—a real job, with real benefits, and a chance to prove to myself and to Kyle that we could have a better life.

In this new beginning, my top priority was ensuring Kyle's well-being. I spent evenings researching daycares, visiting facilities, and finally selecting the best one in College Station. It was expensive, but as I stood in the bright, clean facility filled with warmth and smiling faces, I knew no cost was too high for my son's care.

When I left the daycare that day, I felt a sense of peace wash over me. We were on the right path, and for the first time in a long while, I felt like things were going to be okay.

Dropping Kyle off on that first day was one of the hardest things I'd ever done. My heart felt heavy, almost as if it were breaking, but as I watched the staff greet us with warm smiles and open arms, a sense of reassurance began to settle in. The daycare was more than just a place to leave my child; it was a promise to Kyle of a life filled with opportunities that I had never known.

"Hi there, little guy!" one of the caregivers said, crouching down to Kyle's level. "We're going to have so much fun today."

I forced a smile, trying to push aside the anxiety gnawing at me. "You be good, okay, Kyle?" I whispered, kissing his forehead before handing him over.

Kyle looked at me with wide, trusting eyes, and I felt a pang of guilt mixed with hope. "He's in good hands," the caregiver assured me, sensing my hesitation.

I nodded, my voice barely above a whisper. "Thank you."

I walked out of the daycare and towards my car, unable to shake the mix of emotions swirling inside me. But I knew this was the right decision for both of us. I had to provide for him, and this job was my way of doing that.

My days at the company quickly fell into a steady rhythm. Every morning, as I walked through the office doors, a small part of me still couldn't believe this was my life now. The borrowed clothes I wore each day felt like armor, helping me blend into this new world that still felt foreign to me. But with each passing day, I grew more confident, learning to navigate my role and finding a sense of purpose in my work.

"Morning, PJ!" a colleague called out as I passed by, offering a friendly wave.

"Morning," I replied, managing a smile. I was slowly beginning to feel like I belonged.

I found myself grappling with the physical changes that came with motherhood. The extra weight I had carried since Kyle's birth weighed on my self-esteem, especially with Lenny's cruel remarks echoing in my mind. His cutting words, meant to hurt, often resurfaced during moments of doubt.

But as the days turned into weeks, the hectic pace of work and the emotional stress of my situation began to take a toll. I noticed my clothes fitting differently, the weight slowly starting to come off. It wasn't something I had consciously worked towards; it just happened as a byproduct of my new lifestyle, where work and caring for Kyle left little room for anything else.

One morning, I caught a glimpse of myself in the mirror and barely recognized the woman staring back. There was something different about her—someone stronger, more resilient, emerging from the shadow of who I used to be.

"Wow, you look great," one of my male colleagues remarked one day, his tone half-flirtatious, half-genuine.

I smiled politely, but inside, I felt a mix of emotions. The attention, while flattering, also reminded me of how much my life had changed. I had no interest in their advances, though. My heart was still tender from Lenny's betrayal, and his hurtful comments about my body had left scars that I wasn't ready to heal just yet.

Kyle was my priority. He was the reason I got up every morning, the reason I pushed through the challenges of each day. My love for him was the one thing that kept me anchored in the storm that was my life. As I focused on providing for him and building a new life for us, I realized that this journey was not just about surviving—it was about finding the strength to thrive, for both of us.

Chapter 31

NOT SO CHARMING...YET

Balancing work and motherhood were a challenge, but it was a challenge I embraced. Kyle's laughter and his bright, inquisitive eyes were the best part of my day, washing away any stress or fatigue I felt. Every time I held him, I was reminded why I was working so hard. I often wondered how I'd introduce him to the concept of dating when he got older. The thought of guiding him through the complexities of relationships was something I looked forward to, even if it seemed far off.

At work, I was quickly getting the hang of things. My desk, a small island in the sea of cubicles, became my sanctuary. I sorted through countless messages from clients seeking technical support, creating a system that organized requests from the West Coast and East Coast. It was meticulous work, requiring a level of mindfulness I hadn't realized I possessed. But there was something calming about it, something that made me feel in control in a way I hadn't felt in a long time.

"PJ, you're really getting the hang of this," one of my colleagues remarked as they passed by my desk.

"Thanks," I replied with a smile, feeling a small surge of pride.

The job demanded focus, and in this environment, surrounded by deadlines and technology, I found a strange sense of peace. It was a world far removed from the chaos of my past, a place where I could be someone new, someone capable and in control. Every successful day at the office felt like a victory, a step further away from the pain and uncertainty that had once defined my life.

But just as I was starting to settle into this new phase, a co-worker, Tim, barged into my office one morning, shattering my sense of calm. His dark hair and mustache might have been striking under different circumstances, but the condescension in his eyes made any physical appeal vanish.

He tossed a pile of messages onto my desk, pointing out an error with an air of superiority. "It's moDEM, not moDUM," he stated bluntly.

My cheeks flushed with a mix of embarrassment and anger. How was I supposed to know the correct spelling of 'modem'? I hadn't been in this job long, and the last thing I needed was to be humiliated over a simple mistake.

"Thanks for the heads-up," I muttered, trying to keep my cool.

The tension from the morning lingered, but when Patti, our manager, announced she was taking the team out for lunch, it felt like a small victory. Maybe it was an opportunity to reset the day and gain some favor with the boss.

At the restaurant, we gathered around a large table, scanning the menu. I tried to find something that could yield leftovers for another meal. I settled on a sandwich, savoring each bite as I focused on enjoying the brief escape from the office.

"Wow, that was fast!" Tim exclaimed, drawing attention to my empty plate. He made a point of commenting on how quickly I had devoured my sandwich, making it the topic of conversation at the table.

I forced a laugh, trying to shrug off his remarks, but inside, I felt a sting of humiliation. If only he knew the truth—that I was ravenous, not just for food, but for stability in my life.

The van ride back to the office was filled with casual conversation. Someone asked Tim about his age and marital status.

"I'm 32 and single," he replied, his tone flat.

His quiet demeanor, except when he was picking on me, made his single status unsurprising. Knowing he was single, I wondered if there was a way to get him to stop picking on me. My sister Karen often said we had a way of making people like us. I could use this to create a more peaceful work environment.

Months passed, and I managed to save enough to move into a small apartment with Kyle. I was tired of living under Donna and Rich's roof with their lives, I wanted my own life. It was just the two of us, and I was determined to make it a nurturing home. I converted the only bedroom into a nursery for Kyle, wanting him to have everything a child with two parents would have. I slept on an old daybed in the small living room that Donna gave me to use.

To make ends meet, I juggled multiple jobs. I worked the third shift as a waitress at a pancake restaurant and took on weekend shifts at a hardware store. Thankfully, Donna and Rich were kind enough to watch Kyle while I worked these long hours.

Despite my best efforts, finances were always tight. Rent, daycare, utility bills, and Kyle's constant ear infections strained my budget. Insurance covered some of the medical expenses, but the copays and missed work added up quickly. Lenny offered no support, making every day a struggle.

I refused to compromise on daycare quality for Kyle. He attended the best one I could find, even if it meant working multiple jobs. I was adamant that my son would never experience the hunger, mental, or physical abuse that had shadowed my own upbringing.

One evening, after a particularly long day, I tucked Kyle into bed and sat by his side, whispering, "You're going to have a better life, Kyle. I promise."

Journal entry October 31, 1992

Halloween brings its own magic, a time when costumes and decorations transform the ordinary into realms of fantasy. I can't help but think of my brother Kent, whose love for this spooky holiday always brings a smile to my face. I imagine his home, decorated with elaborate and eerie decorations, ready to entertain and spook the neighborhood kids. Tonight, Kyle wears a charming little dragon costume, complete with tiny scales and a playful tail. Tim, who has been part of our lives for about a year now, will be joining us. His presence has been so comforting, especially in contrast to the problems of my past with Lenny. Tim, with his calmness and maturity, brings a sense of stability that I've desperately craved for so long. There's an age gap of eight years between us, but it's his gentle demeanor and kindness that truly make him stand out. I feel incredibly lucky to have him as a friend, and perhaps more. He adores Kyle and watching them together fills my heart with warmth. Yet, deep down, I often wonder why someone as remarkable as Tim would take an interest in me. Yes, Kyle is irresistibly cute, but there's this lingering doubt about my worthiness. Why would Tim, who comes from a world of etiquette and conventional norms, choose to be with a single mother with a complicated past? These thoughts plague me, casting shadows on the light that Tim brings into our lives. There's a fear that if he learns the full extent of where I come from, the hardships I've faced, and the mistakes I've made, he'll see me differently. He might view me as just a naive girl from the Piney Woods, marked by poor life choices and a broken spirit. The possibility of this revelation scares me, threatening to derail the beautiful relationship that's just beginning to bloom. But tonight, it's about making memories with Kyle and Tim, about embracing the joy of the present moment. As we step out into the night, our little dragon leading the way, I try to push these fears aside. Tonight is for laughter, for pretend scares, and for gathering sweet treats under the October moon. It's a night to cherish the new beginnings and the hope that, despite the shadows of my past, there's light waiting to breathe through. During my last therapy session, Barbara often encouraged me to delve into my sense of self. "Who do you see when you look in the mirror, PJ?" she asks gently, her voice always filled with a warmth that invites honesty. I hesitate, the words catching in my throat. "I see someone who's been through a lot, Barbara," I finally admit. "I come from a place that people often look down on. Labeled as 'poor white trash.' That label... it feels like a heavy cloak I can't shake off." Barbara nods, her eyes meeting mine with an understanding that feels both comforting and daunting. "But those struggles, those labels," she counters softly, "do they define you, or are they just a part of your journey?" I ponder her words, feeling the weight of years of struggle, of being seen as less than, of feeling broken and flawed. "It's hard not to feel defined by them," I confess, my voice barely above a whisper. "Sometimes, I feel unworthy of the happiness I'm reaching for, like I'm not meant to have it." She leans forward, her expression earnest. "Your past, the struggles, the labels—they are chapters in your story, but they don't write your future, PJ. You are more than the hardships you've faced. You're a survivor, a mother, someone who's capable of giving and receiving love. It's okay to embrace the happiness you find. You deserve it, just as much as anyone else." Her words are a comfort, but they also stir a turmoil inside me. Can I really step beyond the shadows of my past, embrace the light of the present, and build a future that's different from where I've come from? It's a question that lingers, even as I write in this journal. As I leave Barbara's office, her parting words echo in my mind. "Remember, PJ, you are not your past. You are the person who has grown from it." Stepping out into the crisp autumn air, I take a deep breath. Tonight, I'll focus on the joy of being with Kyle and Tim, on the laughter and the simple pleasures of Halloween. Just maybe, I can start believing in the person Barbara sees in me.

Chapter 32

A GENTLE MAN

L ife at the office was a mixed bag. At 25, I was friendly
enough to catch the attention of several men around the
workplace. It was flattering, but I wasn't interested in dating.
My heart was still in pieces, slowly being mended, and the only
space I had left was reserved for Kyle. I often thought about
how, maybe when Kyle was older, he could weigh in on my dating life, but for now, it was just the two of us against the world.

My job kept me on my toes as I categorized incoming messages from clients needing technical support. West Coast over
here, East Coast over there—it was routine but required focus.
During one of these routine tasks, Tim, my less-than-charm-
ing colleague, made a memorable entrance into my life. My
relationship with Tim had started on rocky ground. He was
obnoxious and rude, and our early interactions were anything
but pleasant.

One morning, I was at my desk, sorting through the usual
pile of client messages when Tim walked by. He didn't even
bother with a greeting, just dropped a stack of papers on my
desk with a loud thud. "You've got the East Coast mixed in
with the West Coast," he snapped, his tone dripping with irritation. "Try to keep them straight next time, will you?"

Startled, I looked up at him, my cheeks flushing with embarrassment and a bit of anger. "I'm sorry, Tim." I replied, trying to keep my voice steady.

He didn't acknowledge my apology, just turned on his heel and walked away. It wasn't the first time he'd been short with me, and it certainly wouldn't be the last. Every interaction with him seemed to carry that same dismissive tone, as if I were just an inconvenience in his day.

Another time, I was answering a client's call, doing my best to sound professional and helpful. Out of nowhere, Tim's voice echoed from his office next door, mimicking my tone in a loud, exaggerated manner. "What's CHO name! What's CHO name!" he jeered, his mocking laughter filling the office.

Furious, I hung up the phone and marched over to his office, standing firmly in his doorway. "I am not saying it that way. It's 'What is your name?'" I corrected him, my voice steady but tinged with irritation.

Tim just smirked, turning back to his computer without a word. His arrogance was infuriating, and I found myself avoiding him whenever possible, not wanting to deal with his abrasive demeanor.

But everything changed one day, thanks to a dress my mom had sewn for me.

Momma had crafted three dresses in just one afternoon, highlighting her incredible skill as a seamstress. These weren't just any dresses; they were tailored while I wore them, ensuring a perfect fit. I was grateful, especially since Donna and Marley were growing tired of me borrowing their clothes. The dress I chose that day was white with brown polka dots, featuring a tight bodice and a full skirt. It fit beautifully, and it was uniquely mine—very different from the jeans I had once been too ashamed to wear in high school because they lacked a signature tag.

As I was distributing messages at work, I noticed Tim staring at me in the dress. At the time, I was oblivious to his gaze, but he later confessed that he couldn't take his eyes off me. That dress, sewn with love by my mom, seemed to spark something in Tim, shifting his attitude toward me from indifferent to intrigued.

Despite his initial silence and shyness, I found myself inexplicably drawn to him. There was something about Tim that intrigued me, a depth beneath his quiet exterior that I yearned to explore. His change in behavior towards me was unexpected but welcome, marking the beginning of a friendship that gradually evolved into something deeper.

Looking back, I realized just how much I had changed since high school. Those years had been filled with a desperate need to fit in, to be like my best friend Jill. I had spent so much time trying to emulate her, trying to blend in with the crowd. But now, things were different. Standing in that polka-dotted dress, I felt a sense of pride and confidence that I had never known before.

Tim's attention caught me off guard. Though it was subtle, it made me see myself in a different light. His quiet glances and the way he noticed me more than others—these small gestures validated my worth in ways I hadn't expected. It was as if, for the first time, I was being seen for who I truly was, and that realization was both empowering and surprising.

Our relationship began to blossom slowly, built on a foundation of mutual respect and an unexpected connection. The Tim I was getting to know was quite different from the abrasive man I had first met. He showed patience, kindness, and a level of understanding that I hadn't experienced before. It was refreshing, comforting even, and for the first time in a long while, I found myself open to the possibility of dating again.

I remember the evening I decided to invite Tim to dinner. It felt like a pivotal moment in our evolving relationship, a chance to see if the connection I felt was mutual. With Donna kindly offering to watch Kyle for the night, I decided to seize the opportunity.

After getting a fresh haircut—a stylish fresh look with brown locks highlighted with auburn, layered just above my shoulders with wispy bangs framing my face—I stood in front of the mirror, feeling a mix of nervousness and excitement. The new hairstyle was a small but notable change, a symbol of the new chapter I was stepping into.

Taking a deep breath, I picked up the phone and dialed Tim's number. My heart pounded as I waited for him to answer. When I heard his voice on the other end, I tried to keep my tone casual. "Hey, Tim, I was wondering... would you like to have dinner with me tonight?"

There was a brief pause at the other end, and I held my breath. "Sure," he replied without hesitation, his voice warm and easygoing.

I felt relieved, feeling a flutter of excitement. This dinner felt like a step forward, a chance to explore what was blossoming between us. As I hung up the phone, I couldn't help but smile, anticipation bubbling up inside me. Tonight, would be the night I finally tested the waters, ready to see if what we had was real.

But when Tim arrived, I was caught completely off guard. Standing beside him was his roommate, Michael. My surprise must have shown on my face because Tim quickly introduced him as if it were the most natural thing in the world.

"Uh… Hi, Michael," I said, trying to hide my disappointment. This wasn't what I had envisioned. I had planned for an intimate evening to test the waters with Tim, not a gathering with an unexpected guest.

The atmosphere was awkward from the start. The dinner I had so carefully prepared suddenly felt like a casual meal among acquaintances, rather than the special evening I had hoped for. I couldn't help but feel disheartened as Michael's presence changed the dynamic, making it harder to connect with Tim the way I had wanted to.

As the night went on, though, I began to realize something. Tim had brought Michael because he wasn't sure of my intentions either. We were both cautiously feeling our way through this new and unfamiliar territory, unsure of where this connection might lead.

Though the evening didn't unfold the way I had planned, it was still a step forward in our relationship—a tentative beginning that hinted at something more. In those small, uncertain moments, I began to see that there was a future with Tim, a future I hadn't dared to imagine before.

The dinner was an instant disaster. Michael dominated the conversation, his charm and talkative nature filling the room. Tim, on the other hand, remained quiet, almost overshadowed by his roommate's exuberance. As I listened to Michael effortlessly keep the conversation going, a part of me couldn't help but wonder if maybe he would have been a better match, given his outgoing personality.

The evening ended; Michael said his goodbyes, leaving Tim and me alone. Tim offered to drive me to my car, which was parked on the other side of the mall. The moment felt ripe for something more, a step beyond mere co-worker camaraderie. My heart raced as I gathered my courage, turned to him, and asked, "Well, aren't you going to kiss me goodnight?"

I was tired of his shyness and wanted to ignite some spark, to feel that elusive chemistry between us. But his response caught me off guard. "Why do women always expect the man to kiss them after a date?" he asked, matter-of-factly.

I was speechless, my boldness deflated in an instant. All I could manage was a quiet, "I don't know…" before I stepped out of the car. As he drove off, I sat there in the dimly lit parking lot, processing the evening's events with a mix of rejection and frustration.

The sting of his unexpected response lingered as I walked to my car. The idea of dating a single mom might not have been as appealing to him as I had hoped. The rejection was sharp, forcing me to confront those familiar feelings of anger and inadequacy that had plagued me before.

"Maybe we're just meant to be friends," I muttered to myself as I unlocked my car door. Yet, as I sat behind the wheel, a part of me couldn't shake the disappointment. I had wanted more than just a platonic friendship, but now, I was left questioning where we stood, adding another layer of uncertainty to my already tumultuous emotional landscape.

Chapter 33

UNWANTED ADVANCES, UNANSWERED JUSTICE

M r. Corey was a figure who loomed large in the background of the office. As the boss of my manager, Patti, he wasn't someone I interacted with often, but when I did, it was always a mix of intimidation and cautious respect. He was the kind of man who commanded the room with his mere presence—tall, with a stern face and sharp eyes that missed nothing. It wasn't unusual for men in positions of power to make advances, but Mr. Corey's behavior was more than just casual flirting, it was a blatant disregard for decency.

It started subtly, insidiously. He'd make a comment here and there—compliments that felt too personal, lingering looks that made me uncomfortable. But I brushed it off, telling myself that it was just how things were, that I needed this job too much to rock the boat. I had Kyle to think about. But as time went on, his advances became more overt. He'd find excuses to visit my desk, his eyes lingering too long, his comments becoming less about work and more about my appearance.

One day, he called me into his office for what I assumed would be a routine meeting. I was eager, even excited, thinking my hard work had finally caught his attention in a positive way. I had been working tirelessly on troubleshooting computer issues and had even put together a manual on Modem error messages—a tangible piece of proof that I was capable and valuable to the team.

I sat down across from him, filled with anticipation. "Thank you for coming, PJ," Mr. Corey began, his tone too friendly. "I've noticed the work you've been doing. It's impressive," he started.

A sense of pride swelled in my chest. "Thank you, Mr. Corey. I've been working hard to—"

But before I could finish, he leaned forward, his voice dropping to a more intimate tone. "You know, PJ, hard work isn't the only way to get ahead in this company."

I blinked, not understanding at first. "What do you mean?"

He smiled, sliding something across the desk toward me. It was a hotel key. My heart skipped a beat as I stared at it, my mind racing to catch up with what was happening.

"If you want to keep your job, you'll meet me there tonight," he said, his voice as smooth as ever, but there was an edge to it, a threat that was impossible to ignore.

I felt the blood drain from my face. "Excuse me?" I whispered, barely able to get the words out.

"You heard me," he replied, leaning back in his chair, completely at ease. "I think you understand what's at stake here."

I grabbed the key, my hands trembling as I stood up. "I... I have a son..." I stammered, trying to appeal to whatever humanity might be left in him. "I need this job."

He didn't even flinch. "Then I suggest you don't disappoint me," he said.

I walked out of his office in a daze, the key feeling like it weighed a thousand pounds in my hand. My mind was spinning, trying to process what had just happened. This wasn't just a flirtation, this was a direct threat to my livelihood, to everything I had worked so hard to build for Kyle and myself.

I found myself standing in front of Patti's office, my heart pounding in my chest. I needed advice, a lifeline—anything to help me undo this impossible situation. I knocked on the door, and when Patti looked up, I could see the concern in her eyes.

"PJ, what's wrong?" she asked as I stepped inside.

I didn't have the words to explain, so I just handed her the key. "Mr. Corey gave me this," I said, my voice shaking. "He said if I don't go to the hotel tonight, I won't have a job tomorrow."

Patti's face paled as she looked at the key. "Oh my gosh, PJ. Are you serious?"

I nodded, the weight of the situation pressing down on me. "What am I supposed to do? I can't lose this job, but I can't... I can't do what he's asking."

Patti took a deep breath, trying to steady herself. "This is serious, PJ. We need to think about this carefully. It's a misunderstanding?"

"A misunderstanding?" I echoed, incredulous. "He was pretty clear, Patti."

She sighed, running a hand through her hair. "You're right. This isn't something we can just brush off. But you can't go. You know that, right?"

I nodded, tears welling up in my eyes. "But what if I lose my job? How am I supposed to take care of Kyle?"

Patti reached out, taking my hand. "We'll figure this out, PJ. You're not alone in this."

I left her office feeling slightly better, but the fear was still there, gnawing at the edges of my resolve. I couldn't stop thinking about Kyle, about what would happen if I couldn't provide for him. But I also knew that giving in to Mr. Corey's demands would destroy me in a different way. I would never be able to look at myself in the mirror again.

I walked back to my desk, trying to collect my thoughts; Patti suddenly burst into my office, her face a mix of urgency and concern.

"PJ, two more girls have come forward with similar complaints about Mr. Corey," she said, her voice trembling slightly. "Management wants to meet with each of you immediately."

My heart skipped a beat. "Management?" I asked, trying to process what this meant.

Patti, wide-eyed, nodded. "This is it, PJ! This could be our chance to stop him!"

I took a deep breath, feeling a mix of relief and apprehension. The battle lines were drawn, and I knew I had to stand my ground, not just for myself but for Kyle and for every other woman who had been put in this position. As I headed toward the meeting, the weight of what was about to happen settled over me, but there was a newfound determination within me.

"Enough is enough," I whispered to myself, steeling my resolve. "I can't let fear dictate my life anymore."

Patti led me down the corridor to a spacious conference room, the kind reserved for the most serious of meetings. The long, polished table seemed to stretch endlessly, a reminder of the power dynamics at play. As I stepped inside, four individuals, all dressed in sharp suits, sat with an air of authority that made my stomach knot with anxiety. I had never seen them before, but I knew they were the ones who held my career—and my future—in their hands.

Patti introduced me as we entered, her voice steady. "PJ, this is the management team," she said, gesturing to each one.

"We have the Director of Human Resources, the Vice President of Operations, the Legal Advisor, and the Compliance Officer."

They nodded as their titles were mentioned, but their expressions remained serious, almost stern. It was clear this was no ordinary meeting, and I felt like a small fish in a vast, intimidating corporate ocean.

"Please, take a seat," the Director of Human Resources said, her tone professional but not unkind. "We understand this is a difficult situation."

I hesitated for a moment before sitting down, the weight of the situation pressing down on me. The room was silent, the only sound the soft shuffle of papers as the Legal Advisor opened a file in front of him.

"We're here to discuss the incident involving Mr. Corey," the Vice President of Operations began, his voice carrying the authority of someone accustomed to making tough decisions. "This is part of an internal investigation, and we want to assure you that your concerns are being taken seriously."

The words "internal investigation" and "due process" echoed in my mind, but they felt distant, almost detached from the reality of what had happened. I knew they were following the procedure, but it felt like they were speaking a different language—one that was designed to keep emotions at bay.

The Compliance Officer leaned forward slightly, her eyes meeting mine. "PJ, we want to hear from you. Can you walk us through what happened?"

I took a deep breath, trying to steady my nerves. My voice trembled slightly as I began to recount the events. The room was silent as I spoke, the tension thick enough to cut with a knife. I couldn't tell what they were thinking—their faces were unreadable, their expressions carefully neutral. Were they sympathetic? Skeptical? It was impossible to know.

When I finished, the Legal Advisor nodded, making a note in his file. "Thank you for sharing that, PJ," he said, his voice calm. "We are committed to ensuring a safe and respectful workplace."

There was some talk about follow-up meetings, additional training, a review of company policies. It all sounded so rehearsed, so detached from the reality of what I had just experienced. I nodded along, but a sense of unease settled in my stomach.

As the meeting ended, the Director of Human Resources offered a final reassurance. "We appreciate your honesty, PJ. We're going to handle this situation appropriately." They asked me to wait outside the office while they spoke with Patti. After a while, she walked out and we left the room together, her hand resting lightly on my shoulder in a gesture of support. "You did great in there," she said, trying to reassure me. "This is a tough situation, but you managed it well."

"Thanks, Patti," I replied, though my voice was tinged with uncertainty. "But... what now? Do I still have a job here?"

Patti's face softened, and she nodded. "Yes, of course! Management is dealing with Mr. Corey's case. They've decided he'll stay on, but they're taking the allegations seriously."

Her words were meant to comfort, but they only deepened the complexity of the situation. "And what about us? Those of us who spoke out. Are we just supposed to keep working like nothing happened?"

"They've assured me there won't be any repercussions for reporting," Patti said, her tone more reassuring. "You're valued here, PJ. Your contribution is important."

I nodded, my doubt lingering. "I just... I don't know, Patti. It doesn't feel like enough."

Patti sighed, understanding the weight of my concerns. "I get it, PJ. This isn't easy, and it's not fair. But you did the right thing by speaking up." Patti looked at me with kindness and said, "They will pay for counseling if you want it. I would take it," she added.

I looked back down the hallway toward my office, the familiar space now feeling constrictive, almost suffocating. "I guess we'll see," I said quietly, trying to muster some semblance of hope. But deep down, I knew things had changed, and not for the better.

Chapter 34

BREAKING FREE, STEPPING FORWARD

My trust in the company's management was shattered, not just by the incident with Mr. Corey but by their decision to keep him on despite everything. The thought of returning to work, under his management, made my stomach churn. The meeting was over, but my sense of dread and uncertainty lingered. I walked out of the office that day, my mind a storm of emotions—fear, anger, and a fierce determination to protect Kyle's future.

Sitting in my car, I gripped the steering wheel tightly, trying to steady my thoughts. The idea of finding a new job felt overwhelming but staying in an environment where I felt disrespected and vulnerable seemed even worse. In the silence of the car, I whispered a prayer, my voice trembling with desperation. "God, please, show me the way. Help me find a path that will secure a better future for Kyle and me."

The road ahead was uncertain, a dark stretch with no clear direction. But I knew one thing; I would do whatever it took to provide for my son, even if it meant starting over from scratch.

Later that evening, as I sat on the couch with Tim, I could barely hold back my tears. The weight of the day pressed down on me like a heavy blanket, suffocating any sense of hope I had left.

"I can't believe they're letting him stay," I said, my voice cracking as the tears finally spilled over. "It's like they're saying it's okay for him to treat us like that."

Tim wrapped his arms around me, his embrace warm and comforting. "You did the right thing, PJ. It's not easy, but you stood up for yourself. That's what matters."

I nodded, wiping my eyes with the back of my hand. "But what do I do now, Tim? I need a job. I can't let Kyle down. He deserves so much better than this."

Tim pulled back slightly, looking me straight in the eyes. "You won't let him down. You're the strongest person I know, PJ. You've been through hell and back, and you're still standing. You're fighting every single day for Kyle, and that's what makes you incredible."

His words were like a soothing balm to my wounded soul, but the uncertainty of the future still gnawed at me. "But where do I even begin? I have to find something soon. I can't stay there."

"We'll start looking together," Tim said firmly, his voice filled with determination. "You're not alone in this. I'm here for you, and we'll figure it out. Together."

His support was unexpected but deeply comforting. It gave me a glimmer of hope, something to cling to in the middle of this storm. As we sat there, discussing potential job opportunities, I felt a sense of resolve slowly building within me. No matter how challenging the road ahead might be, I was determined to push forward for Kyle's sake. With Tim by my side, the journey didn't seem as daunting as before.

Seeking new opportunities, I turned to Donna and Rich for advice one evening after Kyle had gone to bed. Over a cup of coffee at their kitchen table, Donna mentioned, "You know, PJ, a friend of mine said there's an insurance company hiring. The job involves some travel, but the pay's good, and they offer great benefits."

My ears perked up. "Really? What kind of position is it?"

"It's with a hospital insurance company," Donna explained. "It sounds like a solid opportunity. If you need to travel, don't worry about Kyle. Rich and I can watch him for you."

Relieved by Donna's offer, I decided to go for it. On the day of the interview, I dressed in what Donna called my "power suit"—a bright yellow linen jacket paired with black slacks and a crisp white shirt with lace detailing. As I stood in front of the mirror, I felt a bit overdressed, but Donna assured me, "You look perfect. Go knock 'em dead!"

With a nervous flutter in my stomach, I entered the company's office. The dark wood framing the elegant cubicles gave the place an air of sophistication, and the plush waiting room, complete with a friendly receptionist, helped calm my nerves. My mouth was dry, but I declined the offer of a drink, worried I might spill it on my pristine outfit.

After a few minutes, a short man with striking blue eyes approached me with a warm smile. "Are you PJ?" he asked.

"Yes, that's me," I replied, extending my hand. "You must be John."

"Nice to meet you," John said, shaking my hand firmly. "Let's head to Don's office."

John led me to a spacious office with large windows overlooking a lush golf course. Don, the company's boss, greeted me with a handshake. He was balding and carried an air of someone who had once been quite handsome. His gaze often drifted to the golf course outside, but he seemed friendly enough.

"Please, have a seat," Don said, gesturing to a large conference table surrounded by plush chairs.

As I tried to slide my resume across the sleek table to Don, it unexpectedly shot off to the other side and fluttered to the floor. The moment seemed to stretch in slow motion as my embarrassment grew. Before I could move, John quickly leaped to retrieve it, saving me from the awkwardness of bending down in my suit.

Trying to break the ice, I flashed a smile and quipped, "Well, that was awkward! Someone really needs to have a word with whoever polishes this table so well!"

To my immense relief, the room erupted in laughter. Don and John chuckled heartily, and the tension dissipated in an instant.

As the laughter subsided, I shifted back into professional mode, articulating my skills and experience with confidence. I felt a spark of hope growing within me—this job could be the opportunity I needed, not just for myself but for Kyle's future as well.

Throughout the interview, I couldn't help but think about how I had often felt out of place in professional settings. My siblings had always seemed to possess a natural charisma, a charm my sister referred to as a scent. It was that magical quality that made everyone instantly like them. But during that interview, something changed. Maybe this charm was in me after all. When my resume had flown across the table, turning what could have been a mortifying moment into a room full of laughter, I felt a glimmer of that fabled charm.

By the time John and Don walked me out, they were still chuckling, tears of laughter in their eyes. My accidental resume toss had broken the ice in a way I never could have planned.

As I waited in the lobby, my heart raced with anticipation. Moments later, John reappeared, a smile on his face. "PJ, we'd like to offer you the position. Can you start at the beginning of the month?"

I managed to keep my voice steady as I replied, "Yes, absolutely."

As I reached my car, I let loose, yelling, and snapping my fingers in a burst of joy. Just then, I noticed Don getting into his car, catching a glimpse of my unbridled excitement. His smile told me he might think I was a bit crazy, but there was a twinkle of admiration in his eyes, too.

Chapter 35

A PILLOW AND A PROUD HEART

The next two weeks at my job flew by in a blur of anticipation and nerves. Tim and I were growing closer, and I started to wonder if it was time for him to meet Kyle. The thought filled me with both excitement and anxiety. Introducing Kyle to someone I was dating was a big step—one filled with 'what ifs'—but it felt like the right thing to do. I needed to see if this relationship had the potential I hoped for.

Planning dinner, however, was its own challenge. My latest paycheck had just covered Kyle's daycare and rent, leaving me with barely enough for groceries. But necessity is the mother of invention, as they say. I rummaged through my kitchen and found spaghetti noodles and tomato sauce. After raiding my trusty change jar, I had just enough to buy a loaf of bread and some lettuce. Borrowing a few packets of dressing and parmesan cheese from the grocery store deli felt like a small victory.

As I set the table, I called out to Kyle, "We're eating like royalty tonight, buddy!"

Tim arrived early, just as I was putting the finishing touches on the meal. Kyle, in his beloved Batman underwear, ran up to Tim and hugged his legs with all the enthusiasm of a happy toddler. His silly antics—a mix of things he'd picked up from his cousin and his own vibrant personality—filled the room with laughter. But as I glanced at Tim, I noticed a flicker of discomfort in his eyes. Was he overwhelmed by Kyle's affection, or was I just reading too much into it?

Dinner went smoothly enough, despite the lingering uncertainty. Tim complimented the meal, and Kyle was his usual charming self. But as the evening wore on, I couldn't shake the feeling that Tim was holding back, unsure of his place in our little world. This dinner felt like a test, not just for Tim but for me as well. Could I let someone into the safe little world I had built for Kyle and me?

The night ended with more questions than answers, but I was okay with that. This was unfamiliar territory, and I was learning to take things one step at a time.

But dinner with Tim turned into an adventure of its own. Spaghetti, as it turns out, is not just a meal when you're a toddler like Kyle—it's an art form. He became a little Picasso, using tomato sauce as his paint and the kitchen as his canvas. Noodles dangled from his hair, and sauce splattered across the floor. I tried to keep my composure, reminding myself that messes are just part of life with a child.

Tim, bless his heart, offered to help clean up while I bathed Kyle. It was a small gesture, but it meant the world to me. After the bath, Kyle, now in his pajamas, was all giggles and wiggles as he showed Tim his new toy—a little plastic police car, a thoughtful gift from Tim. Watching them play on the floor, I felt a pang of sadness as I thought about Lenny. He should have been there, sharing these moments with his son. The wound of his absence was still fresh, even after all this time. But then I reminded myself to focus on the present—the gentle man on the floor, making my son laugh.

Once Kyle was tucked into bed with his new car, Tim's observant eyes didn't miss a thing. He noticed the sparse contents of my fridge and my makeshift bed in the living room.

"You don't have a pillow?" Tim asked, concern lacing his voice.

I shrugged it off, trying to sound nonchalant. "I'm fine, really. A pillow isn't necessary for me."

Tim's presence was comforting, yet his questions about my living situation left me feeling exposed, vulnerable. The evening wrapped up with an awkward yet sweet peck on the cheek from Tim. It was clear we were still in the realm of friendship, but his actions spoke of a deeper care and respect.

Lying in bed that night, I found myself praying for the first time in a long while, grateful for Tim's friendship and for Kyle's joy.

The next morning brought a heartwarming surprise. Outside our door lay a brown paper bag filled with food and a pillow with a red bow – gifts from Tim. His note touched me deeply, reaffirming that friendship can be just as powerful and meaningful as any romantic relationship. His gesture showed that he saw beyond my façade, much like Mrs. Kinney back in Huntsville.

As I prepared to take Kyle to the park, I couldn't help but feel blessed. Tim might think he's too good for me, but his kindness was a reminder that goodness still existed in the world. His faith, his regular church attendance, they were parts of him that I admired, even if I felt unworthy at times. Holding the pillow close, I realized that this was more than just a gift—it was a symbol of hope, a reminder that there are people who care, who see the struggles and still choose to stand by you.

As Kyle and I walked through the park later that day, I thought about the journey ahead and the struggles we'd already overcome. The tall trees swayed gently in the breeze, their branches reaching out like the comforting arms of the piney woods where I spent so many days of my childhood. Those woods, with their dense trees and earthy scent, were a place of both adventure and solace for me growing up. Now, in a different part of Texas, I felt that same sense of quiet strength from the woods, as if they were whispering to me that everything would be alright. With a friend like Tim, and the resilience I'd learned from those piney woods, maybe, just maybe, life could be a little sweeter, a little kinder.

Journal Entry December 10, 1992

As the festive lights of the holiday season brighten the world outside, I find myself enveloped in a growing shadow. Thanksgiving has come and gone, leaving behind a trail of memories that weighs heavily on my heart. It was two years ago, on a day much like this, that I saw Lenny for the last time. The anniversary of our parting looms over me, a reminder of what once was. Seeking comfort, I went to my mother's house in Huntsville for a Thanksgiving gathering. The familiar confines of our old metal trailer, now bursting at the seams with family, should have offered comfort. Instead, it felt like stepping into a pressure cooker of emotions, drama, and roaches. Ann, my eldest sister, her life now a whirlwind of five children, including a pair of twins who have boundless energy, was there with her husband, Ernie. The children's lively antics, while endearing, added to the chaos. Kyle, finding friendship in his cousin Josh, my brother Kent's son, was a part of this youthful energy. Richard, our brother, watched over the scene with a stern eye, quick to label the children as future troublemakers. The day spiraled further as a window shattered in the chaos, igniting my mother's anger. Adding to the tension, Daddy arrived with my stepmom, Dorothy, and my half-brother, Jeff. The air, thick with cigarette smoke, seemed to choke any remaining sense of peace. Ernie's efforts to restore order by threatening spankings to his kids made me wonder if Tim grew up with spankings. Meanwhile, Mom, in her unyielding persuasion and shame inducing way insisted that Kyle and I should move back in with her. My attempts to explain my living situation were ignored, drowned out in the chaos of the family gathering. Daddy, never one to mince words, commented on my weight, adding to my discomfort. I yearned to flee from the stifling atmosphere, to return to a life that, despite its challenges, felt like progress compared to the unchanging life I witnessed around me. They seemed unbothered by their circumstances, while I struggled with my own sense of brokenness, constantly striving for something better. Cherrie, my baby sister living next door in her own trailer, faced her struggles. Married to Melvin, a man much older than her, she spoke of her ailments, often dismissed by our siblings. Her longing for acceptance mirrored my own yearning for validation, both of us scarred by Daddy's rejection. Introducing Tim to my family fills me with dread. If he envisions a future with me, this chaos is what he will have to accept. I pray for strength for that day, fearing his reaction might mirror my own desire to escape. Yet, among these shadows, I cling to a flicker of hope, a belief that, just maybe, there's a light waiting to break through the darkness. As I stood in the chaos and disrepair of my family's home during Thanksgiving, my worries about Tim's perception were compounded by a deeper, more personal fear. The state of the trailer— its walls stained and peeling, the floors a canvas of grime and neglect, the air thick with the remnants of cigarette smoke—was a stark reminder of the life I had left behind. This environment, very different from the world I was striving to create for Kyle and myself, not only posed a concern about how Tim might view me but also stirred a profound internal question. Could I ever truly distance myself from this past? The disorder and filth around me were not just physical markers of a life once lived; they were symbols of deeper struggles and hardships. I found myself wondering if I was indeed a product of this environment. Despite my efforts to rise above it, there was a nagging doubt in the back of my mind. Could I ever be more than this? The fear that the chaos and turmoil of my upbringing might somehow define me in Tim's eyes, or worse, in my own, was unsettling. The thought haunted *me – the possibility that no matter how far I ran or how much I changed, the shadows of this trailer life, with its turmoil and neglect, might always be a part of who I am. It was a struggle between the reality of my past and the aspirations for my future, a battle within myself to prove that I could be more than the environment in which I was raised. Was I a terrible person for wanting to be better? I love my family so much, but I want to improve my life.*

Chapter 36

A DANCE OF DESIRE AND RESTRAINT

Growing up, I never had the chance to experience the cultural events that so many others took for granted. Ballets, art galleries, and theaters were as foreign to me as distant lands. So when Tim invited me to see "The Nutcracker" ballet, I was both thrilled and nervous. It felt like a chance to step into a world I had only ever dreamed about, to experience a piece of the culture that had always seemed out of reach.

But excitement quickly turned to anxiety when I realized I had nothing suitable to wear. There was no money for a new dress, and I felt the weight of that reality pressing down on me. Fortunately, Donna, always a source of support, came to my rescue. She lent me a classy black dress adorned with gold buttons. It was simple but elegant, just what I needed. I managed to scrape together enough for a pair of black pantyhose and decided to wear my trusty black dress shoes. I styled my hair into a loose bun, a departure from my usual look, but I hoped it would suit the evening.

"Kyle will be just fine with me," Donna assured me as I got ready. She always had a way of easing my worries, and knowing

Kyle was in her care made it easier to focus on the evening ahead.

"Remember," she added with a wink, "a man who buys you a pillow is a man worth keeping."

I smiled, taking her words to my heart as I finished getting ready. The sound of a car pulling up outside made my heart race. A few moments later, there was a knock on the door.

I took a deep breath and opened it to find Tim standing there, looking sharp in a dark suit. His eyes widened slightly as he took in my appearance.

"You look... amazing," he said, his voice tinged with surprise and admiration.

"Thank you," I replied, a bit shyly, as I grabbed my coat and stepped outside.

Tim offered me his arm as he walked me to the car. He opened the passenger door for me with a gentlemanly gesture that made my heart flutter.

"Ready for the ballet?" he asked, a hint of excitement in his tone as I settled into the seat.

"Definitely," I said, trying to match his enthusiasm, though the butterflies in my stomach were fluttering wildly.

As I glanced into the backseat, I saw Michael and his girlfriend, Malinda, smiling warmly at me. I had met them briefly at a Halloween party, and their presence helped ease some of my nervousness.

"Hey, PJ!" Malinda greeted, her bubbly personality instantly lifting the mood. "You look stunning!"

"Thanks, Malinda. You look great too," I replied, feeling a bit more at ease.

The drive to the theater was filled with light conversation, but I couldn't help but notice how Tim kept glancing at me, as if seeing me in a new light. It was both flattering and a little unsettling, knowing how different this evening was from any-thing I had ever experienced before.

When we arrived at the theater, Tim quickly got out and came around to open my door. The grand building before us, with its sparkling lights and elegantly dressed patrons, took my breath away. It was like stepping into another world.

Tim must have noticed my awe because he gently took my hand and squeezed it. "You're going to love this," he said warmly, his voice full of reassurance.

As we entered the theater, I felt a mix of excitement and nervousness, but also a sense of pride. Here I was, in a beautiful dress, about to experience something I had only ever imagined. And with Tim by my side, it felt like anything was possible.

Tim opened the car door for me, his comment about never having seen my hair up before carrying a subtle hint of irrita-tion. His reaction caught me off guard, but I chose to brush it aside, not wanting anything to dampen the evening.

The ballet was nothing short of magical. As the dancers moved gracefully across the stage, their bodies telling a story with each movement, I found myself transported to a world of elegance and beauty. It was so far removed from the life I had known—one filled with hardship and simplicity. The richness of the culture unfolding before me filled a void I hadn't even realized existed. For the first time, I experienced the joy and enchantment that such cultural events could bring, and it left me longing for more experiences like this.

Sitting there, lost in the spectacle of the ballet, I felt a deep sense of gratitude for this new chapter in my life, one where I was slowly but surely discovering the beautiful complexities of a world I had once thought was not meant for someone like me. As I watched the performance, my mind occasionally drifted to Kyle, imagining how his eyes would light up at the sight of the dancers' graceful movements. It was a moment I wished he could have shared with us.

After we dropped Michael and Malinda off, Tim suggested we grab a late-night steak dinner. The restaurant was cozy and inviting, but Tim seemed distant, lost in thought. I couldn't help but ask, "Are you okay, Tim? You seem... off tonight."

He looked up from his menu, his expression weary. "Just tired, PJ. It's been a long week."

His words were simple, but there was something more lurking beneath the surface, something he wasn't saying. The drive home was filled with a similar silence, leaving me to wonder if I had somehow disappointed him—by not dressing appropriately or by my behavior in front of his friends.

When we arrived at my apartment, I braced myself for the customary quick hug Tim usually gave me before saying goodbye. To my surprise, he hesitated before asking, "Mind if I come in for a while?"

A bit confused but open to his company, I nodded. "Sure, come on in."

We were taking off our coats when Tim suddenly pulled me into an unexpected kiss. Startled, I instinctively stepped back, causing him to quickly apologize. "I'm sorry, PJ. I shouldn't have—"

"It's okay," I reassured him, still catching my breath. "I just wasn't expecting that."

He leaned in again; this time, the kiss was softer, more tentative at first, then growing more passionate. My heart soared with the realization that his feelings for me went beyond friendship. In that moment, all my doubts and worries seemed to vanish, replaced by a happiness I hadn't felt in a long time.

But just as quickly as the moment escalated, it came to an abrupt halt. Tim suddenly stepped back, as if catching himself, and muttered, "I should go."

Confused, I reached out to him. "Did I do something wrong?"

He shook his head, his expression conflicted. "No, it's not you. I just... I need to leave."

Before I could say anything else, he grabbed his coat and hurried out the door, leaving me standing there, leaning against the wall where he had just kissed me moments before. I was left trying to process the whirlwind of emotions. His abrupt departure, following such a tender and passionate exchange, was baffling. I felt a mix of elation and uncertainty, wondering about the complexities of our relationship and where it was headed.

As I dressed for bed that night, my mind was a whirlwind of thoughts, trying to decipher the enigma that was Tim. I noticed my hair was slightly disheveled, a testament to the night's unexpected events. Just as I finished preparing for bed, mulling over the evening's events, my phone rang. It was Tim, his voice tinged with regret.

"PJ, I'm sorry for how I left earlier," he began softly. "I didn't mean to just walk out like that. Can we talk?"

I hesitated for a moment, but then I decided it was time to open up to him, to share the confusion and mixed signals I had been grappling with. Before I could voice my thoughts, Tim started speaking again.

"I've been thinking about tonight... about you," he continued, his voice earnest. "You looked beautiful, PJ. More beautiful than I've ever seen you. It really caught me off guard."

His words were a comfort to the chaos in my mind, soothing the insecurities that had been bubbling up. But then Tim revealed something I hadn't anticipated.

"You should know something about me," he began, hesitating slightly. "I've made a commitment to abstinence until marriage. I'm still a virgin, PJ, and that's something that's really important to me."

His confession stunned me. Here was a man in his thirties, still holding onto his values in a world that often didn't. I couldn't help but feel a pang of unworthiness. My past, marked by early sexual activity, seemed in stark contrast to his principles.

"I respect that, Tim," I finally said, my voice trembling slightly. "But it makes me wonder... Are you sure about me? My life hasn't exactly been... well, it's been complicated."

Tim sighed; his tone was gentle. "Your past doesn't change how I feel about you. It doesn't define who you are now. I care about you, PJ, and I care about Kyle too. We're just different, and that's okay."

His reassurance was comforting, but it also left me in a complex emotional state. I respected and admired his decision to wait until marriage, but I also felt a deep sense of regret that I couldn't bring the same purity to our potential future together.

As we continued to talk, the conversation naturally shifted to lighter topics, and I found myself laughing at some of the stories Tim shared from his day. It was comforting to hear his voice, to feel that connection despite the complexities of our relationship. My past, marked by early sexual activity, was the opposite of his principles. The differences in our backgrounds suddenly loomed large, and I couldn't help but remember the disdain Lenny's family in Florida had shown me. I feared that Tim's family might view me similarly—as someone looking for a provider rather than a partner. It brought back tough memories, especially of the heart-wrenching questions Kyle asked about not having a dad. Explaining those things to a child so young was never easy, and it always left a lingering ache in my heart.

"Tim, I'm scared," I finally admitted, my voice wavering. "I don't want your family to think... to think I'm just after you for a paycheck. I've been judged before, and I don't know if I can go through that again."

He reached out, his hand gently covering mine. "PJ, listen to me. Your past doesn't matter to me, and I don't believe it will matter to my family either. What matters is who you are now and the life we're building together."

His words were comforting, but they left me in a complex emotional state. Here was a man willing to accept me and my history, yet our principles and backgrounds were so different. I respected and admired his decision to wait until marriage, but I also felt a deep sense of regret that I couldn't bring the same purity to our potential future together.

Our conversation ended with an understanding—I would respect and honor his wishes regarding physical intimacy. Despite the complexities of our backgrounds and experiences, there was a mutual recognition of the growing bond between us. As I lay in bed that night, contemplating the future, I knew one thing for certain: Kyle and I were doing fine on our own. Any addition to our little family would have to be someone who understood and embraced our journey, with all its imperfections and beauty.

Chapter 37

SEASONS OF A FLOWER PETAL

As my relationship with Tim evolved, it felt like entering a new season in my life—a season Granny would have called a new flower petal. She always said that each phase in a woman's life was like a petal in a flower, and in the end, these petals would come together to form something beautiful in heaven. This chapter with Tim felt exactly like that—a fresh, unfolding petal in the bloom of my life.

Our journey wasn't without its challenges. There were moments of temptation where either of us felt weak, but we always found strength in one another. When I faltered, Tim was my rock, and when he wavered, I became his stronghold. It was a dance of mutual support and respect that deepened our bond.

Spending more time with Tim, I felt a sense of contentment and hope. Here was a man who valued me for more than just a physical relationship. He genuinely cared for both me and Kyle, treating us with a kindness and respect that made me feel truly valued. Tim's acceptance and understanding of everything about me reinforced my belief that we could build a life together.

His bond with Kyle grew stronger too. It was evident in the way they interacted, a genuine affection forming between them. Kyle's laughter and joy around Tim filled my heart with happiness and a sense of relief. Perhaps, I dared to believe, happiness was within my grasp once again.

But doubts lingered. What if our sexual compatibility wasn't there? What if Tim didn't fully understand the realities of living with a toddler like Kyle? These thoughts would occasionally cloud my mind, casting a shadow on the bright future I envisioned.

One incident at a store brought these fears to the forefront. Kyle, in typical toddler fashion, threw a tantrum—falling to the floor, kicking, and screaming. I managed it as I always did, keeping a close eye on him while continuing my shopping. When I finally scooped Kyle up, struggling with his arched-back resistance, I noticed Tim's embarrassment. He quickly exited the store, a clear sign that the realities of parenting were still new to him.

Later that evening, I asked Tim if he was okay. He hesitated, clearly searching for the right words.

"I just... wasn't expecting that," he admitted. "I've never seen a tantrum like that up close before."

I nodded, understanding. "It's part of being a parent, Tim. Kids have their moments, and we just have to ride them out."

He gave a small smile, but I could see the uncertainty in his eyes. "I know. It's just... a lot to take in sometimes."

The differences in our experiences also surfaced in small, everyday moments. Tim was surprised to learn that I referred to Kyle's underwear as "panties" and that I taught Kyle to sit down to pee.

"Panties? Isn't that what girls wear?" Tim asked one day, looking at me curiously.

I laughed, shrugging. "That's just what I've always called them. And teaching him to sit down... well, I never really thought about it. I didn't know how else to do it."

Tim's blank stare made me realize that these were roles he would have to assume, teaching Kyle the things I couldn't.

The next day, while I was at work, my phone buzzed with a notification from Kyle's daycare. It was an emergency.

"PJ, it's about Kyle," the daycare worker's voice crackled through the line. "He's got a pencil eraser stuck in his nose, and we're having trouble getting it out. Every time we try to get him to blow it out, he just sucks it in further."

My heart raced. Kyle had always struggled with blowing his nose—he would suck in air instead of blowing out, making situations like this even more difficult. I couldn't afford an emergency visit to the hospital, so I had to think fast.

"Don't worry, I'm on my way," I said, trying to stay calm. I quickly informed my manager and left work, driving straight to the daycare.

When I arrived, I found Kyle sitting in a small chair, looking scared but trying to be brave. Tim had insisted on coming with me, and he watched anxiously as I knelt in front of Kyle.

"Okay, buddy," I said softly, trying to keep him calm. "Mommy's going to get that eraser out of your nose, but I need you to stay very still, okay?"

Kyle nodded as his big eyes filled with tears. I carefully inserted a pair of tweezers into his nostril and, with a steady hand, managed to grab hold of the eraser. Slowly, I pulled it out, and the relief on Kyle's face was immediate.

"There we go, all done," I said, smiling at him and wiping away his tears.

Tim, who had been standing nearby, let out breath he didn't realize he was holding. "PJ, that was... incredible. I don't know how you stayed so calm."

I shrugged, trying to downplay it. "It's just part of being a mom, I guess. You do what you have to do."

But inside, I felt a surge of pride. Despite the many challenges and doubts I faced as a single mother, moments like this reminded me of my strength and capability.

As we left the daycare, Tim was quiet for a moment before finally speaking again. "You're amazing, PJ. Truly. I don't know how you do it, but I'm in awe of how you handle everything."

I smiled, feeling a warmth in my chest that hadn't been there in a long time. "Thanks, Tim. It means a lot to hear that."

Despite these hurdles, our love and understanding continued to grow. Tim and I were learning, adapting, and embracing the complexities of our blended lives. Each challenge, each moment of uncertainty, was an opportunity to strengthen our bond and deepen our commitment to each other.

It was clear that this new petal in my life was one of growth, learning, and love—a beautiful addition to the flower that my life was becoming. But navigating the waters of a budding relationship while raising a child was a journey filled with complexities. The enormity of such responsibility could be overwhelming even to the natural parent, so the thought of stepping into an instant family was undoubtedly daunting.

These challenges and fears weren't just mine; I could see they weighed on Tim, too. His hesitations and concerns were evident, especially during the moments when we parted ways after spending a weekend together. There were times he admitted to feeling overwhelmed by the continuous presence of Kyle and me.

"I never imagined it would be like this," Tim confessed one evening as we sat on the porch, watching the sunset. "It's not that I don't want to be with you, PJ. It's just... a lot to take in all at once."

I squeezed his hand, offering a reassuring smile. "I know, Tim. It's a big adjustment, and it's okay to feel that way. We're figuring this out together."

He looked at me, gratitude in his eyes. "Lenny screwed up when he let you and Kyle go. I am so lucky to have you both in my life."

As we sat there, side by side, I felt a deep sense of connection with Tim. We were both learning as we went and growing stronger together.

Chapter 38

UNDER ONE ROOF, UNDER PRESSURE

Kyle, at the tender age of three, struggled with the idea of sharing my attention. His possessiveness flared up whenever Tim showed me affection, his little voice asserting, "No, my mommy!" whenever Tim came close. It was clear that Kyle was uncomfortable with the idea of anyone else taking up space in our little world. Tim, for all his patience, found it difficult to accept this rejection, even though it came from a child. I could see the strain it placed on his attitude towards Kyle, and it pained me to witness the tension growing between them.

One evening, after Kyle had been particularly resistant to Tim's presence, I tried to explain things to my son. "Kyle, sweetie, Tim's our friend. He's here to help us, to make sure we're happy."

He just pouted, clinging to me. "No, just Mommy and Kyle."

Tim sighed, standing awkwardly in the doorway. "Maybe I should give you two some space," he offered, though his tone suggested he was tired of doing just that.

I was caught in an emotional struggle, torn between wanting to protect Kyle from any form of discipline or correction from Tim, and yearning for a deeper commitment in our relationship. I knew that for me to fully trust Tim and to see if we could truly build a life together, we needed to live under the same roof. But this idea clashed with Tim's beliefs, beliefs that were deeply rooted in his faith and upbringing. He would have to hide such an arrangement from his visiting parents, and the thought weighed heavily on him.

One night, as we sat on the porch, I broached the subject again. "Tim, I just think that if we're serious about this... about us, we need to know if we can live together. We need to be sure."

Tim stared out into the night, lost in thought. "PJ, you know how I feel about this. Living together before marriage... it's just not something I believe in. It's not right."

I took a deep breath, trying to keep my voice steady. "I understand, but I need some kind of assurance. I need to know that we're compatible in every way before we take that big step. I've been hurt before, Tim. I can't go through that again."

Tim turned to me; his expression was conflicted. "But at what cost, PJ? If we go against what I believe in, what does that say about us? About our future?"

I looked away, my mind drifting back to the shadows of my past, where I had learned about survival but never truly understood love or self-worth. I didn't want to repeat those mistakes, yet here I was, pushing for something that felt all too familiar.

"I don't want to lose you," I whispered, more to myself than to him. "I just... I need to feel secure."

After a long pause, Tim finally gave in. "Alright," he said, his voice heavy with resignation. "We'll try it your way."

But even as the words left his lips, I knew this victory was hollow. I had pushed him into something that went against his principles, driven by my own fears and insecurities. In my desperation to secure our future, I had ignored the foundation we were supposed to build it on.

As we walked back inside, the night air felt heavy with the weight of my decisions. I couldn't shake the feeling that I was perpetuating the very cycle I wanted to break. I realized that I was still trapped in the shadows of my past, much like the shadows that linger in the piney woods—a place where I had learned to survive but not to thrive. It was a reminder that without true self-love, any relationship I tried to build would stand on shaky ground.

That night, as I lay in bed, the weight of my actions pressed down on me. I was searching for a way out of the legacy of my upbringing, but I hadn't yet found the path to self-love or to Jesus. I didn't understand then that loving myself was crucial before I could truly love someone else. My past and my family had not equipped me with this wisdom.

This realization marked the end of a significant chapter in my life, one that had started with hope and ended with introspection. As I stood at the crossroads of my journey, I knew I had to find a way to heal and grow, to break free from the patterns that had shaped me. The path ahead was uncertain, but it was one I had to take, for my sake and for Kyle's.

Journal Entry December 21, 1992

As Christmas approaches, my heart is a mix of anticipation and anxiety. I'm determined to make this holiday special for Kyle, his second Christmas but the first since I've started to pull my life together. Last year, his innocence was blissfully unaware of Lenny's absence, an absence that still haunts me. My life has changed drastically in a year. Now, I'm with Tim, a man who is everything Lenny wasn't. But with Tim's presence, Lenny's absence becomes even more pronounced. I had a conversation with Tim about this. "I just wish Lenny could see what he's missing out on," I told him one evening, the frustration evident in my voice. Tim, always patient, replied, "But PJ, Kyle has you, and now he has me. Isn't that enough?" I knew Tim was right, but the pain of Lenny's rejection still stung. "It's not just about us," I said. "It's about Kyle having a father. And I'm scared... what if you decide this life isn't for you?" Tim took my hand, a reassuring presence. "I may not have been prepared for fatherhood but being with you and Kyle... it's opened my eyes to a new kind of love and responsibility. I'm here for the long haul." Yet, doubts linger. Tim's family holds a significant place in his life, and I worry about their perception of me, especially with the upcoming wedding of a family friend where I'll meet them for the first time. "I'm nervous about meeting your family," I confessed to Tim one night. "What if they don't like me?" Tim was silent for a moment before responding. "My family's opinion is important, but so is ours. I just want them to see the amazing person I know." His words offered some comfort, but I couldn't shake the feeling of impending judgment. As I write this, I realize the complexity of our situation. Tim has integrated into our lives, but the specter of Lenny and the potential disapproval of Tim's family loom large. I'm caught between my fears and the hope of creating a new family with Tim. This Christmas, more than ever, feels like a turning point, a step into either a brighter future or a reinforcement of my deepest fears.

Chapter 39

HIGH STANDARDS

Tim invited me to a family friend's wedding in Seguin. It was his way of introducing me further into his world, a gesture that felt both thrilling and intimidating. I hadn't been to many weddings, especially not one in a place like Seguin, where Dwyer family roots run deep. The invitation wasn't just about attending a wedding; it was about stepping into his life more fully, meeting the people who mattered to him, and being part of an event that held significance for his family.

"Are you sure you want me to come?" I asked hesitantly as Tim handed me the invitation.

"Of course, PJ," he said, giving me one of his reassuring smiles. "I want you to meet more of the people I care about. Plus, I think you'll enjoy it."

I nodded, though a part of me felt a little nervous. I knew this was a big step for us, and I didn't want to mess it up.

The day of the wedding arrived; we dropped Kyle off at Aunt Donna's house and as we drove to Seguin, I couldn't help but admire the scenery. The town had a charm to it, with its historic buildings and tree-lined streets. When we pulled up to the venue, a wave of anxiety hit me. The place was stunning, far more elegant than anything I was used to. The reception hall was filled with twinkling lights, beautifully arranged flowers, and an atmosphere of refined celebration.

As we walked inside, Tim greeted several people with ease, introducing me to a few of his friends and relatives. They were polite, their smiles warm, but I still felt a little out of place. This wasn't just a wedding; it was a glimpse into the life Tim had known all his years, a life so different from my own.

Taking in the glamour and elegance of the reception, I couldn't help but let my thoughts drift to my own family. What would they think of such a posh event? I could almost hear their wide-eyed wonder, with a touch of skepticism, as they took in the grandeur surrounding me.

I watched as the Dwyer family mingled with ease; I imagined Karen's reaction to the lavish décor. "Can you believe this?" she'd probably say, her voice filled with a mix of awe and disbelief. I pictured Momma fussing over the extravagance, comparing it to our simple, modest celebrations back home in the piney woods. "This is nice and all," she'd say, "but give me a good old-fashioned barbecue any day."

Daddy would feel uneasy, shifting in his chair, uncomfortable with all the pomp and formality. I could see him tugging at his collar, longing for the familiarity of our backyard gatherings. And Ann, well, she might be caught between admiration and discomfort, not quite sure where to go.

The thought of my family in this setting brought a bittersweet smile to my face. Here I was, in a world so different from the one I grew up in, yet I couldn't shake the feeling of being an outsider. In one world, I was too refined; in the other, perhaps not refined enough.

As I watched the guests laughing and chatting, a part of me longed for the unpretentious, straightforward manner of my family. "You know," I could almost hear Momma saying, "we'd be the talk of the town if we brought our trailer park ways here."

There was an authenticity in their simplicity, a raw honesty in their interactions that was missing in the polite small talk around me. I could imagine Karen saying, "It's all just for show," and part of me would agree.

The contrast between my life now and the one I left behind was significant, and suddenly I couldn't help but feel caught between two worlds.

The evening, filled with beauty and celebration, left me feeling like I was walking a tightrope—one end was where I had come from and the other was where I was trying to fit into. It was a constant balancing act, trying to merge these two parts of my life into something that made sense. The acceptance of Tim's family was crucial to our relationship, but so was staying true to who I was and the life I had lived before I met him.

We arrived at Jack and Dot's home on the Guadalupe River, and I couldn't help but be struck by its elegance. The two-story house, with its sprawling backyard and a swimming pool framed by vibrant hibiscus flowers, took my breath away. It quickly became clear that Tim's family didn't just live comfortably—they lived with a level of affluence that was completely foreign to me.

"This place is something, isn't it?" Tim said, noticing my wide-eyed wonder as he guided me upstairs.

"It's beautiful," I replied, trying to keep the awe out of my voice.

Tim smiled and led me to the "girls" room, just down the hall from where the "boys" would be staying. It was there that I met his niece, Shannon. With her striking blue eyes and lively personality, she immediately made an impression.

"Hi, I'm Shannon," she said, greeting me warmly, her eyes sparkling with curiosity. "It's so nice to finally meet you! Tim's told us so much about you."

I smiled, trying to push aside my nerves. "It's great to meet you too, Shannon."

We chatted, Shannon mentioning she was close to completing her college education, a milestone that seemed to come naturally to everyone in the Dwyer family. Doctors, lawyers, and professionals in prestigious fields filled their family tree, each branch representing a level of success and stability that I had rarely seen up close.

"That's really impressive," I said, trying to hide the pang of self-doubt that crept in. "You must be excited to graduate."

"Oh, absolutely! It's been a lot of work, but it's worth it," Shannon replied with a confident smile, clearly at ease in her world.

My sense of being out of place heightened. Despite Tim's comforting presence, I couldn't shake the feeling that I was a fish out of water. Their world was so vastly different from mine—so far removed from the simple, often chaotic life I had known. It reminded me of my childhood friend Jill's family, another example of success and stability that seemed so foreign to my own experiences.

As I watched Tim's family laugh and chat, without care, I couldn't help but wonder aloud, "Tim, what makes one family so successful while another struggles so much?"

He looked at me, his brow furrowed in thought. "I don't know, PJ. It's a mix of opportunities, choices, and sometimes just plain luck."

I nodded, but his words didn't fully ease the questions swirling in my mind. I was caught in a dilemma—should I distance Kyle from my family in the piney woods to ensure his success?

Or would doing so mean denying him a part of his identity and roots? It was a heavy question, one that weighed on me more than I cared to admit.

That night, as I lay in bed in a house so different from any I had ever known, I stared at the ceiling, my thoughts racing. The softness of the sheets, the quiet hum of the ceiling fan, everything about this place was the opposite of what I was used to.

Tim's world was one of opportunity and stability, something I desperately wanted for Kyle. But I also wanted him to know where he came from, to understand the strength of our roots in the piney woods. The challenge of finding that balance, of breaking the cycle of dysfunction without losing touch with our identity, was one I was now more determined than ever to meet.

As I drifted off to sleep, I knew I had a long road ahead, but I was ready to face it, for Kyle's sake and for mine.

Chapter 40

SHADOWS OF SHAME

The atmosphere at the Dwyer household was lively and charged, especially around the dining room table where all the Dwyer men congregated. Their discussions ranged from politics to hunting stories, each topic eliciting loud, passionate responses. Voices rose and fell as they debated and disagreed, creating a boisterous backdrop to the evening. Shannon, being the only female in their midst other than Dot, seemed right at home among them. I wondered where Dot was, given her absence from the spirited discussions.

Soon enough, Dot emerged from the kitchen, arms laden with snacks to appease the animated crowd. She was a vision of elegance and beauty, her blonde hair perfectly styled, her intense blue eyes framed by high cheekbones, and her makeup flawlessly applied. Her red-painted fingernails gleamed as she moved, a testament to her attention to detail. Her expensive clothes, tailored to fit her slim figure, only added to her movie-star aura. It was easy to see that she had been a stunner in her youth, with beauty that could have graced the silver screen.

With no Kyle by my side, I felt a bit adrift amid the family dynamics. Seeking a purpose, I wandered into the kitchen, hoping to assist Dot with the preparations. The kitchen was a hive of activity, with an array of dishes being cooked and baked.

"Can I help with anything, Dot?" I asked, stepping up to the counter.

Dot glanced at me, her intense blue eyes taking in my offer with a mix of surprise and mild curiosity. "Of course," she said, her voice as polished as her appearance. "Why don't you start with these avocados?"

She handed me a large pile of the dark green fruits, and as she did, she began to explain her meticulous process of selecting the perfect avocados from the local store. "I'm very particular about my avocados," she said with a slight chuckle. "If they're not just right, I'll take them back to the store without hesitation."

I smiled, though inside I felt a bit out of my depth. "I've never actually prepared an avocado before," I admitted sheepishly, trying to keep my tone light.

Dot's eyebrows arched in surprise, her expression betraying a hint of disbelief. "Never?" she asked, her eyes narrowing slightly.

"No, never," I replied, forcing a laugh, while internally I wondered, I bet she's never prepared squirrel dumplings either.

Dot's attention to detail was impeccable. She explained everything from the best plate to use for serving bread to the importance of keeping the food hot until the moment it was served. As I began peeling the avocados, I encountered their gooey, slimy texture, which I found utterly repulsive. Dot noticed a few that were slightly rotten and immediately expressed her intent to return them to the store.

I hesitated to mention my aversion to slimy textures, knowing it would reveal a less polished side of me. I imagined the look on her face if I confessed that even wiping Kyle's runny nose was a challenge. Instead, I kept quiet, suppressing my gag reflex with every avocado I hollowed out, determined to make a good impression. I smiled through the discomfort, but it was clear that each moment in Dot's kitchen was a test of my ability to adapt and belong.

The evening was becoming an exercise in fitting into a world so different from mine. Every action, every interaction, felt like a silent evaluation. How much of myself am I willing to compromise to be a part of this family? I wondered, shelling yet another avocado.

Dot's gaze occasionally flicked to me as we worked side by side, her demeanor polite but distant. Her subtle reserve made me feel as though she were carefully measuring my place in their family. Her refined etiquette and meticulous standards for everything from food to table settings were worlds away from the life I had known. It wasn't that she was unkind, but there was a guardedness in her manner, a quiet scrutiny that suggested she was still weighing whether I truly belonged.

As I prepared the avocados, I couldn't shake the feeling that Dot was observing me with a hint of judgment. Her presence reminded me of the vast differences between us, of the simple life I had lived in the piney woods compared to the privilege and polish of the Dwyer family.

That evening, in the presence of Dot's subtle scrutiny, I felt the weight of my past pressing down on me. The resilience I had developed growing up in the piney woods was something I was proud of, but here, under Dot's watchful eye, it seemed almost inadequate. I was proud of my roots, but in that moment, I couldn't help but feel a pang of inadequacy.

The evening continued, and I found myself trying to bridge the gap between my world and theirs. It was a delicate balancing act, trying to find common ground while wrestling with the feeling of being an outsider. The Dwyers' world was one of affluence and education, so different from the humble beginnings that had shaped my early life. I forced a smile despite the internal struggle, realizing this was more than just adapting to a new family. It was about reconciling the different parts of who I was—the resilience and simplicity of my past with the new possibilities and challenges of my present.

Dot's kitchen felt like the epicenter of this balancing act. "You're doing great," Dot said, her voice smooth as she floated around the room, checking on various dishes.

"Thanks," I replied, trying to keep my voice steady as I opened another avocado. I wanted to do well, to prove that I could fit in, but each task felt like a test of my adaptability.

"It's a bit different from how we do things back home," I added, hoping to ease the tension I felt building inside me.

Dot nodded politely, her blue eyes scanning the kitchen. "Different can be good," she said, though her tone suggested she wasn't entirely convinced.

As the gathering transitioned to the dining area, everyone formed a circle for prayer. Jack led the prayer, his voice strong and steady, while Dot, with tears in her eyes, added her heartfelt thanks for having all her sons home. I couldn't help but think of my family's more raucous gatherings. I imagined Dot's reaction if she saw my relatives playing corn cob catch with our dogs—she'd probably have a heart attack! Back home, our prayers were more along the lines of "Rub a dub dub, thanks for the grub!"—a far cry from the solemnity of the Dwyers' grace.

Dot had set the table meticulously, with twelve matching plates and a story for every piece of silverware. As she shared the history of her pewter goblets, I offered to help by filling them with ice.

"Here you go," Dot said, handing me a crystal container with a pair of tongs. "Use these, dear. It's more... hygienic."

"Of course," I said, trying not to feel out of place as I carefully placed single ice cubes into the goblets, trying not to clink the ice too loudly. Back home, we just grabbed handfuls of ice—this was a whole new level of formality.

The seating at the table was its own strategic game, with everyone trying to avoid the dreaded middle seats and their treacherous table legs. Dot was in her element, buzzing around the table, piling more food onto everyone's plates despite their polite protests.

"Dot, really, I'm full," one of the guests said, holding up his hands as she tried to add another scoop of mashed potatoes to his plate.

"Nonsense," Dot replied with a warm smile. "You need your strength."

As I watched her, I wondered if she ever got a chance to sit down and enjoy her own meal. The woman was a whirlwind of energy, making sure everything was perfect. My mind drifted to the mountain of dishes that awaited us, and I remembered Momma's advice about always helping to clean up after a meal. I was mentally rolling up my sleeves when a woman I hadn't met entered the kitchen.

"Who's that?" I whispered to Tim.

"She's the help," Tim explained. "She comes in to clean up so the family can relax."

The concept was so foreign to me that I half-joked, "Maybe I should start doing dishes for payment!"

Later, as the evening began to wind down, Tim asked if I had brought a swimsuit.

"No, I didn't," I replied quickly, my self-consciousness about my body ruling out any notion of parading around in a bathing suit. Instead, I settled comfortably at a patio table, under a brightly colored umbrella.

As I watched the Dwyer family enjoy themselves by the pool, I couldn't help but feel like a spectator in their world. It was beautiful, yes, but also foreign and, in some ways, a little intimidating. I sipped my drink and tried to focus on the positives—after all, I was here with Tim, who cared about me. But no matter how hard I tried, the feeling of being caught between two worlds lingered, reminding me of just how far I had come—and how far I still had to go.

The Dwyer men made their grand entrance to the pool, each dive sending tidal waves across the water. They quickly set up a volleyball net in the middle and began what could only be described as the most aggressive aquatic volleyball game I had ever seen. I watched, trying to keep my expression neutral, but I couldn't help but notice the sight of their hairy chests and backs—unlike the hairless men in my own family. Inside, I was both fascinated and slightly horrified by the sheer amount of hair.

"Come on, PJ, join in!" one of the Dwyers called out, his voice booming across the pool.

I shook my head with a polite smile. "I think I'll just watch for now, thanks."

As they continued their game, splashing and shouting with every point scored, I found myself reflecting on the day. It was an endless series of cultural shocks, humorous in hindsight but overwhelming in the moment. Being with the Dwyers was like stepping into a different world, one where each action, each tradition, was steeped in a formality and propriety that was completely alien to me.

The swimming pool itself was an oasis of sparkling blue water, offering more than just a setting for their boisterous game. From where I sat under the umbrella, I could see a breathtaking view of Lake Placid, one of the many picturesque rivers in the area. The pool's edge seemed to merge seamlessly with the horizon, where the tranquil waters of Lake Placid stretched out before me, glistening under the sun and mirroring the sky above. It was like a painting come to life.

"Isn't it beautiful?" I heard Tim say as he walked over to me, towel draped around his neck. He had taken a break from the game to check on me, his wet hair dripping onto his shoulders.

I nodded, still captivated by the view. "It's incredible. I've never seen anything like it," I replied in awe.

Tim smiled, taking a seat beside me. "I figured you might enjoy the view. It's one of my favorite spots."

Leading down from the pool area was a set of stone steps, carefully crafted to accommodate the steep incline of the property. The steps descended into a lush, green lawn that stretched out like a plush carpet, inviting anyone to walk barefoot and feel the softness of the grass. At the end of this verdant expanse, a small pier jutted out into the water, its wooden planks weathered but inviting. Moored to the pier was a charming little blue rowboat, perfect for two. It sat there quietly, a promise of tranquil adventures on the water to contrast the vigorous pool games.

Tim followed my gaze. "We could take the boat out later if you'd like. It's a nice way to unwind."

I smiled at the thought, but the idea of relaxing in such an idyllic setting felt almost foreign. "Maybe," I said, not committing to the idea just yet.

As I sat there, taking in the scene. My childhood didn't include picturesque landscapes and leisurely pursuits like this. The Dwyers' world was one where relaxation and beauty were woven into their daily lives, a concept that was both new and overwhelming to me.

I watched the sun dance on the water's surface, creating ripples of light that played on the boat. The peaceful, almost ethereal escape made me wonder about the different lives people led and how some places could feel like a dream, far removed from the struggles and hardships that were more familiar to me.

Tim reached over and took my hand, bringing me back to the present. "You, okay?" he asked gently, concern in his eyes.

I nodded, squeezing his hand in return. "Yeah, I'm just... taking it all in."

Tim smiled, and we sat there in comfortable silence, both of us gazing out at beautiful Lake Placid, the sounds of distant laughter and splashes from the pool echoing in the background. I felt both enchanted and intimidated by this new world I was stepping into. The Dwyers' lifestyle, with all its elegance and charm, felt like a dream—a dream that might remain just out of reach for someone like me.

There at the Dwyer residence, I wrestled with a mix of emotions. A part of me felt an odd sense of relief when I noticed the Dwyers weren't as flawless as they initially seemed. It's a terrible thing to admit, but seeing their imperfections made them more relatable, more human. Yet, being in such an affluent setting was still incredibly daunting. Everything they did appeared so meticulous, so deliberate, and their conversations often revolved around topics that held little interest for me.

Their world felt like a maze of unspoken rules and expectations—an intense love for football (which I didn't share), regular church attendance (not part of my routine), higher education (I had only attended trade school), a carefully curated way of speaking (I was known to swear when I was hurt), and topics like Botox (something completely foreign to me). Each of these differences felt like a strike against me, widening the gap between our worlds.

I couldn't help but worry about bringing Kyle into this environment. The Dwyer home was a treasure trove of expensive, delicate items—a potential disaster zone for an energetic, curious toddler like Kyle. And then there was the swimming pool and the river. Kyle, with his love for water, would be drawn to them like a magnet, and the thought of him running off the pier into the murky river terrified me. I knew I'd have to be extra vigilant, packing his toys and games to keep him occupied and safe.

As I reflected on the day, I remembered what Momma used to say about having "a million-dollar itch with only a penny to scratch it." Material comfort was nice, but it came with its own set of challenges. Sure, it could be comfortable, but in some ways, it could be unbearably dull. I realized that while I admired certain aspects of their lifestyle, I didn't necessarily yearn for it. I valued the simplicity and authenticity of my own upbringing, despite its hardships. These high standards and sophisticated ways of living were a world away from the unembellished life I knew—the life of a "hillbilly from the piney woods" and her little boy.

As I considered these differences, I began to understand that it wasn't just about fitting into Tim's world; it was about finding a way to blend our worlds without losing who we were. It was a delicate balance I hoped we could achieve together.

On the drive back to College Station with Tim, I found myself reflecting and planning. We talked about the possibility of bringing Kyle to his parents' house for Christmas, a thought that filled me with both excitement and anxiety. The contrast between my past life with Lenny and my current journey with Tim was obvious; now, I was surrounded by people who not only believed in me but saw me as someone of worth. This newfound sense of belonging and appreciation was uplifting. Tim's family had welcomed me with open arms and, despite my anxiety and the endless comparisons I made between their lives and mine, their eagerness to meet Kyle felt like a validation of my place in their world.

I realized that I, too, had high standards, especially when it came to Kyle. Finding someone who could be a good father to him was paramount, and Tim was that person. But only time would tell if our worlds could truly blend into one.

Chapter 41

ROADBLOCKS AND RESCUES

My initial anxieties subsided, and our relationship flourished; Tim's willingness to watch Kyle while I traveled for work was a clear sign of his commitment. My upcoming work trip to Colorado would be a new experience for both Tim and Kyle. I could see the nervousness in Tim's eyes as we talked about it.

"You'll do great, Tim," I reassured him, placing a hand on his arm. "And remember, Donna is just a call away if you need any help."

Tim nodded, though his uncertainty lingered. "I know, but it's still a bit daunting. I've never been on my own with him for so long."

"He adores you," I said with a smile. "You two will be fine. Just stick to his routine, and he'll be happy."

The plan was set—after I returned from Colorado, we would take a trip to Huntsville to meet my family. It was a necessary step for us to move forward, though I couldn't help but feel a knot of apprehension in my stomach.

As I packed my suitcase, Kyle wandered into the room, his big eyes watching me carefully. "Mommy, why do we have two homes?" he asked, his innocent question, catching me off guard.

I paused, trying to find the simplest way to explain it to him. "Well, sweetie, just like we visit Granny's house or Aunt Donna's, we also visit Tim's house. It's like having different places to go to, but we always come back home."

Kyle seemed satisfied with the answer and nodded, going back to his toys. His contentment was a relief, but it also underscored the need for a serious discussion with Tim about our living arrangements. That conversation, I decided, would have to happen after our trip to Huntsville.

As I zipped up my suitcase, I felt a mix of anticipation and anxiety. Colorado would be a good break, a chance to focus on work, but the upcoming visit to Huntsville weighed heavily on my mind. It was time for Tim to see where I came from, to meet the people who shaped me, for better or worse. And after that, we would need to talk about what came next for us.

The Colorado trip marked my first solo business journey without my colleague, John. It was to be quick but significant, to represent another step in my growing independence and confidence. Instead, it was a comedy of errors, starting with the realization that I didn't have a credit card to rent a car. As a senior executive tasked with training me, John had always teased me about being "green," and here I was, proving him right. At the airport, I made the rookie mistake of trying to use the official phone instead of the payphones—a clear sign of my limited flying experience.

Navigating inside the airport turned into a nightmare. I hadn't understood the importance of packing light, and so I went, lugging all my belongings while dressed in a business suit and heels, struggling to make it to the terminal to catch my connecting flight. By the time I reached my destination, I was already exhausted and frazzled.

To make matters worse, I ended up in a rundown airport hotel, waiting for the credit card Tim was sending overnight. The hotel was far from comforting—a door that wouldn't close properly, a broken heater, and a bathroom that was too grimy for me to even consider using. I spent the night huddled in my coat, with a chair against the door for some semblance of security, counting the hours until I could leave.

The next day, with Tim's credit card finally in hand, I managed to rent a car and make it to my first meeting. My first appointment was with the administrative group in the hospital's meeting room, and it felt like another test of my endurance. The heels I wore were killing me as I wandered around the hospital, completely lost. I just kept walking, stopping random people in the hallway to ask where this mysterious meeting room was.

By the time I finally found the room, my feet were screaming, and my nerves were frayed. I opened the door to find a table full of people staring at me, clearly waiting for some sort of video presentation.

Video presentation? I felt my stomach sinking to my aching feet. I was just planning to leave my business card and talk about our great insurance. The looks on their faces told me they were expecting far more.

Feeling a wave of panic, I stammered out a greeting, trying to cover my lack of preparation. But the embarrassment lingered, making it hard to focus as I did my best to salvage the situation. I could feel the judgment in their eyes, each one wondering why I wasn't as prepared as they had anticipated.

After what felt like an eternity, I left the meeting room, my confidence in tatters. Feeling a small sense of accomplishment for surviving the ordeal, I decided to reward myself with some fast food. But even that turned into a challenge—driving in snow for the first time, I ended up backing into another car at the drive-thru.

I hastily covered the damage with dirty snow before returning the car, and to my immense relief, there were no repercussions. The trip was a steep learning curve, but it also made me realize my own resilience and capability. I survived, albeit with a few bumps along the way.

When I got back home, I found out that Tim had had a rough time looking after Kyle. He had fallen ill, and despite his best efforts, he was struggling to cope. Donna had to step in to help, and the guilt of having left them weighed heavily on me, especially when I saw the exhaustion and distress in Tim's eyes.

"Are you okay?" I asked, watching Tim as he sat on the couch, rubbing his temples.

He looked up at me, managing a tired smile. "I'm fine. It was just... harder than I expected."

"I'm so sorry, Tim," I said, sitting beside him. "I didn't mean for you to have to deal with all of that alone."

"It's not your fault," he replied, his voice soft but strained. "I just wasn't prepared for how much work it would be."

Donna, who had just put Kyle to bed, came into the living room and joined us. "You did great, Tim," she reassured him. "It's tough, but you managed it."

I could see the relief in Tim's face, but I also saw the weariness. It was clear that this experience had taken a toll on him, and it made me realize how much I was asking of him.

"Thank you," I said, looking between Tim and Donna. "I don't know what I would have done without you both."

Tim reached over and took my hand, giving it a gentle squeeze. "We're a team, right? We'll figure this out together."

His words brought a sense of comfort, but they also under-scored the challenges we were facing. As much as our relation-ship was flourishing, moments like this reminded me that there was still a lot we needed to learn—together.

Chapter 42

BEAUTY IN THE BROKENNESS

The upcoming trip to Huntsville to meet my family weighed heavily on my mind. As much as I tried to prepare Tim, I knew there was no way to fully explain the reality of where I came from. The anxiety gnawed at me the entire drive, making my stomach churn with nerves. I kept glancing over at Tim, wondering how he would react to it all. My worst fears seemed to manifest when I suddenly felt sick.

"Tim, pull over," I blurted out, my voice shaky.

Without hesitation, he steered the car to the side of the road. I barely got the door open before I was sick, the anxiety overwhelming me. Tim was beside me in an instant, handing me a bottle of water, his hand gentle on my back.

"Are you alright?" he asked, concern lacing his voice.

I nodded, wiping my mouth and taking a shaky breath. "Just nerves," I admitted, trying to force a smile. "It's... it's going to be a lot."

Tim squeezed my hand, offering a reassuring smile. "We'll get through it together."

As we continued the drive, my mind raced with thoughts of how Tim would perceive my family, and whether our relationship could survive the stark contrast between our worlds. The closer we got, the more I dreaded what was to come.

When we finally pulled into the driveway of my childhood home, the disrepair was worse than I had remembered. More dogs than I could count roamed inside the gate, barking loudly as we approached. Before we could even get out of the car, Cherrie's two boys came running out, completely naked, screaming in excitement. Cherrie yelled, "Put some pants on or I will whoop your asses!" I glanced over at Tim, who was trying to keep his expression neutral. "Welcome to my childhood home," I said, forcing a laugh, though I could feel the tension in my voice.

Tim gave a small nod, his eyes scanning the chaos in front of him. "It's... something," he replied, his tone unreadable.

Before we could step out of the car, Momma appeared at the trailer door, still in her nightgown even though it was well into the afternoon. She was holding up a hand to caution us. "Wait a minute! I gotta get this dog on a leash. He's a biter."

The sight of Momma and Cherrie, both still wearing their nightgowns with no bras underneath, their large busts swaying as they moved, made me cringe inside. This was not the impression I wanted to make. Cherrie's nightgown was almost sheer, leaving little to the imagination, and I felt a wave of embarrassment wash over me.

Once the dog was secured, we cautiously made our way inside. The smell hit us first—a potent mix of animals, cigarettes, and something else that was harder to place. Roaches scurried across the countertops, and the table was littered with dirty dishes and an overflowing ashtray. Flies buzzed around our heads, landing on everything they could find.

As I sat down, trying to keep Kyle close to me and away from the mess, one of Cherrie's boys climbed up on the kitchen counter, dropping his pants and peeing into the sink. I shot Tim a mortified look, but he just stared in disbelief, not saying a word.

Momma seemed unphased by it all. "He's got good aim, that one," she said with a chuckle, making no move to stop him.

As if things couldn't get any worse, a cat jumped up onto Tim's lap, and before he could react, it puked up a dead mouse right there on his jeans. Tim jumped up in shock, trying to brush the mess off while the cat nonchalantly hopped back down.

I felt like the room was spinning. Every worst-case scenario I had imagined was playing out right in front of me, and I could see the discomfort in Tim's eyes.

"Kyle, no!" I suddenly exclaimed as I noticed my son trying to eat cigarette ashes out of the overflowing ashtray on the table. I quickly grabbed him, pulling him away from the dirty tray.

Momma just shrugged. "He's probably missin' some kind of vitamin. You ought to just let him have it."

I stared at her in disbelief, unsure whether to laugh or cry. I could see Tim was doing his best to stay calm, but the horror of the situation was evident in his expression.

After what felt like an eternity, I finally stood up. "We really need to get going," I said, desperation in my voice. "Tim has to get back."

Momma and Cherrie seemed disappointed but didn't argue. We made our way back to the car, and as soon as we were inside, I felt like I could finally breathe again. Kyle dozed off in his car seat, leaving Tim and me in silence. He didn't say anything until we stopped at a gas station.

"I... I've never seen anything like that," he said quietly, his voice shaking slightly. "I can't believe you grew up in such conditions."

I felt tears welling up in my eyes as I turned to him. "I knew you'd think less of me," I whispered.

Tim reached over and took my hand, his eyes softening. "No. Seeing where you come from only makes me admire you more. The strength you've shown, the life you're giving Kyle... it's incredible."

Tears spilled over as I leaned into him, feeling a mix of relief and love. We held each other for a long moment, the tension and fear of the day finally melting away.

When we got back to Tim's place, Kyle quickly fell asleep on the couch, exhausted from the day's events. Tim led me to his bedroom, his arms wrapped around me protectively. He kissed my forehead softly.

"Stay with me tonight?" he asked, his voice gentle.

I nodded, agreeing without hesitation. The warmth of his embrace felt like the safest place in the world after the chaos of the day.

The next morning was blissful. Kyle joined us in bed, giggling and playing between us, a picture of a happy family. For a moment, everything felt perfect.

As the day wore on, Kyle's energy began to wane, his mood souring with the afternoon heat. His crankiness was growing more intense by the minute, and I could sense Tim's unease. We had shared a blissful morning, but now, the weight of the previous day's visit to my family's home in Huntsville seemed to settle heavily over us.

Tim watched Kyle fuss, his brow furrowing slightly. "Maybe it's time for him to take a nap," he suggested gently. "It might be better if he naps at your place."

His words hit me like a punch to the gut. My heart sank, and a wave of fear washed over me. Was this it? Was Tim going to end things after having time to process what he had seen at my mom's place—the chaotic mess, the overwhelming smell, the animals, the roaches—everything that screamed "poor white trash" in my mind? I couldn't help but compare it to the pristine, organized world Tim had grown up in.

I swallowed hard, trying to keep the disappointment from showing on my face. "Of course," I replied, forcing a smile. My voice was strained, betraying the emotions I was trying to suppress.

Tim looked at me, his eyes searching mine as if he could sense the turmoil brewing beneath the surface. "PJ, it's not... I just need some time to think," he said, his tone soft but firm. "Yesterday was... a lot to take in."

I nodded, my throat tight with unshed tears. "I understand," I whispered, but in my heart, I didn't. I felt like my world was crumbling around me, and I was powerless to stop it.

As I started packing up Kyle's things, my mind raced with a thousand thoughts, each one more painful than the last. I could feel the gap between our worlds widening, the difference between the life I had come from, and the life Tim was accustomed to. The thought of losing him because of where I came from was unbearable.

Tim, sensing my distress, stepped closer. "PJ," he said softly, placing a hand on my arm. "Yesterday... I don't want you to think it changes how I feel about you. It doesn't. It's just... it made me realize how strong you are. What you've overcome."

His words were meant to comfort, but they only deepened my self-doubt. "But it's not just about me, Tim," I said, my voice trembling. "It's about Kyle too. I need to know that you can handle this—handle us. My life isn't... it's not easy, and I don't want you to feel trapped."

Tim shook his head, his grip on my arm tightening slightly. "I don't feel trapped, PJ. I'm just trying to process it all. I grew up so differently... it's hard to wrap my head around it."

I looked down at the clothes I was packing for Kyle, my hands shaking slightly. "I don't want to be a burden to you," I admitted, my voice barely above a whisper. "I don't want you to regret being with us."

Tim's expression softened, and he lifted my chin so that I had to meet his gaze. "PJ, you're not a burden. Neither is Kyle. You two mean the world to me," he said, his voice filled with sincerity. "But I need you to know that I'm in this for the long haul. I just… I need to take it one step at a time."

I nodded, though the knot of fear in my stomach didn't loosen. "Okay," I managed to say, though my heart was still heavy with doubt.

Tim kissed my forehead, lingering for a moment as if trying to convey everything he couldn't put into words. "Let's give Kyle a break, and then we'll figure things out together," he said quietly.

As I gathered the last of Kyle's things, I couldn't shake the feeling that this might be the end of Tim and me and our journey together. The doubts and fears loomed large, overshadowing the morning's happiness, and I braced myself for the possibility that our worlds were just too distant to bridge.

Journal Entry January 12, 1993

As the crisp pages of the new year turn, I find myself sitting on the edge of anticipation. My therapy sessions with Barbara have become a cornerstone of my journey towards healing. She always has a knack for steering the conversation towards introspection, especially around the new year. This time, she's curious about my resolutions, and I have one that feels both daring and necessary: to cautiously open my heart to forming new relationships. For so long, my world has revolved around Kyle and Tim. They are my sanctuary in the chaos, the steady shores to my tumultuous sea. Yet, I've come to realize that in anchoring myself so firmly to them, I've drifted away from the possibility of fostering deeper connections with others, particularly with other women. It's a vulnerability I've shied away from, fearful of the complexities and potential pains it might unveil. Barbara encourages me to explore this avenue, to embrace the discomfort that comes with vulnerability. It's a daunting thought, opening up about my past, my mistakes, and the fears that haunt me. I'm afraid of being judged, of not being accepted for who I am, flaws and all. Barbara explains that honesty and vulnerability are the foundations of meaningful connections. I yearn for a space where I can be myself, unguarded, and find understanding and acceptance. The holiday season in Seguin was a comfort to my soul. Being surrounded by Tim's family, experiencing their warmth and acceptance, was a beautiful reminder of the joy and comfort that comes with being part of a larger community. Through Kyle's eyes, I rediscovered the wonder in the world, the magic in the small moments that often go unnoticed. Now, as I look ahead, I'm cautiously optimistic. I know the path to building new relationships won't be without its hurdles. The fear of being hurt again, of trusting and being let down, lingers in the back of my mind. Yet, there's a part of me that's hopeful. Hopeful that, by allowing myself to be vulnerable, I can find a sense of belonging and connection that I've been missing. This year, my resolution isn't just a statement of intent; it's a commitment to myself to be brave, to be open, and to embrace the potential for new friendships and deeper connections. It's a journey I'm ready to embark on, with all its uncertainties and possibilities.

Chapter 43

THE TRUTH HURTS

The air in the living room buzzed with anticipation as Tim prepared his surprise. Kyle, wiggling excitedly in my lap, was a bundle of energy, his love for surprises matching my own.

"Are y'all sitting down?" Tim called out from the other room, his voice brimming with excitement.

"Yes!" Kyle and I answered in unison, our curiosity piqued.

Tim stepped into the room, holding a single red rose, which he gently handed to Kyle. Then, in a moment that felt suspended in time, he got down on one knee in front of us.

Looking at Kyle, he asked softly, "Would you be okay if I became your Daddy? I want to marry your Mommy and become a family."

Kyle's eyes sparkled with delight. "Sure, Tim! Can I call you Daddy now?" he asked, his innocence shining through.

Tim then turned to me, his eyes full of love and hope. He opened a black velvet box, revealing the most beautiful engagement ring I had ever seen.

"Will you marry me?" he asked, his voice tender, "and give me the honor of being your husband and raising Kyle together?"

Overwhelmed with emotion, tears welled up in my eyes and spilled down my cheeks. I could only nod, my heart too full to speak, as I accepted the ring and the promise of a life together.

Tim slipped the ring onto my finger, and Kyle, with his innocent excitement, repeated his question, eager to start calling Tim 'Daddy.' Tim smiled at him and explained gently, "You can call me Daddy after we get married in the church, Buddy." Kyle's eyes lit up, and from that moment on, he asked about the wedding every day, curious and excited about this new chapter in our lives.

After the proposal, Tim and I embraced tightly, my heart swelling with gratitude. "Thank you," I whispered, tears in my eyes. "Thank you for loving me."

Tim held me close, his voice warm. "I love you, PJ. I can't wait to start our life together."

Overjoyed at the thought of becoming his wife, I could see the happiness in Tim's eyes as well. He was eager to announce our engagement to his family, partly to quell their constant questions about when we would finally get married. We had been living together, but we kept my apartment for appearances, especially for his family. Whenever his parents visited, we went through the charade of "moving out" and pretending we weren't cohabiting. It was a ridiculous situation, but it mattered to Tim, so I went along with it. My biggest worry was Kyle accidentally spilling the beans. I didn't want him to think that lying was okay.

As we packed for our trip to Seguin to celebrate Tim's and his father's birthdays, and to share our engagement news, the reality of planning a wedding hit me. Tim and I had talked about having a Christmas wedding, a year away, giving me time to save for a dress and, I hoped, lose some weight. As we loaded the car, excitement and apprehension swirled inside me. The wedding, managing our relationship, and dealing with everyone's expectations—it felt overwhelming. But I was deter-mined to make it work.

"I can do this," I murmured to myself, trying to summon all the resolve I could muster.

I took a moment to reflect on how far we'd come, remem-bering a conversation with Tim that had planted seeds of doubt in my mind. During one of our more vulnerable moments, I asked him, half-joking, half-serious, "You'd never actually marry me, would you?" At the time, I was struggling with my own self-worth, haunted by the differences in our backgrounds. Deep down, I had convinced myself that someone like Tim, with his upbringing and values, would never seriously consider marrying someone with my history and baggage.

But, as we headed to Seguin with the news of our engage-ment, I realized how wrong I had been. Tim had not only chal-lenged my assumptions but shattered them entirely with his proposal. The ring on my finger was a symbol of his commit-ment, his belief in us, and his willingness to face whatever chal-lenges came our way.

As we drove, I found myself lost in thought. The journey to this point had been anything but smooth; filled with doubts, insecurities, and the baggage of past experiences. But Tim's proposal was more than just a promise of marriage; it was a testament to his faith in us, a lesson in trust, and an invitation to let go of my past fears and embrace the future we were build-ing together.

I had been thinking a lot about the idea that everyone truly has their cross to bear, and it's all a matter of perspective. If Christ's life were measured by the standards of what people today admire—wealth, success, power—it might not appear to be very influential or "successful." And yet, His life was unde-niably powerful and transformative. It was a thought that had been lingering in my mind, pushing me to see things differently, to measure my own life and worth by a new standard.

This growing understanding of my faith was something entirely new, something that had quietly begun to take root in my heart. I realized that the effectiveness of a life isn't about worldly success or the things we often chase after. It's about the impact we have, the love we give, and the strength we find in carrying our crosses, just as Christ did.

I felt a newfound sense of purpose and clarity. No matter what lay ahead, I knew that we would face it together, with love, patience, and understanding. And I knew that, just as Jesus carried His cross with grace and strength, I could carry mine, with Tim by my side, and a growing faith in my heart to guide me.

As we neared Seguin, the familiar sights and sounds of the Dwyer household greeted us, filling me with a mix of anticipation and nerves. I knew where I'd find Dot—right in the kitchen, preparing her famous roast beef and mashed potatoes. Sure enough, there were the avocados, waiting just for me to peel them, a task that had somehow become my unofficial job. I sighed inwardly, resigning myself to it. Peeling those avocados was a small task, but it symbolized the ongoing challenge of fitting into this new world.

As the family gathered in the dining room, I could feel the energy building. Everyone formed a circle, holding hands in preparation for the prayer before the meal. Dot stood next to Tim, her hands gently clasping those of her sons, and there was a warmth in the room that I couldn't help but feel a part of, even as an outsider.

Tim cleared his throat, his hand squeezing mine just a bit tighter. "Before we pray, I have some news to share," he began, his voice steady but full of emotion. I could feel the anticipation in the room as everyone turned their attention to him.

"I wanted to let you all know that PJ and I are getting married," Tim announced, his eyes meeting mine with a look of love and commitment. The room erupted in joyous congratulations, the circle tightening as everyone pulled us in for hugs and best wishes.

Kyle, standing beside me, was practically bouncing with excitement. "Can I call you Daddy now?" he asked, looking up at Tim with wide, hopeful eyes.

Tim knelt to Kyle's level, smiling. "Soon, Buddy. Right after we get married in the church."

Kyle beamed, and the room filled with laughter and chatter as everyone congratulated us. The warmth and acceptance from Tim's family were overwhelming, and I couldn't help but feel both joy and a bit of nervousness for what lay ahead.

Tim's father Jack led the prayer, and I couldn't help but think about my own family and how different this moment would be with them. Jack's words were heartfelt, and when he mentioned his gratitude for "all the love and new beginnings," I felt a tear slip down my cheek. There was a sincerity present that touched me deeply.

After the prayer, the questions about the wedding started almost immediately. The excitement was apparent, but as they asked about dates, venues, and details I hadn't even begun to think about, I felt a pang of insecurity. These were things I wasn't entirely prepared for, but I nodded and smiled, taking it all in stride.

Later, as we drove back to College Station, the car was quiet with Kyle fast asleep in the backseat. I turned to Tim, feeling the need to talk about everything that had just happened.

"So, a Christmas wedding?" I asked, trying to gauge his thoughts.

Tim nodded, a smile playing on his lips. "Yeah, I've always loved the idea of a wedding around Christmas time. The church will be beautifully decorated, and there's just something special about that time of year."

I thought about it for a moment, imagining the scene he described. "December 11th then?"

"That sounds perfect," Tim agreed, reaching over to take my hand.

As we continued to discuss the details, I couldn't shake the feeling of being overwhelmed. The thought of planning such an elaborate event in less than a year was daunting, and I wondered how I would manage to meet the expectations set by his family. But I was determined to make it work, to blend our worlds together as best as I could.

The next day, back at home, I sat down with a notebook to start planning. It was one of the few times I made a list, a clear sign of how important this was to me. I even bought a book on wedding planning, thumbing through it and realizing just how much there was to do—and how much it would cost. Hosting a rehearsal dinner seemed almost impossible on my budget, and I half-joked to myself about serving beans and rice with cornbread, knowing that wouldn't fly with the Dwyers.

In the process of all the planning, I felt a deep yearning for my father's approval. I decided to call him, hoping he might agree to walk me down the aisle.

"Daddy, it's me," I began, trying to keep my voice steady as I reached out to him by phone. "I'm getting married, and I wanted to ask if you would walk me down the aisle."

There was a long pause on the other end of the line before he finally responded, "I don't think I can do that, PJ."

His refusal hit me like a ton of bricks. I mumbled a quick goodbye before hanging up, but the tears had already started to flow.

Just then, Tim and Kyle walked in, catching me in the middle of my breakdown. Kyle rushed to my side, his little hands trying to wipe away my tears. "Mommy, don't cry," he whispered, his eyes wide with concern.

Tim was there in an instant, pulling me into his arms. "What happened?" he asked softly, his voice full of concern.

I buried my face in his chest, my voice breaking as I told him. "My dad... he won't walk me down the aisle."

Tim held me tighter, his voice firm but gentle. "I'm so sorry, PJ. What about your brother, Richard? You always tell me he has been like a father figure in your life."

Later that evening, after I calmed down, I decided to call my brother Richard, asking if he would walk me down the aisle instead.

"Richard, would you do me the honor of walking me down the aisle?" I asked, trying to keep my voice steady.

Richard didn't hesitate. "Of course, PJ. I'd be honored," he said.

His willingness to step in brought a sense of relief and joy, reminding me that I still had unwavering support in my life, even when it felt like the world was crumbling.

As the day ended, I found myself reflecting on the contrasting worlds I inhabited—the love and acceptance I found with Tim and the lingering pain of my past. My journey was a testament to resilience, a balancing act between embracing the future and coming to terms with the shadows of my history. Despite the challenges, I held onto the hope that our wedding, our union, would be a beautiful amalgamation of all the facets of my life—a celebration of love's triumph over adversity.

Journal Entry February 4, 1993

Today marks a milestone as we celebrate Kyle's third birthday, a joyful occasion filled with laughter and the innocent chatter of his little friends. With the festivity, Tim and I are busy with the delightful yet daunting task of planning our wedding for December 11th. It's a season of joy and anticipation, yet within me, there's a trace of inexplicable sadness, a shadow lingering in the corners of my heart. I grapple with a persistent fear, an anxiety that whispers doubts about my deserving of happiness. It's as if happiness is a fragile thing, easily shattered by the slightest mistake. This fear, this unease about fully embracing joy, puzzles me. I often find myself wondering when I will be able to shed this apprehension and fully trust in the steadfast love and blessings that life has offered me. In therapy, Barbara has been a guiding light, helping me navigate these complex emotions. She points out how fear has been a dominant force in my life, shaping my perspectives and actions. She gently suggests that there's a part of me that unconsciously undermines my own happiness, more accustomed to struggle and dysfunction than to stability and contentment. The very thought of self-sabotage is unsettling, yet I'm committed to self-reflection and growth. I'm learning to recognize these patterns and work through them. I'm gradually realizing the depth of God's love and grace in my life, allowing it to heal the wounds of my past. Barbara encourages me to lean into my faith, to find strength and comfort in the knowledge that I am not alone. With each session, I feel a little more empowered, a little more hopeful. I'm starting to believe that I can overcome this ingrained fear, to truly embrace and cherish the blessings of my life. I'm learning to trust in God's plan and God's timing, to let go of the reins of control, and to believe that I am deserving of happiness and love. As I watch Kyle surrounded by joy and innocence, I'm reminded of the purity and simplicity of a child's love. It's a love unburdened by the complexities of the adult world, a love that I yearn to embody. I hope to nurture this same purity and simplicity within myself, embracing life's blessings with an open heart, free from the shackles of fear and doubt. As I close this entry, I look forward to what lies ahead. A wedding, a new chapter as a wife, a new life for Kyle with a loving father figure in Tim. It's a journey of healing, of new beginnings, and of faith—faith in love, in happiness, and in the divine plan that guides us all.

Chapter 44

KYLE'S TRUE HERO

Dot's efficiency in planning our wedding continued to astound me. She had an incredible network in Seguin and the surrounding areas, and she knew exactly who to call to get things done. One afternoon, I found myself sitting in her kitchen, where the scent of fresh coffee filled the air as she laid out her plans.

"I've secured the Sangerhalle in New Braunfels for the reception," Dot announced, her voice full of pride. "It's such a charming venue, perfect for the kind of wedding I know you'll love."

I nodded, a little overwhelmed by how quickly everything was coming together. "Wow, Dot, that sounds wonderful!"

"And for the rehearsal dinner," she continued, "we've got the Chapparelle Country Club. It's a lovely place with excellent food, and they're very accommodating. I think it'll be perfect."

I couldn't help but smile, grateful for her help. "Thank you so much, Dot. I don't know how I would have managed all this without you."

She waved off my thanks with a smile of her own. "It's my pleasure, PJ. I want everything to be exactly right for you and Tim."

As Dot moved on to discussing caterers and other details, I felt a wave of anxiety wash over me. The costs associated with such an elaborate wedding and rehearsal dinner started to weigh heavily on my mind. I wasn't used to this level of extravagance, and the idea of covering all these expenses made my stomach twist in knots.

Later that day, as I left Dot's house and headed back home, I tried to shake off my worries. There was so much to do, and I needed to stay focused. But amidst all the wedding planning chaos, there was one event on the horizon that brought me genuine joy—Kyle's birthday on February 4th. I decided to keep it simple, something fun and manageable, given everything else going on. I chose a McDonald's with an indoor playground for the party, a perfect spot for Kyle and his friends to run wild, regardless of the weather.

One evening, as I was finalizing the guest list for Kyle's party, I picked up the phone to call Donna. She answered on the second ring.

"Hey, PJ! What's up?"

"Hey, Donna. I was wondering if you could do me a favor," I said, twirling the phone cord in my fingers. "Could you remind Lenny about Kyle's birthday? I don't want Kyle to feel like his dad forgot about him."

There was a brief pause before Donna spoke again, her voice gentle. "I'll give him a call, PJ. But you know how Lenny is... I don't want you to get your hopes up."

"I know," I replied quietly, trying to keep the disappointment out of my voice. "It's just hard, seeing him be there for his other kids and not for Kyle."

"I get it," Donna said softly. "It's not fair, and I'm so sorry you have to deal with this. But you're doing a great job with Kyle, and he's so lucky to have you."

"Thanks, Donna," I said, feeling a lump form in my throat. "I just don't want Kyle to grow up feeling the way I did... abandoned."

After I hung up, I couldn't stop thinking about the parallels between Lenny and my own father. The sense of abandonment I had felt as a child was something I never wanted Kyle to experience. The thought weighed heavily on me, and I worried about how all this would affect him as he grew older. Would he understand why his father wasn't there? Would he feel the same hurt I did?

But I knew I had to focus on what I could control. I was determined to make Kyle's birthday special, to surround him with love and joy, and to make sure he knew how much he was cherished. Planning his party became a way for me to channel my emotions into something positive.

On the morning of Kyle's birthday, I woke up early, excitement bubbling up inside me. I tiptoed into his room, where he was still asleep, his little face peaceful and content. I leaned down and kissed his forehead.

"Happy birthday, my sweet boy," I whispered, my heart swelling with love.

Later, as we arrived at McDonald's, Kyle's eyes lit up at the sight of the playground. The other kids soon joined, and the room filled with the sound of laughter and excited chatter. Watching Kyle play, surrounded by friends and family who loved him, filled me with a deep sense of contentment.

When it was time for the cake, Kyle's face was covered in ketchup, his hair sticking up in all directions, but he was grinning from ear to ear. As everyone sang "Happy Birthday," I caught Tim's eye across the table, and he gave me a warm, loving smile.

The party wound down and we started packing up the presents. I felt a sense of peace wash over me. Despite all the challenges and uncertainties, I had managed to create something beautiful for Kyle. This was his day, a celebration of the joy he brought into our lives. And in that moment, I knew that no matter what the future held, I was doing everything I could to give Kyle the love and happiness he deserved.

I watched Kyle happily playing with his new toys, his laughter filling the room. Tim walked over, a smile on his face as he watched Kyle too.

"You did a great job today," Tim said, his voice warm with admiration.

I smiled, though my thoughts were elsewhere. "Thanks. I just wanted it to be special for him."

"It was more than special." Tim replied, reaching out to gently squeeze my hand.

I looked up at him, the weight of all my worries and doubts suddenly feeling lighter. "I just... I get so caught up in thinking about what's missing, you know? Lenny, my father... I worry about what Kyle might feel, what he might be missing."

Tim knelt beside me, his eyes meeting mine with a sincerity that took my breath away. "PJ, Kyle isn't missing anything. He has you. And he has me. We're his family, and that's more than enough."

Tears welled up in my eyes as I looked over at Kyle, who was now showing off his new toy to one of the other kids. "I guess I've been so focused on the voids, on what's not there, that I've missed what's right in front of me."

Tim nodded, understanding. "I know it's hard. But look at him. He's happy, PJ. He's loved. And that's what matters. God has a way of filling the empty spaces in our lives with better things. Sometimes, it just takes a little time to see it."

I nodded, wiping away a tear that had escaped. "You're right. I've been so blind to it. Kyle has you, loving him as your own, better than Lenny ever could."

Tim smiled, pulling me into a gentle hug. "And I'm the lucky one. You both have filled the voids in my life too, more than I ever thought possible."

We stood there in each other's arms, the noise of the party fading into the background. Kyle ran over, holding up his toy with a big grin. "Look, Mommy! Look, Tim! Isn't it cool?"

Tim bent, ruffling Kyle's hair. "It's the coolest, buddy. Just like you."

Kyle giggled, and I felt a warmth spread through me, melting away the last remnants of doubt. God had indeed filled the voids in my life, not with what I thought I needed, but with something far better.

"Ready to go home?" Tim asked, his hand resting on Kyle's shoulder.

I nodded, a smile spreading across my face as I looked at the two of them. "Yeah, let's go home."

As we walked out, I knew, deep in my heart, that this was where we were meant to be—together, filled with love, and surrounded by the blessings that had quietly grown in place of the things I once thought I had lost.

Chapter 45

GIFTS, GOWNS, AND GROWING PAINS

It was wedding preparation time, and Dot's resourcefulness in securing venues and caterers for our December 11th wedding was a godsend, especially with the holiday season rush. One afternoon, as we sat together going over details, Dot casually mentioned, "We'll need about 300 invitations just for our side."

I nearly dropped my pen. "Three hundred? Really?"

Dot nodded as if it was the most natural thing in the world. "Yes, Dear. And you'll also need to find accommodation for your family. Our house will be full of relatives coming in from Mexico."

"Mexico?" I echoed, my mind spinning. I hadn't anticipated that. The scale of the wedding was starting to feel overwhelming, not just emotionally but financially, too, especially when it came to the rehearsal dinner.

As the wedding planning progressed, Tim and I found ourselves scaling a mountain of decisions. Some nights, the intensity of it all was too much, and my insecurities would creep in. One evening, as we lay in bed, I finally voiced my fears.

"Tim, do you ever worry about us? I mean, I sometimes fear you might call everything off."

Tim turned to me, his expression serious but tender. He took my hand and said, "PJ, I'm committed to this, to us. I'm not going anywhere."

His words were comforting, but the doubts still lingered. I couldn't shake the nagging feeling that my love for Tim might be tainted by the bitterness and hatred I still felt toward Lenny. These emotions haunted me, so much so that I brought them up during one of my therapy sessions with Barbara.

"Do you think my feelings for Tim are somehow... tainted by all the unresolved anger I have toward Lenny?" I asked, searching for guidance.

Barbara gave me a thoughtful look. "It's natural to have complicated emotions, especially when you've been through as much as you have. But your love for Tim is separate from that. It's important to acknowledge your feelings about Lenny but not let them define your relationship with Tim."

As the wedding plans took shape, the differences in our families' backgrounds became more apparent. I chose Donna as my matron of honor because I knew she understood the dynamics at play, especially with my family. Tim asked his brother Kevin to be his best man, with his other brothers and close friends filling the roles of groomsmen.

Finding my wedding dress turned into an adventure of its own. I had lost fifteen pounds by then but still needed a dress that could accommodate my fuller figure. After much searching, I finally found a taffeta gown in a beautiful champagne color. The only downside? It cost three times what I had budgeted.

At my first fitting, the seamstress seemed a bit frustrated with my continued weight loss. "You're making my job difficult," she said with a sigh as she adjusted the dress.

I couldn't help but smile. "I can't help it. I'm proud of how far I've come," I said, admiring my fitter physique in one of the most important dresses a woman can wear. The moment was transcendent.

When Donna saw me in the dress, her eyes widened, and she let out a soft gasp. "PJ, you look stunning," she breathed, her voice filled with genuine admiration.

I looked at myself in the mirror, seeing a reflection of someone who was finally beginning to feel worthy of the happiness that was within reach. As I turned to face her, I felt a renewed sense of confidence. The doubts and fears, while still present, seemed a little less daunting in that moment.

The wedding drew closer, and the reality of marrying Tim and becoming part of his family started to sink in. Despite the challenges that lay ahead, I felt a sense of anticipation and hope that grew stronger with each passing day. This wedding wasn't just about Tim and me; it was about the merging of our worlds, the beginning of a new life as a family. I could see the excitement in Kyle's eyes whenever we talked about the wedding, and that filled me with even more determination to make this work. Tim, Kyle, and I were embarking on a journey that promised love, learning, and a brighter future.

As plans progressed, the bridal showers started lining up. "Aunt Teenie is organizing a yard and garden shower," I mentioned to Tim one evening as we were going over the calendar. "And Marie is planning a Christmas ornament shower."

Tim raised an eyebrow, smiling. "That sounds like a lot of showers."

"Tell me about it," I said, shaking my head with a half-smile. "Donna already threw one in College Station. I honestly thought that would be it. This whole whirlwind of events is so... alien to me. I'm not used to this much attention."

Tim reached over, taking my hand. "It's because people care about you, PJ. They want to celebrate this moment with you."

I sighed, letting his words sink in. "I just hope I can balance everything. Work at CC is already so demanding, and now with all these wedding activities, I might get fired for not focusing enough."

Tim chuckled softly, his grip on my hand tightening. "Your colleagues are excited for you, too, PJ. They'll understand. You've worked hard to get here. You deserve to enjoy this time."

I looked at him, feeling the warmth of his reassurance. "I hope you're right. I don't want to mess this up."

"You won't," Tim said firmly. "We're in this together, remember? No matter what, we'll figure it out."

His confidence was contagious, and I found myself smiling back at him. "Okay," I agreed, feeling a bit lighter. "We'll figure it out."

Days went by and the showers came and went, each one a reminder of the community we were building around us. The wedding was no longer just a distant event; it was becoming real, tangible. And with each step, my confidence in our future grew stronger.

The complexity of our living situation added another layer of stress to everything. Dot, completely unaware that Tim and I were already living together, would relay messages through Tim. One night, after yet another one of these conversations, Tim sighed heavily as he tossed his keys onto the kitchen counter.

"I wish we could just tell everyone, "He said, frustration clear in his voice.

I leaned against the counter, feeling the weight of the secret we were keeping. "Me too. It would make things so much simpler."

Our weekend was swallowed up by registering for wedding gifts, a task that felt both exciting and overwhelming. As we wandered through the aisles, scanning everything from kitchen appliances to bedding, I couldn't help but feel a bit lost.

"Where are we going to put all this in the apartment?" I wondered aloud, holding up a set of fancy dinner plates that seemed out of place in our little home.

Tim chuckled, trying to ease my concerns. "It's just part of the process, PJ. We'll figure it out."

I nodded, trying to share his optimism, but a nagging doubt lingered in the back of my mind. Growing up in the piney woods, life had always been about practicality and making do with what we had. Registering for all these new things felt foreign, like I was stepping into a world I wasn't sure I belonged in.

As the bridal showers approached, I found myself wrestling with the decision to invite my family. "I'm just worried about them feeling out of place," I confided in Tim one evening as we sat on the couch. "Your family's gatherings are so different from ours."

Tim squeezed my hand gently. "But they're your family, PJ. They should be there, no matter what."

I knew he was right, but the thought of my family mingling with his filled me with anxiety. In therapy, I was working through these feelings, learning how to manage the social situations that triggered my insecurities.

"It's about adapting your responses," Barbara, my therapist, advised during one of our sessions. "But it can be exhausting, I know."

And it was exhausting. I spent so much time analyzing my words and actions, trying to make sure I didn't offend anyone or make my family feel out of place.

"I don't want my family to feel hurt or inferior," I said to Tim one night, my voice thick with worry. "They're not used to these kinds of events."

Tim listened; his expression thoughtful. "We'll make sure they feel welcome, PJ. We'll do it together."

Preparing Tim's family for me felt like walking a tightrope. I wanted to be honest, to give them a sense of what to expect, but I also didn't want to paint my family in a negative light.

"It's a challenge, growing up the way I did," I admitted to Tim as we talked about the upcoming events. "You learn to switch roles depending on who you're with, but it's draining."

Tim's eyes were filled with empathy as he looked at me. "You're doing your best, PJ. That's all anyone can ask for."

"But sometimes I wonder," I mused, staring down at my hands, "will I ever overcome these insecurities from my past? Will I ever stop feeling like I have to please everyone?"

Tim wrapped his arms around me, pulling me close. "You've come so far already. We'll keep working on it together. You don't have to do this alone."

His words were comforting, but the doubts still lingered, a reminder of the struggles I carried from growing up in the piney woods. I knew this journey wasn't just about planning a wedding or blending into our families; it was about finding peace with my past and learning to embrace the future with confidence.

Chapter 46

TWO WORLDS ON A TIGHTROPE

O ur wedding day loomed closer, and the pressure of merging two vastly different worlds weighed heavily on me. I found myself constantly trying to bridge the gap, to find some harmony between the life I came from and the life I was stepping into with Tim. It was a relentless struggle, testing my resilience and determination in ways I hadn't anticipated.

One day, amid the chaos of wedding preparations, I took Mom dress shopping. The task seemed simple enough, but it quickly became another point of tension. "What about this one?" I asked, holding up a soft blue dress that I thought would be perfect for her.

Mom shook her head, her eyes settling on a sleek black dress instead. "This one feels right," she said with finality.

"Black... Mom? For a wedding?" I tried to hide my surprise. It wasn't exactly the color I had in mind for such a joyous occasion.

Mom shrugged. "It's elegant. And you know I'm not one for frills."

But I didn't push her. "Okay, if that's what you want."

The financial strain of the wedding preparations became more apparent when I found myself buying Cherrie's bridesmaid dress and shoes. She simply couldn't afford it, and I didn't want her to feel left out or embarrassed. But as I swiped my card, I felt the weight of every dollar spent. The idea of taking out a small loan crossed my mind more than once, especially after I learned just how many guests Dot had invited to the rehearsal dinner.

"How many did you say?" I asked, trying to keep the shock out of my voice.

"Quite a few," Dot replied, her tone casual, as if it were no big deal.

The number of guests was overwhelming, and I could feel the anxiety gnawing at me as Tim and I packed for another trip to Seguin. I was zipping up my suitcase when Tim asked me to sit down, his tone unusually serious.

My heart skipped a beat. This is it, I thought, dread settling in. He's going to end things.

But instead of the dreaded conversation, Tim handed me a small card with my name on it. I opened it to find a check for $2,500 tucked inside.

I looked up at him, speechless, my emotions a whirlwind of relief and gratitude. "Tim, I... I don't know what to say."

He gave me a reassuring smile, his eyes full of sincerity. "I know you're stressed about the money," he said gently. "I want you to enjoy our wedding without this burden."

His generosity was overwhelming, but it stirred up a mix of emotions within me. While I was incredibly grateful, I couldn't help but worry about appearing financially dependent. What would others think? How would my family react?

"Thank you," I finally managed, my voice thick with emotion. "I'll use it to cover Kyle's daycare, the hotel for my family, and maybe even get some Christmas gifts."

Tim nodded, understanding the complexities of what I was feeling without me needing to say it. "Just say you'll let me help," he said softly, sincerely.

As our wedding day inched closer, my nerves were stretched thin. It wasn't the marriage itself that had me on edge, but the impending reactions of my family. At the rehearsal dinner, my worst fears began to materialize.

Richard, who was stepping in as the 'father of the bride,' seemed hurt that I hadn't prepared a special gift for him. He pulled me aside after dinner, his face a mask of disappointment. "I thought there might be something, you know, a gesture," he said, his voice tinged with sadness.

I winced, guilt washing over me. "I'm sorry, Richard. I just... I've been so caught up in everything."

He nodded, but the hurt in his eyes lingered.

Meanwhile, Mom was fuming over the seating arrangements. "I've never been treated so poorly," she confided in me, her voice laced with bitterness.

"Mom, it's not like that," I tried reassuring her, but she wasn't having it. Her complaints only added to the mounting stress, making me feel like I was being pulled in a thousand different directions.

The actual rehearsal was a disaster. We got lost on the way to the church, arriving over an hour late. By the time we finally made it, I was so frazzled that I could barely focus on what the pastors were saying. Everything felt like it was spiraling out of control.

After the chaotic rehearsal, Tim and his friends left for his bachelor party. He kissed me goodbye, and I tried to muster a smile. "Have fun," I told him, though my mind was still reeling from the day's events.

"I will," he promised, squeezing my hand before he walked out the door.

But as I watched him leave, I couldn't help but feel a pang of unease. The day had been so overwhelming—the rehearsal dinner, the family chaos—and the bachelor party plans only added to the complexity of the situation.

Yet, as I sat there, alone with my thoughts, I remembered Tim's reassurances and the love that had brought us this far. It wasn't going to be easy, but I was determined to face whatever challenges lay ahead knowing that, with Tim by my side, we could find a way to make it work.

My friends insisted on throwing me a bachelorette party, but I was hesitant. My mind was still wrapped up in the worries about the wedding and the way things had gone during the rehearsal dinner. They wouldn't take no for an answer, though, promising that a night out would do me good.

"We're going to have fun tonight," Donna said, grabbing my arm with a grin. "No stress allowed."

We started at a quaint, cozy restaurant downtown. They had arranged a private area just for us, and the inviting atmosphere was a welcome respite. As we sat down, I couldn't help but feel a bit of the tension begin to melt away.

"Surprise!" Donna announced as the lights dimmed slightly and a slideshow began to play on a screen they had set up. Pictures from my childhood flashed by, followed by snapshots of my time with Kyle and my journey with Tim. Each photo brought a mixture of laughter and tears. Seeing those memories come to life reminded me of how far I'd come and how many blessings I had in my life.

After dinner, they had another surprise in store. "We're not done yet," my friend Dana from work said, a twinkle in her eye as she led me out of the restaurant.

"Where are we going?" I asked, curiosity piqued.

"You'll see," she replied, her smile widening.

We arrived at a nearby salon, where they had booked spa treatments for all of us. The moment I walked in, the soothing scents and calming music began to work their magic on me. As I lay down for a massage, I felt the tension in my shoulders start to ease under the gentle hands of the massage therapist.

"This is exactly what you needed," one of my friends said, her voice relaxed and content as we all enjoyed our treatments.

I nodded, feeling the truth of her words. For the first time in what felt like weeks, I could finally relax, if only a little.

Later, we moved on to a lounge that featured live music. The place was lively, the music upbeat, and everyone around me was having a wonderful time. My friends chatted and laughed, but despite their efforts, I found it hard to fully immerse myself in the festivities. My thoughts kept drifting back to Kyle and the never-ending list of wedding preparations.

"Are you okay?" Donna asked, leaning in close to be heard over the music.

"Yeah, just a bit tired," I admitted, forcing a smile. "It's been a long day."

She squeezed my hand. "It's your night, PJ. Try to enjoy it. Everything else will sort itself out."

I nodded, but as the night wore on, my exhaustion grew. The idea of going back to the hotel, where the heavy smell of cigarette smoke lingered in the air, was less than appealing. I couldn't help but worry about how it might affect my wedding dress. It was a small concern in the grand scheme of things, but it felt significant with the whirlwind of emotions I was feeling.

Finally, we decided to call it a night. As we headed back to the hotel, my friends continued to chat and laugh, their spirits still high. I felt a wave of gratitude for them, knowing how much they cared and wanted to make this time special for me. But underneath it all, the weight of the upcoming wedding and all the worries that came with it remained, lingering in the back of my mind like a persistent shadow.

When we finally returned to the hotel, I slipped off my shoes and sat on the edge of the bed, my thoughts racing.

Donna glanced at me as she tossed her purse onto the chair. "You okay, PJ?" she asked, concern in her voice.

I nodded, though my mind was far from settled. "Yeah, just... tomorrow's a big day, you know?"

She smiled warmly. "You're going to be a beautiful bride, PJ. Everything's going to be perfect."

I forced a smile, but deep down, I realized where most of my stress originated—from my own gnawing sense of unworthiness. I couldn't shake the feeling that I didn't quite belong in this world of bridal showers, elaborate weddings, and happy endings. It all felt so foreign, so far from the life I had known.

As I got ready for bed, I couldn't help but think about how much had changed. Just a few years ago, I never would have imagined myself here, on the brink of marrying a man like Tim—kind, patient, and willing to take on the responsibility of loving Kyle and me. But with that love came a nagging fear that I wasn't enough, that I didn't deserve any of this.

Donna must have sensed my unease because she came over and sat beside me on the bed. "PJ, you know Tim loves you, right? And you deserve every bit of this happiness."

I looked at her, my eyes misting over. "Sometimes, I don't know if I do," I admitted, my voice barely above a whisper.

"You do," she said firmly, squeezing my hand. "You've been through so much, and you've come out stronger. You're not just marrying Tim—you're starting a new life, a better life. And you deserve every bit of that."

I took her advice to heart and tried to push the persistent doubts that had plagued my mind throughout what should have been the happiest moment of my life aside. Tomorrow wasn't just about the wedding; it was about celebrating a love that had grown stronger through every challenge we'd faced. It was about starting a new chapter with Tim and Kyle, one filled with hope, love, and the promise of a brighter future. Moreover, it was about a woman who had grown stronger and surer of herself, of her own worth. And that woman was me.

I closed my eyes and took a deep breath, trying to find some peace to quiet my tumultuous mind. "I can do this," I whispered to myself, though the words felt more like a plea than a declaration.

As I drifted off to sleep, I clung to that hope—the hope that despite all the hurdles and the lingering doubts, tomorrow would be a day of joy for Tim, for Kyle, and for me.

The bridal suite buzzed with activity; everyone focused on making sure everything was perfect for my wedding day. I sat in front of the mirror, trying to keep calm, but my thoughts kept drifting to Kyle. He had been so excited to be the ring bearer, but now I could see the anxiety and confusion building in his little face as he tried to stay close to me. Every time he managed to get near, someone would scoop him up and move him away.

"Kyle, you need to stay out of Mommy's way," one of the bridesmaids said, lifting him off the floor as he tried to hug my leg.

"But I want Mommy!" Kyle cried, squirming in her arms.

"She's getting ready, sweetie," another voice chimed in. "Let's go outside for a bit."

"No! Mommy!" Kyle screamed, kicking his legs as they tried to carry him out of the room. His cries echoed through the suite, and I could feel my heart breaking.

I turned sharply in my chair, my patience snapping. "EVERYBODY OUT! NOW!" I commanded, my voice ringing with authority.

The room fell into a stunned silence as everyone froze. All eyes turned to me, but I was only focused on Kyle, who was still reaching out for me, tears streaming down his little face.

"I said, OUT!" I repeated, my voice firm but calm.

The bridesmaid who was holding Kyle quickly set him down, and one by one, everyone started to file out of the room, leaving me alone with my son. As the door closed behind the last person, I rushed over to Kyle and scooped him into my arms. He clung to me tightly, sobbing into my shoulder.

"Shh, it's okay, baby. Mommy's here now," I whispered, stroking his hair and rocking him gently.

"They wouldn't let me stay with you," he sniffled, his small body trembling with emotion.

"I know, sweetheart," I said softly, holding him closer. "But I am here now. No one is going to take you away from me."

He looked up at me with his big, teary eyes, still unsure. "Mommy, are we getting married today?" he asked, his voice shaky.

I smiled, kissing the top of his head. "Yes, sweetie. We're getting married to Tim today, and he's going to be your Daddy. How does that sound?"

Kyle's face lit up, his earlier distress melting away. "You look like a princess, Mommy," he said, his voice full of wonder as he looked at my dress.

"Thank you, baby. And you're going to be the best ring bearer ever."

Holding him close, I sent up a silent prayer. "God, please bless this day. Bless our wedding and give Kyle the peace he needs today. Watch over us all as we start this new life together."

As the time to walk down the aisle drew closer, Kyle's mood completely shifted. He was back to his cheerful self, ready to take on his key role. I took one last look in the mirror and noticed the wrinkles in my dress from holding Kyle, but instead of feeling frustrated, I felt a deep sense of contentment.

"Those are the sweetest wrinkles ever," I murmured to myself, smiling at the thought. They were a reminder of what truly mattered today: the love I had for my son and the new beginning we were about to embark on together.

I thought back to the piney woods where I had grown up, surrounded by challenges and hardships. Those woods had shaped me, taught me resilience, and brought me to this very moment. They had given me the strength to face life's trials head-on, without breaking. And now, as I prepared to walk down the aisle, I realized just how thankful I was for every twist and turn that had led me here. My existence was no longer about shame or feeling unworthy; it was about gratitude. The piney woods had given me strength, and God had filled the voids in my life with better things than I ever imagined. Tim loved Kyle as his own, better than Lenny ever could, and that was a gift I would never take for granted.

With Kyle by my side, ready to walk down that aisle, I felt an overwhelming sense of peace and I was thankful for every moment that had led us there.

Chapter 47

NEW DADDY, NEW LIFE

I walked toward the entrance of the church, my heart racing with a whirlwind of emotions. It was a moment of transition, a crossing from what was into what could be. I thought of the therapy sessions with Barbara, where I shared my thoughts on this new chapter of my life.

"I'm excited for my future with Tim," I admitted to her, "but it feels like I'm severing the last tie to my past with Lenny."

Barbara, with her usual calm wisdom, nodded in understanding. "It's a significant transition, PJ. Embracing this new chapter also means letting go of what was."

Her words echoed in my mind as I neared the church doors, my hands trembling slightly. I found myself offering up a prayer, not just for the future that awaited Tim and me, but surprisingly, for Lenny's happiness as well.

"Wishing him well means you've truly forgiven," Barbara had said once. And standing there, I realized that I wanted to forgive, to let go, to move forward without the weight of the past holding me back.

At the entrance, Richard stood waiting, his presence a comforting reminder of family. He looked at me with soft eyes and a gentle smile.

"You look beautiful," he whispered, his voice filled with sincerity.

"Thank you for being here, Richard," I replied, squeezing his arm. "It means the world to me."

The grand doors of the church swung open, and the organ's music swelled, filling the space with a sense of sacredness. As I stepped forward, I felt the weight of every gaze upon me, yet my focus was on Tim, standing at the altar. His expression was a blend of nerves and awe, his eyes reflecting the emotions that mirrored my own.

As I walked down the aisle, I spotted Kyle sitting with family, his small face lighting up when he saw me. My heart swelled with love for him, for the life we had shared so far, and for the new future we were about to build.

Finally, I reached the altar, and Tim took my hand, his touch warm and steady. We exchanged our vows and rings, the words binding us together in a promise that felt both fragile and strong. I could sense Tim's anxiety about speaking in front of everyone, so I gently rubbed his hand, silently letting him know I was with him, supporting him.

"Introducing Mr. and Mrs. Timothy Dwyer," the pastor declared, his voice ringing with finality and joy.

As we turned to walk back down the aisle, hand in hand, a small hand reached up to grab mine. I looked down to see Kyle, his face beaming with happiness, walking proudly between us. The three of us stood there, together, a new family.

When we reached the back of the church, Kyle tugged at Tim's hand, looking up with eager eyes. "Now, Tim?" he asked, his voice filled with anticipation.

Tim smiled down at him, nodding. "Yes, Kyle. Now."

Kyle's face broke into the biggest grin as he shouted, "DADDY!!" Tim scooped him up into a warm embrace.

And in that moment, Barbara's words from one of our sessions came back to me: "Your past forms the person you are today. It's important to acknowledge it and to be thankful for it."

This was the beginning of our new life, one built on the lessons of the past and the love we had found in each other. I smiled at Tim and Kyle, both halves of my full heart. We were a family now, ready to face whatever the future held, together. And as I looked back at the life I had come from, the shame of being from the piney woods was no longer there—only pride in the strength it had given me.

UNSHACKLING THE HEART

PJ Hamilton

In the quiet garden of the soul, where shadows linger.
Beneath the heavy burdens of shame, where doubts reside.
There blooms a fragile flower, a whisper of light.
A promise of healing, from the pain we hide.
For long we've walked in silence, under shame's cold gaze.
Chains of our own making, binding us in haze.
But within each heart lies a flame that never dies,
A spark of sacred courage, where our true strength lies.
Let us journey inward, where the healing waters flow,
In the depths of our being, where true selves grow.
Unshackle the heart, let go of the yoke,
Embrace the light within, let it rise and evoke.

In the mirror of forgiveness, see your true reflection,
unmarred by imperfection, but in grace's perfection.
For you are more than the sum of past mistakes,
You are a tapestry of hope, with every breath you take.
So, dance in the rain of redemption, let it wash away the pain.
Turn your face to the sun, let go of the chain.
For in each moment of forgiveness, in every act of love,
We find the path to freedom, and the peace we're worthy of.

Healing is a journey, through time it unwinds,
In the chambers of the heart, and the corridors of the mind.
Step by step, with each tear and each smile,
We walk the road of healing, mile by mile.
In the garden of tomorrow, where new dreams take flight,
May you find your peace and joy, in love's eternal light.
For you are born of stardust, a miracle, a song,
In the symphony of life, where you truly belong.

ACKNOWLEDGMENTS

As I bring this second edition of *From the Piney Woods* into the world, my heart overflows with gratitude. First and foremost, I want to thank God, my Heavenly Father. Without His grace and guidance, none of this would be possible. He is the true source of my strength and resilience, and I am eternally grateful for His love, presence, and hand in all things.

To my dedicated team—Lisa, Susie, and Ania—thank you. Your insights, expertise, and unwavering belief in this story helped shape it into something even more meaningful. I couldn't have done this without you guiding and challenging me every step of the way.

To my loving husband, Tim, my children, Kelsey, Kyle, and Sarah, and my wonderful grandchildren, Tucker, Tavin, and Natalin—you are my heart. Thank you for your steadfast support, for always standing by my side and encouraging me to see this dream through. I hope this book shows you that dreams are always worth pursuing and never forget the Plus One Theory! A reminder to reach a little further and embrace life fully.

To my family—Kent and Toni Bates, Karen Chapin, and Ann Randolph—thank you for your love and belief in me. You remind me of where I come from and of the resilience and strength that our family shares.

I also want to honor those no longer with us—Mom, Dad, my sister Cherrie, and my beloved Granny Koonce. Their lives impacted mine in ways I'll never forget, and though our journey was complex, they loved me the best way they knew how. Granny Koonce's wisdom and grace live on in my heart, and her presence is woven into the fabric of my life and this story.

And finally, to the teachers, friends, and families from my childhood who saw potential in me before I could see it myself, thank you for the lasting impact you've made on my life.

This edition of *From the Piney Woods* has come alive because of each of you. Thank you for being part of this journey.

ABOUT THE AUTHOR –
PJ HAMILTON

PJ Hamilton, author of the *From the Piney Woods* series, writes with a heartfelt passion for stories that inspire hope, resilience, and personal transformation. Growing up in East Texas, PJ experienced firsthand the struggles of a difficult childhood, marked by abandonment, neglect, and the challenges of finding her place in the world. It was through these hardships that she discovered a powerful truth: our past does not define us, it prepares us.

Her writing reflects this journey, weaving together deeply personal experiences with universal themes of healing, growth, and redemption. PJ's goal is to empower readers to see their own struggles as stepping stones to a brighter, purpose-driven future. Through her storytelling, she shows that even in the darkest of times, there is always hope, strength, and the ability to rise above.

In addition to writing, PJ is a motivational speaker who shares her message of courage and transformation with audiences across the country. She believes in the power of kindness, connection, and the idea that everyone has the potential to turn their past into a foundation for a better tomorrow.

When she's not writing, PJ's favorite pastime is telling stories to her grandchildren—after all, she is, at heart, a storyteller. She lives with her family in Texas and continues to write stories that inspire and uplift readers from all walks of life.